Jonathan Miller is one of the most important and prolific directors of theatre and opera today. Written with Miller's full cooperation and with access to rehearsals, this is the first book to explore his work in depth. Michael Romain examines this significant career in theatre through a series of interviews with Miller and his collaborators. It is rare that a director is willing or able to discuss his craft and rarer still to find colleagues who can recount their impressions of rehearsals and productions. In a series of conversations with actors, conductors, designers, singers, directors, and writers, a fascinating portrait of Miller emerges.

A profile of Jonathan Miller

A profile of

JONATHAN MILLER

Michael Romain

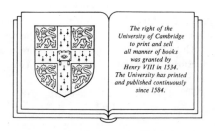

The right of the
University of Cambridge
to print and sell
all manner of books
was granted by
Henry VIII in 1534.
The University has printed
and published continuously
since 1584.

CAMBRIDGE UNIVERSITY PRESS
Cambridge
New York *Port Chester*
Melbourne *Sydney*

Published by the Press Syndicate of the University of Cambridge
The Pitt Building, Trumpington Street, Cambridge CB2 1RP
40 West 20th Street, New York, NY 10011, USA
10 Stamford Road, Oakleigh, Melbourne 3166, Australia

© Cambridge University Press 1992

First published 1992

Printed in Great Britain at the University Press, Cambridge

British Library cataloguing in publication data
Romain, Michael
A profile of Jonathan Miller
1. Great Britain. Theatre. Directing. Miller, Jonathan,
1934–
I. Title
792.0233092

Library of Congress cataloguing in publication data
Romain, Michael.
p.   cm.
Includes index.
ISBN 0 521 40137 2. – ISBN 0 521 40953 5 (pbk.)
1. Miller. Jonathan. 1934–   . 2. Theatrical producers and
directors – Great Britain – Biography. 3. Opera producers and
directors – Great Britain – Biography. I. Title.
PN2598.M536R66 1991
792'.0233'092 – dc20   90–20076   CIP
[B]

ISBN 0 521 40137 2 hardback
ISBN 0 521 40953 5 paperback

To my parents

Contents

Contents

Illustrations

Foreword

The Earl of Harewood

For much of his life, certainly since it started to become public at the time of *Beyond the Fringe*, Jonathan Miller's achievements, not least because of their multiplicity, have invited superlatives in such quantity that to praise him has been seen as a cliché. This is nothing short of ludicrous, because a man's versatility does not diminish what he's done or make it less worthwhile.

I first met him at the time of *Beyond the Fringe*, when his sense of the ridiculous, both verbal and physical, permanently enlarged my vocabulary, but it has been in his capacity to illuminate other men's work, in the theatre primarily but also in the field of painting and visual imagery, that I have found him at his most stimulating. A description of his activities suggests a dilettante, but the reality is far from that. In the field I know best he is an outstanding professional, and his operatic productions are among the best of our day. I was lucky enough to meet Janáček's *Cunning Little Vixen* in the production of Walter Felsenstein in East Berlin, and quite mistakenly thought it so nearly definitive that no other would stand comparison. But Jonathan Miller's production for Glyndebourne quite swept that notion away, and it was a great pleasure when he agreed to direct Mozart's *Marriage of Figaro* for English National Opera while I was Managing Director. *Figaro* was an outstanding success, full of accurate observation – Marcellina picking Susanna's new bonnet to bits at the start of Act I; pointed business – the Countess going into a faint when Susanna emerges from the dressing-room;

new light on old situations – the Countess teasing Cherubino in Act II with more erotic overtones than I had previously encountered. At a small party after the first night, I asked Jonathan whether he would consider Britten's *Turn of the Screw* for his next venture with ENO, and he hardly had time to accept before he was describing medical theories which make the Governess's hallucinations (if that is what they are) horribly plausible.

Nobody has a greater sense of what's publicly ridiculous, and the *Mikado* he directed for ENO found things in text and music which had never been discovered before, all delivered with a disciplined timing which would have delighted W. S. Gilbert, even if some of the goings-on would have surprised him. I have the happiest memories of *Rigoletto* in his production, but almost as bright are recollections of the discussions we had about projects which never came to fruition. *Those* would have enlivened any Festival programme.

Perhaps Jonathan Miller's greatest quality is the ability to inspire whoever he's working with. When the by no means short rehearsal period for *Figaro* was over and the first night had arrived, I went, before the performance, into the singers' dressing-rooms, and the Countess said straight out: 'I'm so unhappy it's all over. I've never enjoyed anything as much as these rehearsals!' You don't very often hear a director praised like that.

Chronology

Jonathan Miller was born in London on 21 July 1934. He was educated at St Paul's School, London, and read Natural Sciences at St John's College, Cambridge (MB, B.Ch.1959; Hon. Fellow 1982); he qualified as a Doctor of Medicine in 1959.

PERFORMANCES

1954   *Out of the Blue* (Cambridge Footlights), Phoenix Theatre, London
1957   *Tonight*, BBC TV
1960   *Beyond the Fringe*, Lyceum Theatre, Edinburgh Festival
1961   *Beyond the Fringe*, Arts Theatre, Cambridge
1961–2   *Beyond the Fringe*, Fortune Theatre, London
1962–4   *Beyond the Fringe*, John Golden Theatre, New York
1964   *One Way Pendulum*, Woodfall Films, dir. Peter Yates
1976   *Pleasure at Her Majesty's*, Her Majesty's Theatre, London
       (Amnesty Benefit)

STAGE PRODUCTIONS

1962   *Under Plain Cover* (Osborne), Royal Court Theatre, London
1964   *The Old Glory* (Lowell), American Place Theatre, New York
1966   *Come Live with Me* (Minoff and Price), New Haven, Connecticut
1967   *Prometheus Bound* (Aeschylus/Lowell), Yale Repertory Theatre,
       Connecticut
       Richard II (Shakespeare), Ahmanson Theater, Los Angeles
1968   *Benito Cereno* (Lowell) Mermaid Theatre, London
       The School for Scandal (Sheridan), Nottingham Playhouse

1969 *The Seagull* (Chekhov), Nottingham Playhouse
      King Lear (Shakespeare), Nottingham Playhouse
1970 *Twelfth Night* (Shakespeare), Arts Theatre, Cambridge
      Julius Caesar (Shakespeare), Arts Theatre, Cambridge
      Hamlet (Shakespeare), Arts Theatre, Cambridge
      The Tempest (Shakespeare), Mermaid Theatre
      King Lear, National Theatre at the Old Vic, London (Nottingham
          production)
      The Merchant of Venice (Shakespeare), The National Theatre at the Old
          Vic (also ATV film)
1971 *Prometheus Bound*, Mermaid Theatre
      Danton's Death (Büchner), The National Theatre at the Old Vic
1972 *The School for Scandal*, The National Theatre at the Old Vic
      The Taming of the Shrew (Shakespeare), Chichester Festival Theatre
1973 *The Malcontent* (Marston), Nottingham Playhouse
      The Seagull, Chichester Festival Theatre
1974 *Measure for Measure* (Shakespeare), The National Theatre at the Old Vic
      The Freeway (Nichols), The National Theatre at the Old Vic
      The Marriage of Figaro (Beaumarchais), The National Theatre at the Old
          Vic
      'Family Romances': *Ghosts* (Ibsen); *The Seagull*; *Hamlet*, Greenwich
          Theatre
      Arden Must Die (Goehr), Sadler's Wells Theatre, London
      Noyes Fludde (Britten), Roundhouse Theatre, London
1975 *The Importance of Being Earnest* (Wilde), Greenwich Theatre
      All's Well that Ends Well (Shakespeare), Greenwich Theatre
      Measure for Measure, Greenwich Theatre
      Così fan tutte (Mozart), Kent Opera
      Rigoletto (Verdi), Kent Opera
      The Cunning Little Vixen (Janáček), Glyndebourne
1976 *Orfeo* (Monteverdi), Kent Opera (also BBC TV)
      The Three Sisters (Chekhov), Cambridge Theatre, London
1977 *The Cunning Little Vixen*, Frankfurt Opera
      The Cunning Little Vixen, Australian Opera
      Eugene Onegin (Tchaikovsky), Kent Opera
1978 *The Marriage of Figaro* (Mozart), English National Opera at the London
          Coliseum
1979 *La Traviata* (Verdi), Kent Opera
      She Would if She Could (Etherege), Greenwich Theatre
      The Flying Dutchman (Wagner), Frankfurt Opera
      A Midsummer Night's Dream (Shakespeare), Vienna Burgtheater
      The Turn of the Screw (Britten), English National Opera

1980   *Arabella* (Strauss), English National Opera
      Falstaff (Verdi), Kent Opera
1981   *Otello* (Verdi), English National Opera
1982   *Rigeletto*, English National Opera (also Metropolitan Opera, New York
        and Thames TV/Channel 4)
      Così fan tutte, St Louis Opera, Missouri
      Hamlet, Donmar Warehouse, then Piccadilly Theatre, London
      The School for Scandal, American Repertory Theater, Harvard University
      Fidelio (Beethoven), Kent Opera (also subject of Channel 4 series)
1983   *The Magic Flute* (Mozart), Scottish Opera
1985   *Don Giovanni* (Mozart), English National Opera
1986   *The Magic Flute*, English National Opera
      Tosca (Puccini), Maggio Musicale, Florence
      The Mikado (Gilbert and Sullivan), English National Opera (also Thames
        TV)
      Long Day's Journey into Night (O'Neill), Broadhurst Theater, New York,
        then Haymarket Theatre, London (also BBC TV)
1987   *Tosca*, English National Opera
      The Emperor (Kapúscínski/Miller and Hastings), Royal Court Theatre
        (also BBC TV)
      Measure for Measure, Teatro Ateneo, Rome
      The Mikado, Los Angeles Music Center Opera (also US TV)
      The Barber of Seville (Rossini), English National Opera
      Tristan and Isolde (Wagner), Los Angeles Music Center Opera
      The Taming of the Shrew, Royal Shakespeare Company,
        Stratford-upon-Avon, then Barbican Theatre, London
1988   *Andromache* (Racine), The Old Vic
      One Way Pendulum (Simpson), The Old Vic
      Bussy D'Ambois (Chapman), The Old Vic
      The Tempest, The Old Vic
      Candide (Bernstein/Voltaire), The Old Vic (also Scottish Opera and BBC
        TV)
1989   *King Lear*, The Old Vic
      La Traviata, Glimmerglass Opera, New York State
      Mahagonny (Brecht and Weill), Los Angeles Music Center Opera
      The Mikado, Houston Grand Opera
      The Liar (Corneille), The Old Vic
1990   *Don Giovanni*, Maggio Musicale, Florence
1991   *The Girl of the Golden West* (Puccini), La Scala, Milan, Teatro Regio,
        Turin
      Katya Kabanova (Janáček), Metropolitan Opera, New York
      Così fan tutte, Maggio Musicale, Florence

Tosca, Houston Grand Opera
The Turn of the Screw, Los Angeles Music Center Opera
The Magic Flute, Mann Auditorium, Tel Aviv
Fidelio, Glimmerglass Opera, New York State
The Marriage of Figaro, Vienna State Opera
1992 *The Marriage of Figaro*, Maggio Musicale, Florence
The Makropulos Case (Janàček), Glimmerglass Opera, New York State

FILM AND TELEVISION

1962 *What's going on Here?*, NBC New York (Director)
1964–5 *Monitor*, BBC TV (Series Editor/Presenter)
1965 *Profiles in Courage: Anne Hutchinson*, TV New York (Writer)
The Drinking Party (Plato's *Symposium*), BBC TV (Producer/Director)
1966 *Alice in Wonderland*, BBC TV Film (Producer/Director)
The Death of Socrates, BBC TV Film (Producer/Director)
1967 *Scotch*, Documentary Film For John Walker and Sons (Writer/Director)
1968 *Oh Whistle and I'll Come to You*, BBC TV Film (Producer/Director)
1970 *Take a Girl like You*, Columbia Pictures (Director)
1973 *Clay*, BBC TV Film (Director)
1975 *King Lear*, BBC TV (Director)
1977 *The Body in Question*, BBC TV 13-Part Series (Writer/Presenter)
1980 *The Taming of the Shrew*, BBC TV Shakespeare (Producer/Director)
The Merchant of Venice, BBC TV Shakespeare, Dir. Jack Gold (Producer)
All's Well that Ends Well, BBC TV Shakespeare, Dir. Elijah Moshinsky
(Producer)
The Winter's Tale, BBC TV Shakespeare, Dir. Jane Howell (Producer)
Antony and Cleopatra, BBC TV Shakespeare (Producer/Director)
1981 *Timon of Athens*, BBC TV Shakespeare (Producer/Director)
Othello, BBC TV Shakespeare (Producer/Director)
Troilus and Cressida, BBC TV Shakespeare (Producer/Director)
A Midsummer Night's Dream, BBC TV Shakespeare, Dir. Elijah
Moshinsky (Producer)
Henry VI, BBC TV Shakespeare, Dir. Jane Howell (Producer)
1982 *King Lear*, BBC TV Shakespeare (Producer/Director)
States of Mind, BBC TV 15-Part Series (Writer/Presenter)
1984 *The Beggar's Opera*, BBC TV (Producer/Director)
Ivan, BBC TV *Horizon*, Documentary (Writer/Presenter)
1985 *Così fan tutte*, BBC TV Film (Director)
1986 *Origins*, BBC TV (Writer/Presenter)
Equinox: Prisoner of Consciousness, Channel 4 (Writer/Presenter)

1988　*Four Virtuosos*, Channel 4 (Writer/Presenter)
1989　*Dialogue in the Dark* (by Michael Ignatieff), BBC TV (Director)
　　　Who Cares?, BBC TV 6-Part Series (Presenter)
　　　Equinox: Moving Pictures, Channel 4 (Writer/Presenter)
1990　*QED: What's so funny about that?*, BBC TV (Writer/Presenter)
1991　*Museums of Madness*, BBC TV (Writer/Presenter)

PUBLICATIONS

1963　Film Critic for *The New Yorker* (also contributor to the *New York Review Of Books* and the *Partisan Review*)
1971　*McLuhan*, Fontana Modern Masters
1972　*Freud: The Man, His World, His Influence* (Editor), Weidenfeld & Nicolson
　　　Censorship and the Limits of Permission, British Academy
1978　*The Body in Question*, Jonathan Cape
1982　*Darwin for Beginners* (With Boris Van Loon), Unwin and Writers and Readers Publishing Co-op
1983　*States of Mind*, BBC Publications, London/Pantheon Books, New York
　　　The Human Body (with David Pelham), Jonathan Cape
1984　*The Facts of Life* (with David Pelham), Jonathan Cape
1985　*Bodyworks*, Genesis Computer Program
1986　*Subsequent Performances*, Faber & Faber
1990　*The Don Giovanni Book: Myths of Seduction and Betrayal* (Editor), Faber & Faber

POSITIONS HELD

1970　Contributory Member of the Royal Society study group on non-verbal communication
1970–3　Research Fellow in the History of Medicine at University College, London
1973–5　Associate Director of The National Theatre
1975–6　Member of the Arts Council
1977　Visiting Professor in Drama, Westfield College, London
1978–87　Associate Director of the English National Opera
1981　Fellow, University College, London
1983　Visiting Professor of Medicine at McMaster University, Ontario
1984　Research Fellow in Neuropsychology at the University of Sussex
1988–90　Artistic Director of the Old Vic

AWARDS

Jonathan Miller's awards include Director of the Year for *The Three Sisters*, Society of West End Theatre 1976; the Silver Medal, Royal Television Society 1981; the *Evening Standard* Opera Award for 1982 for *Rigoletto*; and the CBE in 1983.

Acknowledgements

My thanks to: Jonathan Miller, for his unfailing co-operation; the Earl of Harewood; Philip Prowse, Richard Hudson and Patrick Robertson and Rosemary Vercoe, for their assistance with illustrations; Emma Harris at the Old Vic; Caro Newling and Zoe Mylchreest at the Royal Shakespeare Company; Mary Fulton at Town House Publicity; Jane Livingston and David Ritch at the English National Opera; Norman Platt at Kent Opera; Jessica Ford and Nick Matthias at Harold Holt; Joy Garnham at Lord Harewood's office; Paul Kellogg and Stein Bujan at Glimmerglass Opera; Peter Hemmings at the Los Angeles Music Center Opera; Wynn Handman at The American Place Theatre; and Elijah Moshinsky; and last, but by no means least, Victoria Cooper, my editor at Cambridge University Press, for her constant support and sage advice.

All the interviews were conducted between March 1989 and June 1990.

Michael Romain   Hampstead, London

I

JONATHAN MILLER:
WORK IN THE
EUROPEAN THEATRE

MME RANYEVSKAIA: 'Are you still a student?'
TROFIMOV: 'I expect I shall be a student to the end of my days.'
Anton Chekhov, *The Cherry Orchard*[1]

Like Trofimov, Jonathan Miller is the eternal student. For him, as for
Montaigne, the world exists as a school of inquiry. Able to find significance in
all things, he has – in its original secular sense – *Ozeanisches Gefühl*, which
Freud defined as 'a sensation of "eternity", a feeling of something limitless,
unbounded – as it were, "oceanic" … a feeling of an indissoluble bond, of
being one with the external world as a whole'.[2] Few – if any – other directors
have such a range of interests and breadth of experience. Apart from being a
theatre, opera, film and television director, he is also a doctor, neuro-
psychologist, research fellow, lecturer, author, presenter and producer.
Miller's work as a director reflects his polymath predilections. His productions embrace psychology, psycholinguistics, anthropology, sociology
(particularly the work of Erving Goffman and Rom Harré), philosophy (most
notably Plato, and the Enlightenment thinkers), history (with special emphasis on the eighteenth century), literature (Kafka's vision is a recurring motif),
photography, art and architecture. His versatility extends to both his repertoire – he has moved directly from *The Mikado* to *Long Day's Journey into
Night*, from Racine to N. F. Simpson – and to his style – after exhausting the
stage crew at the Coliseum with the demands of his spectacularly large-scale
Tosca, he retired to the tiny studio space of the Royal Court Theatre Upstairs

---

1 Translated by Elisaveta Fen (London: Penguin Books), p. 349.
2 Sigmund Freud, *The Standard Edition of the Complete Psychological Works*, ed. James Strachey
(London 1953–74), vol. XXI, pp. 64–5.

to stage his austere, intimate, dream-like production of *The Emperor*. He is fascinated by the possibilities of mixing mediums in his work: casting John Cleese and Alexei Sayle in Shakespeare, Roger Daltrey in John Gay, Jack Lemmon in O'Neill and Eric Idle in Gilbert and Sullivan; or drawing on the films of Chaplin for *Mahagonny*, Rossellini for *Tosca* and the Marx Brothers for *The Mikado*.

Although Miller draws on a huge variety of sources and references, they never dictate the direction of his work. He may *refer* to Darwin, Klein or structuralism, but his work is never derivative. The one theme that can be discerned throughout his directorial career is the Renaissance concept of 'renovatio', the idea of an apparently ancient object being transformed into something new. This idea reveals itself in the way that Miller's work startles an audience into looking at a play or an opera in a new, unexpected, light, so that the piece itself is refreshed in the process. 'Renovatio', or renewal, informs Miller's work to such an extent that it can often capture the public imagination in productions like his *Merchant of Venice*, with its late nineteenth-century setting, his season of inter-related 'Family Romances', his (Edward) Hopper-esque 'Mafia' *Rigoletto*, his chiaroscuro, Goya-esque *Don Giovanni* and his dazzling white vision of *The Mikado*, set in the foyer of a grand hotel in an English seaside resort *c.* 1929. Miller achieves this artistic restoration and renewal in his work by reappraising and redefining plays and operas. He is not held back by a reverence for a work's status as a classic: when he began rehearsing *Long Day's Journey into Night*, he told the cast to forget that it was a play reputed to be a masterpiece, so that they could shake off the weight of its Aeschylean aura and play it simply for what it was – an intimate, naturalistic American study in family life. Such an approach has frequently earned Miller accusations of iconoclasm or avant-gardism from traditionalists. Yet Miller has always been guided by a firm adherence to the 'deep structure' (to borrow Noam Chomsky's phrase) of a work.

In addition to his reappraisal of the repertoire, Miller also interprets works and moulds productions through scientific analysis. Science, as Leonardo realised, is an art, and Jonathan Miller is a contemporary example of a European tradition that stretches back through Büchner and Chekhov to Goethe (reflected in his creation, Wilhelm Meister). Miller's own symbiosis of the arts and the sciences derives from his parents. His mother, Betty Bergson (her great-uncle was the philosopher Henri Bergson), was a writer and novelist, as well as a biographer of Browning. His father, Emanuel Miller, trained as a philosopher before becoming a doctor and neurologist, and later moved into psychiatry. He initiated the child guidance movement in England, setting up its first clinic in 1924 and subsequently founding the

Institute for the Scientific Treatment of Delinquency. Miller's own interest in medicine and science lies in research rather than treatment. He has always been fascinated by the psychology of human expression, something he can work on equally well in the clinic and rehearsal studio – directing a play or an opera, he is dealing all the time with behaviour and language:

I was interested in the 'ordinary' way people carried themselves, and their nuances of behaviour, which had an influence on what I observed when I was at the bedside of patients who had neurological damage. Noticing what people actually do, instead of accepting the clichés of what we think they do. Theatre tends to clone all sorts of habits that seem to come from nineteenth-century melodramas. There's a reciprocity between working as a clinician, which makes you look very carefully at behaviour, and working in the theatre, which concentrates me on getting the details right. There are tiny things that people do – the apparent rubbish of posture and gesture – which get eliminated from performance but are actually what gives performance its texture. Maybe knowing this was one of the reasons I was a good comic performer. I just saw things, and much of my success was simply getting it right.[3]

Theatre and opera provided Miller with a natural extension of his research into the mechanics of behaviour, and his productions display acute attention to psychological detail (Erving Goffman's *The Presentation of Self in Everyday Life* and *Behaviour in Public Places* are important references for him). His views on medicine have always been humanistic, and this notably informs his approach to works such as *The Tempest* and *The Magic Flute*, leading him to replace their traditionally metaphysical fantasy worlds with the social and cultural frameworks of the seventeenth and eighteenth centuries respectively. As a doctor, he knows how emotion can be convincingly – rather than histrionically – portrayed, and the results are often startlingly realistic:

My approach to Ophelia has been influenced by the work of R. D. Laing, and it was not until I worked with Kathryn Pogson in 1982 that I was able to realize the full effect of schizophrenia on stage. I gave her a lot of clinical information but also simply reminded her of behaviour and mannerisms while she was constantly on the lookout for characteristics she could use on stage.[4]

When he directed *The Taming of the Shrew* for the Royal Shakespeare Company, Miller pointed out that Kate's violent and unpredictable outbursts are symptomatic of her unhappiness and isolation as an unloved and neg-lected daughter – what she needed, he said, was a child therapist. Fiona Shaw's Kate was initially a withdrawn, jerky and disordered figure, bran-dishing a pair of scissors with which she scraped the walls or distractedly cut

---

[3] 'Doctor in Spite of Himself', Jonathan Miller interviewed by Penelope Gilliatt in *The New Yorker*, 17 April 1989.
[4] Jonathan Miller, *Subsequent Performances* (London: Faber & Faber, 1986), p. 116.

off locks of her rapidly diminishing hair. Like a disturbed child, she greeted Petruchio (Brian Cox, burly and imperturbable) with a slap in the face. Her gradual awakening to him proved literally therapeutic.

Miller's *Othello* for his BBC TV Shakespeare cycle pitted Bob Hoskins' Iago – a combination of 'the rough army sergeant, the puritan trooper at Naseby, and the mischief-making fairy-tale dwarf – a primal trickster like Rumpelstiltskin' – against the exotic, near-operatic Moor of Anthony Hopkins. Ever since Coleridge puzzled over Iago's 'motiveless malignity', the dynamics of his personality have proved to be a problem for actors and directors. One of the ways in which Miller approached Iago's characterisation with Hoskins was to focus on his motivating envy:

I began by asking about the nature of envy itself and found that there are several ways of approaching the question. At an almost psychoanalytic level you can ask what it is that makes people destructively envious. To find an answer I turned to the most revealing line that Iago speaks almost inadvertently, towards the end of the play when he is waiting in the shadows for the murder of Cassio, and remarks 'He hath a daily beauty in his life / That makes me ugly.' This seems to summarize for me the nature of envy.[5]

Miller's approach resulted in a frighteningly convincing – and, at rare moments, oddly touching – characterisation from Hoskins, far removed from the usual pantomime villain, and one which emphasised Iago's pivotal role in the play rather than allowing it to become a one-man firework display of jealousy.

A further example of Miller's work in psychology which illuminates his work in theatre is his use of speech act theory, which he will often employ in rehearsals to discover the real meaning of a speech or sentence, instead of using the traditional interpretation based on the written word. When it comes to orchestrating the rhythms of conversation on stage, he will draw on his research into psycholinguistics and behavioural psychology, as he did to remarkable effect in *Three Sisters*:

Chekhov is quite clearly more realistic than Shakespeare. The characters speak lines that are very like those that ordinary people speak when conversing with one another. There are ways of enhancing that sense of being in the presence of reality, and it is most important to attend to what are called 'the rules of conversation'. These have been identified only in the last twenty years or so by psycholinguistics who are very interested in what is called 'turn-taking' in conversation. Conversation has a certain internal structure which is determined by rules that we all somehow know without understanding how we acquire this knowledge ... It is also useful to allow for things that Chekhov has not written; by this I mean interruption, reduplication and overlap

---

[5] Jonathan Miller, *Subsequent Performances*, p. 149.

with people starting to talk when the previous speaker has not finished and then having to apologize. All these little characteristics of speech take a long time to re-create on stage but when actors manage it the audience feels as if it is in the presence of a real conversation ... It was an intuitive awareness that prompted me to rehearse Chekhov in this way.[6]

The 'rhythm of ordinary speech' has distinguished much of Miller's work, from the irritable exchanges of the shipwrecked courtiers in *The Tempest* to the philosophical debate between the dying Hume and the drunken, tortured Boswell in *Dialogue in the Dark*. When he used the technique of overlapping dialogue for *Long Day's Journey into Night* (particularly appropriate for the Tyrone household, where the same old lines are repeated again and again until – as in so many families – the characters simply stop listening to each other), the play's running time was reduced from four and a half hours to just over three, with hardly any textual cuts, and to the surprise of Broadway audiences accustomed to marathon performances. Played at the speed of normal speech, the production achieved a Chekhovian sense of ensemble, adding the piece to Miller's series of 'Family Romances'. (As with Violetta in *La Traviata*, the tubercular Edmund Tyrone benefited from the doctor-director: while audiences and critics usually expect Edmund to look as if he is at death's door, Miller knew that this was not medically accurate for someone just beginning to develop tuberculosis and boldly went against the stereotype by casting the physically strapping, but *emotionally* fevered, young American actor Peter Gallagher in the role.)

Anthropology informed Miller's interpretation of *The Tempest*, in which he cast black actors as Ariel and Caliban, bringing the racial issue to the forefront of the play:

My approach to *The Tempest* was very largely guided by *Prospero and Caliban*, a book by O. Mannoni. He gave an anthropological interpretation of the Malagasy revolt and emphasized the effect of the paternal white imperial conqueror on an indigenous native population. So, instead of making Caliban and Ariel personify natural principles, I simply made them into native people, the rightful inhabitants of the island. I was guided not only by this book, but also by reference to the imperial themes of the late sixteenth and seventeenth century and the notion of the New World. There are accounts of the journey that describe the behaviour of British sailors on the shore of Massachusetts making the Indians drunk. This made me want to see what would happen if I liberated Caliban from his fishy scales, and mythical monstrous identity, and made him monstrous simply in the eyes of those who arrive on the island. Caliban's servitude was a social one.[7]

---

[6] Jonathan Miller, *Subsequent Performances*, p. 170.
[7] Jonathan Miller, *Subsequent Performances*, p. 160.

Noting that Shakespeare wrote the play only a few years before Galileo developed his telescope, Miller presented Prospero (first Graham Crowden, mysterious and tortured, at the Mermaid; then the melancholy Max von Sydow at the Old Vic, all his power overshadowed by the impending loss of his daughter) as an embryonic scientist, rather than the traditional magus with a repertoire of party tricks, even placing an early telescope at the front of his cubic cell.

As well as the interpretations gleaned from scientific analyses, Miller also draws inspiration from the visual arts. Caravaggio gave him the dramatic balance of light and shadow for *King Lear*; Edward Hopper's *Nighthawks* evoked the eerie sense of late-night loneliness for the third act of *Rigoletto*; and Poussin provided the classical pastoral backgrounds and poised, controlled style of movement for *Orfeo*. Miller's staging of the final scene of *Mahagonny* resembled a *pietà* by Rogier van der Weyden. The Kafka-esque atmosphere of 1920s Vienna for his *Measure for Measure* was derived from the photographs of August Sander, while those of the Count de Primoli characterised the background of his late nineteenth-century *Merchant of Venice*. In this way, Miller is able to make connections between social history and art history – between the society of Sheridan's *The School for Scandal*, for example, and that of Hogarth's *Marriage à la Mode*. He will often bring prints and art books to rehearsals to illustrate the mood or style he is aiming for (a large part of Miller's direction works through metaphor). The writer and critic Penelope Gilliatt, a long-standing colleague of Miller, recorded his description of his use of art in the theatre for her *New Yorker* profile:

He talked about Wölfflin's work on the organization of space in pictures, and Panofsky's on iconography. 'I take jobs in Italy and France and Germany so as to be able to go to galleries and churches. I did *Measure for Measure* in Rome last year, and rehearsed in a beautiful old triumphal arch on top of the Gianicolo. We didn't rehearse until four-thirty, when the heat began to subside, which meant that I could get up at nine o'clock and go to churches and do sketches, and visit most of the galleries ... The pleasure of looking at paintings and exploring Roman churches feeds back into the theatre all the time, of course.'[8]

Although Miller's productions always observe the 'deep structure' of plays and operas, his work has nothing to do with the 'authentic' school of direction produced in period costume. Miller's approach to works informed by the culture of their own time (such as *Orfeo*, or the Mozart operas) aims not at the literal re-creation of a bygone age but at an examination and recognition of the past informed by the sensibility and staging techniques of the present. Yet his treatment of works from the past is characteristically flexible. The

[8] 'Doctor in Spite of Himself', *The New Yorker*, 17 April 1989.

approach varies from play to play, from opera to opera: if the work reflects the period of its composition, Miller will root it in that context; but if it has no connection with its own period or that specified in the text or libretto, then he will feel free to relocate it as he sees fit. He will also strike a balance between these two courses of action by using what he describes as 'historical parallax' to present one area of the past through the eyes of another.

Miller's reputation in some quarters as an 'updater' is inaccurate, as only a tiny percentage of his overall output is actually transposed in time – *Prometheus Bound*, its unwieldy literal setting replaced by a seventeenth-century limbo; the nineteenth-century *Merchant of Venice* with Laurence Olivier as Shylock, a Rothschild-like Victorian businessman; the 1920s *Measure for Measure*, set to pastiche Schoenberg in Freud's Vienna; the two *Rigolettos*, the first set in the Dickensian world of the 1850s, the period of composition, the second set famously in the Mafia underworld of 1950s New York; a *Tosca* set in 1944 as the Allies advance on Mussolini's crumbling Rome; and the thoroughly English 'Roaring Twenties' *Mikado*. All dramatically valid transpositions, bringing Miller's 'renovatio' to bear on mostly familiar works.

'I think contemporary connections are legitimate for most nineteenth-century operas', Miller told Penelope Gilliatt. 'Between about 1830 and 1880, composers and librettists dealt carelessly with the past. The anchorage of the work to the period in which it's said to happen is loose and very provisional anyway. Sometimes it can be remoored with much more effect ... When you make these theatrical distortions, the mapping has got to be almost one for one.' By 'mapping' he means making sure that the characters and motives and social drives of a work transposed in time will fit onto 'the deep structure' of the original.

Miller's approach to works which, like *The Taming of the Shrew*, are rooted firmly in the past is influenced by the Annales school of French historians, who use sociological and anthropological techniques in an effort to reconstruct the *mentalité* of the past. Miller uses a similar approach to illuminate the society and culture reflected in the play or opera. Only by exploring the *mentalité* of the past can a Mozart opera or most of Shakespeare be fully understood (while works like *Rigoletto* or *Tosca* have nothing to do with Renaissance Mantua or Rome in 1800, hence Miller's temporal transpositions).

Aware that the Mozart operas are anchored in the world of the Enlightenment, and embody the values and concerns of the late eighteenth century, Miller accordingly staged them in their own context (rather than imposing contemporary themes over those of the Age of Reason, as have Peter Sellars and David Freeman). His *Figaro* was set in the household of a minor rural

7

aristocrat, the relationships defined by the social conditions of the eighteenth century; Goya's dark, late eighteenth-century Spanish world provided the background for *Don Giovanni*; and *Così fan tutte* took place in a Neapolitan villa of 1790, the year of composition, with Don Alfonso as a philosopher in the Enlightenment tradition of Diderot, Voltaire and Johnson, his study cluttered with books and scientific instruments, all lit in the chiaroscuro manner of the eighteenth-century English painter Joseph Wright of Derby. When he directed *The Magic Flute* Miller brought out its Enlightenment themes by replacing its traditional ancient Egyptian setting with a multi-layered and intricately detailed panorama of the Age of Reason, embracing freemasonry and the French Revolution as well as the American Declaration of Independence, Rousseau's Man of Nature, and the Habsburg Empress Maria-Theresa with her Catholic retinue.

Miller set his production of *The Tempest* in the seventeenth-century context of Europe reaching out to the New World, *Othello* amidst the splendour of Renaissance Venice, and *Hamlet* against an austerely evoked Tudor background. This reconstitution of the *mentalité* of the past not only releases the full significance of the plays and operas, but also strips away the traditional stereotypes and clichés that surround them. Miller's *King Lear* ruled a Stuart kingdom, where the play's seventeenth-century themes of statecraft and Christian imagery could be realised, rather than a primitive, pagan society governed by Druids. His *School for Scandal* avoided the usual West End representation of Georgian London, all fluttering fans and silk handkerchiefs, and presented an accurate picture of the minor gentry in the 1770s, living in dank houses, with unwashed, pregnant servants, lice-infested wigs, and a suitably Hogarthian atmosphere.

When confronted with a work set by a playwright or composer in the distant past or mythical antiquity, Miller will use a central image to align and express several different periods. For Monteverdi's *Orfeo*, Poussin's paintings bridged the gap between the seventeenth century, when the opera was composed, and the period to which it refers, classical/mythical antiquity, as well as matching the formal, poised style of the opera itself.

With Shakespeare's Greek and Roman plays, Miller points out that the playwright

is not writing about a literal, historical past, and the more we learn about the Elizabethan period the more striking the discrepancy between what he writes and the supposed date of the play's action becomes ... it is much better either to set them in some kind of sixteenth-century Renaissance limbo or any setting that makes allowance for the past.[9]

[9] 'Doctor in Spite of Himself', *The New Yorker*, 17 April 1989.

8

Thus for his television production of *Antony and Cleopatra* Miller re-created 'a syncretic appearance showing fragments of antique dress, and figures in sixteenth-century armour alongside ordinary stage costumes reflecting the time at which the play was written'.[10] When he directed *Julius Caesar*, Miller attempted

to reconcile in one format all the conflicting themes – Roman antiquity, the Renaissance and the faint implications of modern Italian Fascism which I did not want to make explicit but to hint at. The format that brought all this together – and highlighted that strange sense of surrealist premonition which runs throughout the language with its peculiar dream images and its stabbed bleeding statues – was given to me by the paintings of de Chirico. The setting was based on his work, which is full of Roman piazzas, classical statues and long shadows, and enabled us to bring the surrealist ingredients of the play to life.[10]

The long-term significance of Miller's work begins with only his second production: when *The Old Glory* opened New York's American Place Theatre in 1964, Miller's innovative direction was acclaimed by Robert Brustein as heralding the start of a Renaissance for the American theatre. Not only did its success ensure the survival of the American Place Theatre, but it also launched Frank Langella into the forefront of American actors and introduced a mixture of stillness and stylisation onstage that was later to be developed in the United States by Robert Wilson and Andrei Serban. A few years later, Miller's startlingly Hogarthian *School for Scandal* came as a revelation in the treatment of eighteenth-century drama after decades of polished and plush revivals.

The updating of plays and operas forms only a tiny percentage of Miller's work, but a prominent part, from *The Merchant of Venice* and *Measure for Measure* early on in his career right up to his recent *Tosca* and *The Mikado*, setting a precedent for dozens of younger directors. Of his work in this vein, it is undoubtedly his *Rigoletto* which has made the most resounding impact. Struck by the inconsistency between Verdi's nineteenth-century score and the opera's literal setting in Renaissance Mantua, Miller realised

how consistent the plot was with something that could have taken place in another Italian community where people have absolute power of life and death over others, namely the world of the Godfather and the Italian Mafia. Since the music of the nineteenth century continues to be played, and is influential in the Italian communities of the twentieth century, it seemed much less anachronistic, and a perfectly obvious and effortless transposition.[12]

---

[10] Jonathan Miller, *Subsequent Performances*, p. 123.
[11] Jonathan Miller, *Subsequent Performances*, p. 128.
[12] Jonathan Miller, *Subsequent Performances*, p. 183.

Replacing the dusty trappings of the sixteenth-century court of the Gonzagas with Lugers, Ray-Bans and juke-boxes, Miller set his 1982 production of *Rigoletto* for the English National Opera in the Mafia underworld of 1950s New York. The Duke became a Mafia Boss with Rigoletto as his hunchback barman, an ever-present joker; the settings ranged from a neon-lit hotel bar to a shadowy street of looming tenement blocks, and finally to the lonely diner reminiscent of Edward Hopper's *Nighthawks*.

English National Opera conductor Peter Robinson recalls:

Jonathan had already done a *Rigoletto* set in the mid-nineteenth century for Kent Opera, and I remember sitting with him in a Melbourne restaurant shortly after that and hearing him say, 'One day I want to set it in 1950s New York – the characters could be members of the Mafia.' There were several of us there with him, and he kept exploring this idea, thinking how it would work for Gilda and where Rigoletto himself would fit in – 'Maybe he would be the bartender?' So it had been ticking over in his mind for some time before he actually staged it for Lord Harewood, who was running the ENO at the time. He first dreamed up the idea after seeing *Some Like It Hot* and picking up on the line – 'I couldn't have been at the St Valentine's Day Massacre. Me? I was at *Rigoletto*.'

The plot of *Rigoletto* actually fits the Mafia setting perfectly, with Monterone as the head of a rival family, and so on. Jonathan's updating makes so much sense, as there is a very strong contrast between the nineteenth-century music and the sixteenth-century setting if you do it in Renaissance Mantua, whereas a Mafia community in the 1950s would be full of nineteenth-century Italian opera. For the whole of this century, that kind of music has been the Italians' folk music. Having 'La donna è mobile' come out of a juke-box was an inspired touch.

We watched videos of *The Godfather* during rehearsals, as Jonathan wanted the cast to get the right physical gestures rather than 'operatic' acting. He wanted them to imitate the relaxed style of American social life – the way that they slap each other on the back and shake hands without really looking at anyone in particular as they move around a room, the way that they smoke or hold their cigarettes, and so on. It was a very strongly cast production – John Rawnsley fulfilled Jonathan's conception of Rigoletto perfectly, and Arthur Davies was ideally suited to the Duke. (*personal communication*)

The originality – and validity – of Miller's concept, the sheer panache with which it was staged, and the way that it instantly seized the public imagination made *Rigoletto* a landmark in modern opera production comparable to Patrice Chéreau's *Ring* cycle or Peter Brook's pared-down *Carmen*.

Like *Rigoletto*, *The Barber of Seville* is also a standard work in the repertoire and Miller points out the problem for directors faced with the challenge of staging it afresh:

The Barber has been done many times before, and everyone thinks they know how it should be done. There are lots of traditional views about how it ought to be presented, what it ought to look like, how it ought to sound, and how jolly it ought to be. If you are going to produce it responsibly you have to take note of that, but at the same time not feel enslaved by it. I know that because of productions of mine like *Rigoletto* and *Tosca* people view me with foreboding and relish, thinking 'What's he going to do with it this time?' as if I'm this vandal whose actions are deplorable and delightful. In fact, only a small number of my productions have been updated, but people tend to notice those more. But I had no intention of updating *The Barber of Seville*.

I saw the opera as an Italian comedy. It's only very incidentally set in Spain, but people always take the setting very literally. You often get a lot of bullfighter costumes and castanets, and extremely vulgar Marbella views of Spain. It actually comes out of the world of Goldoni's comedies, the *commedia dell'arte*. And that's what I emphasised, without being too literal about it.

I used *commedia* elements, Venetian dolls and marionettes, and, above all, the world of Venetian comedy as a basis. But people are so enslaved by title and name that they say indignantly, 'Well Seville, unless I'm very much mistaken, Seville is in Spain, but no doubt the good doctor knows better!' You have to put up with all that sort of nonsense. The opera has got that quality of the clockwork automata which were so popular at the end of the eighteenth century. I wanted it to look like that – highly artificial. (*personal communication*)

Tanya McCallin's set reflected this artificiality: the walls of the sun-baked street of the opening scene opened up to reveal the interior of Dr Bartolo's house mounted on a raised stage. Almaviva serenaded Rosina accompanied by a band of musicians, tumblers and jugglers clad in *commedia* garb, while the passing citizens looked as if they had just stepped out of the eighteenth-century Venice of Pietro Longhi.

When Miller directed *The Mikado*, he set out to blow away all its oriental cobwebs, with the result that it emerged crisp and fresh – and, in the hands of the designer Stefanos Lazaridis, dazzlingly white. Bearing out G. K. Chesterton's view that not a single joke in *The Mikado* fits the Japanese whereas all the jokes fit the English, Miller's production revealed the operetta as a satire on the sheer silliness of English society and customs, replacing the traditional setting of mythical Japaneserie with the foyer of a grand hotel in an English seaside resort *c.* 1929, where the only echoes of the East were the faint outlines of Mount Fuji through the windows and the occasional Kung-fu burlesque.

Lazaridis reflected the fantasy world of the piece in his surrealist set design. His hotel foyer was a cream-coloured architectural collage of outsize objects and mismatched masonry – fragmented brickwork and crazy angles, chairs and musical instruments suspended halfway up the walls, and huge champagne bubbles floating over white palm trees. Rows of doors in the background recalled Miller's *Measure for Measure* and *The Emperor*; while the doll-like black and white make-up and the elegant cream decor anchored the action in a *Vogue* world of 1920s chic.

With their morning-dress, monocles and red carnations, the chorus were gentlemen of English clubland rather than of Japan. Nanki-Poo became a classic buffoon clad in striped blazer, flannel bags and straw boater; Ko-Ko entered straight from the tennis court; and the 'Three Little Maids' were giggling schoolgirls in gymslips, sucking lollipops and brandishing lacrosse racquets, with perfectly enunciated Kensington vowels. Miller's direction captured the light, frothy essence of *The Mikado*, paralleling its lunatic humour and spontaneous eruption of song and dance with Marx Brothers movies and Hollywood musicals of the 1930s. Gilbert's 'cuckoo-land' town of Titipu is not so far removed from the Marx Brothers' equally imaginary Freedonia, and Ko-Ko's entrance number here took the form of Groucho's first appearance in *Duck Soup*.

When he directed *Tosca* for the Maggio Musicale in Florence, Miller released the opera from the Zeffirelli-esque world of florid costume melodrama by updating it to 1944, as the Allies advance on Mussolini's crumbling Rome. The fascist regime was already tottering, and the social and political instability was reflected in the distorted perspective of Stefanos Lazaridis' darkly oppressive set design: the towering walls of a decaying church lurched at precarious angles over the steeply raked stage, with tattered red curtains hanging forlornly from the proscenium, and scaffolding thrusting out into the auditorium. Angelotti was a member of the Resistance movement aided by the Underground sympathiser Cavaradossi, while Scarpia was the Chief of the Fascist Police, surrounded by menacing grey-suited henchmen.

The supernatural elements of plays and operas are usually represented in heavily clichéd style, but Peter Robinson, who conducted Miller's *Don Giovanni* for the ENO, was struck by the way that Miller avoided this:

At the climax, instead of having a heavy statue lumber on, Jonathan presented the Commendatore as a rather dusty corpse – wearing the dressing-gown that he had been killed in – who actually came in and sat down at the Don's dinner table. That was an inspired touch – it's much easier to believe in that as a spectre than the great clanking statue on a horse that you usually get. Then Jonathan followed that with a wonderful *coup de théâtre*: instead of having the traditional devils and demons with horns and pointed tails running around, he had the Don dragged off to Hell by these unearthly women, the spirits of his former victims, clutching dead babies and so on. (*personal communication*)

Challenging the received view of familiar works – 'renovatio' in action – has inevitably earned Miller a maverick image among the critical fraternity. Tyrone Guthrie was a comparable figure. Although Guthrie did not possess Miller's intellectual range and breadth of vision, he did have many characteristics in common with him (even physically – Guthrie was also well over six feet tall, informally dressed and prone to displays of perpetual motion in rehearsal). Like Miller, Guthrie began his career as a performer (until J. B. Fagan advised him to give up acting and try directing) and quickly became a 'star' director (whose name alone could fill a theatre) on the international stage, moving from project to project with seemingly limitless energy. He, too, branched out into writing and lecturing.

As with Miller, Guthrie's work was noted for its originality, imagination, playfulness and invention – neither director could ever be accused of producing uninteresting work. In productions as diverse as *The Mikado* and *Mahagonny*, Miller has proved his theatrical flair, and Guthrie displayed similar skill at choreographing crowd scenes or devising detailed characterisation and intricate comic 'business' for minor roles. He excelled at spectacle and pageantry – as seen in his *Peer Gynt* (1944), *Cyrano de Bergerac* (1946), *Tamburlaine the Great* (1951) and *Henry VIII* (1953).

Above all Guthrie, like Miller, was an innovator and non-conformist, never afraid to experiment and take risks, never reverent in his approach to the classics or inhibited by the weight of tradition surrounding them. He was equally celebrated for his 'updatings', which ranged from the modern-dress *Hamlet* (1938) with Alec Guinness to productions of *Troilus and Cressida* (1956) and *All's Well that Ends Well* (1959), set in what Kenneth Tynan described as 'Shavian Ruritania'; his *School for Scandal* – for John Gielgud's 1937 season at the Queen's Theatre – anticipated Miller's by avoiding the tradition of fluttering fans in favour of a more down-to-earth approach.

Guthrie, too, moved back and forth between the opera house and the theatre, where he worked mainly in the classical repertoire. Like Miller, he tried everything from Aeschylus to Chekhov, the rare as well as the familiar – two of the first plays he directed were Euripides' *Iphigenia in Tauris* (1929) and Ibsen's *Rosmersholm* (1929), returning repeatedly to the same works that have preoccupied Miller: *Hamlet, Measure for Measure, The Taming of the Shrew, La Traviata*, the Chekhov quartet.

His working methods were also similar to Miller's. He did not believe in beginning rehearsals with the ritual of a formal read-through, nor did he ever impose rigid blocking on a cast, but preferred to allow the production to develop as cast members grew more confident with each rehearsal. Totally uninterested in dogmas, whether Method acting or pedantic, over-academic verse-speaking, Guthrie prized spontaneity in performance above everything else. Performers found that he gave them great freedom and created lively, stimulating rehearsals, and they, in turn, were devoted to him. Although he worked mainly with leading actors – Olivier, Laughton, Wolfit, Guinness – he always managed to achieve a strong sense of ensemble in his productions.

Mainstream British theatre has long suffered from a certain insularity. (During the National Theatre's first decade on the South Bank, the playwrights whose work was most frequently staged were Shakespeare, Shaw, Ayckbourn, Pinter and Hare – there were no plays at all, for example, by Racine, Corneille, Goethe, Schiller, or Ostrovsky.) In the classical repertoire, Shakespeare holds sway at the expense of other dramatists. An exception to this has been the Old Vic under Miller's direction, a post he held from January 1988 to July 1990. There, he demonstrated that 'there is a world elsewhere', staging plays that would be considered standard repertoire in other European centres but which have largely been absent from the British stage. In his three seasons as Artistic Director, Miller presented a remarkably diverse and wide-ranging repertoire at the Old Vic: Racine's *Andromache*, Lenz's *The Tutor*, N. F. Simpson's *One Way Pendulum*, Ostrovsky's *Too Clever by Half*, Chapman's *Bussy D'Ambois*, *The Tempest*, Bernstein and Voltaire's *Candide*, *King Lear*, *As You Like It*, Feydeau's *A Flea in Her Ear*, Corneille's *The Liar*, Isaac Babel's *Marya*, Corneille's *The Theatrical Illusion*. Many of the plays were receiving their British or London premières – Chapman's *Bussy D'Ambois* had not been revived since 1604, and Miller's production proved a revelation in Jacobean political drama. The seasons were a return to the days when Laurence Olivier and Kenneth Tynan were running the National Theatre Company at the Old Vic, where they aimed 'to give a spectrum of world drama'. (Miller himself directed *The Merchant of Venice* for them at the Old Vic early in his career.)

Under Miller's artistic direction, the Old Vic engaged European artists as a matter of principle: Angelika Hurwicz from the Berliner Ensemble re-created her production of *The Tutor*, which Miller had seen and admired in Vienna; Max von Sydow came to play Prospero in Miller's *Tempest*; Peter Zadek, the Artistic Director of the Deutsches Schauspielhaus in Hamburg, was scheduled to direct Wedekind's *Lulu*, until serious illness forced him to withdraw; and the theatre also played host to the Katona Jozsef Theatre from Hungary with its productions of *The Government Inspector* and *Three Sisters*, and to Yuri Lyubimov's internationally touring production of *Hamlet*.

Although British theatre largely remains resolutely text-based, Miller developed a distinctive visual style at the Old Vic with the aid of his resident designer for the first season, Richard Hudson. Their first collaboration, *Andromache*, heralded a striking balance between text and image, more commonly seen in Paris and Berlin than in London: Hudson's set – a crumbling classical façade hanging precariously over the cast, with shadowy corridors leading off into infinity, all seen through a distorted perspective on the steeply raked stage – not only made an immediate visual impact, but also reflected the structure and mood of Racine's play, creating a poised and powerfully oppressive background to the action. With Hudson leading the way (combining painterly and sculptural elements in his designs to dramatic effect), the Old Vic provided an outlet for the talents of a new generation of designers – Antony McDonald, The Brothers Quay, Peter J. Davison, Nigel Lowery. Their work, whether abstract or expressionist, maintained an emphasis on the freedom of the imagination from the constraints of literal representation: in short, a European style.

By the end of his first season at the Old Vic (15 January 1988 – 7 January 1989), Miller (like Olivier and Tynan, Guthrie and Baylis before him) had given the theatre a firm artistic identity – one which pioneered a consistently stimulating, daring, intelligent and innovative approach to the repertory of world drama: a European theatre in the Waterloo Road. What is it in Miller's work that characterises him as a European, rather than a British, director? A combination of several factors: his international repertoire (typified by his Old Vic seasons), in both theatre and opera; his visual style (cultivated with a series of designers – Philip Prowse, Stefanos Lazaridis, Richard Hudson and Robert Israel – whose skill at matching text and image equals that of Richard Peduzzi, Karl-Ernst Herrmann, Lucio Fanti and Ezio Frigerio); his ability to tap into European history, culture and thought to create an informed background to a production; his refusal to submit to the demands of tradition or the limitations of naturalism; and his deep commitment to 'renovatio' and innovation, particularly in the classics. To consider Miller's work in its proper context, it must be set alongside that of his peers in the European theatre – Patrice Chéreau in France, Peter Stein in Germany, Giorgio Strehler and Luca Ronconi in Italy. Indeed, Miller's Old Vic had much in common with Chéreau's Théâtre des Amandiers, Stein's Schaubühne, Strehler's Théâtre de l'Europe and Ronconi's Teatro Stabile di Torino.

Like Miller, Patrice Chéreau is an actor-turned-director with a reputation for revitalising the classics in a strikingly visual manner, and a strong affinity with the eighteenth century – displayed in Mozart operas and a series of Marivaux plays. His production of Marivaux's *La Dispute* (1976) demonstrated many directorial characteristics which he shares with Miller. The atmospheric lighting became part of the dramatic action – hauntingly chiaroscuro, with vivid side-lighting, as in Miller's *King Lear*. The mobile pillars and high walls of Richard Peduzzi's architectonic set were echoed in Richard Hudson's designs for Miller's *Bussy D'Ambois*, while the setting itself – a moonlit château garden, where lovers flirt amidst shrubs and hedges – evoked the Fragonard air of Miller's *Marriage of Figaro* at the Coliseum.

Chéreau's evident taste for the epic – *Peer Gynt* (1981), a four-and-a-half-

hour *Hamlet* (1988), a spectacular semi-underwater *Massacre at Paris* (1972)
– reached its apotheosis with his famously controversial *Ring* cycle at Bayreuth (1976), an 'updating' as effective as Miller's 'Mafia' *Rigoletto*. Taking
his cue from Shaw's view of *The Ring* as an anti-capitalist, revolutionary tract,
Chéreau replaced its traditional mythical world with an abstract mix of the
late nineteenth (the first staging of the complete *Ring* cycle was in 1876) and
twentieth centuries. The director and his regular designer, Richard Peduzzi,
exploited Bayreuth's vast technical resources to the full to make a series of
dramatic visual statements onstage – the hydro-electric dam on the Rhine,
the 'Industrial Revolution' of Mime's forge – similar to those achieved by
Miller in his work with Richard Hudson and Robert Israel.

A comparison can also be made between Miller and Peter Stein. Stein ran
the Schaubühne in Berlin as a collective where the political ideology
governed everything from the choice of repertoire to an emphasis on the
ensemble. His politically based interpretations always ran the risk of having a
reductive effect on the play, whereas Miller's concerns operate on a much
broader cultural level. Stein's political commitment is partly responsible for
his serious (and respectful) attitude to theatre production – he lacks the
playful, irreverent spirit which distinguishes Miller's work even in Racine or
Ibsen. Like Brook, Stein requires unusually long rehearsal periods (two
months minimum), which produce seamless ensemble work and perfectly
choreographed effects. Miller generally uses four and a half weeks for
rehearsals, which enables the cast to retain a certain spontaneity of performance, and gives it freedom to develop further once the production has
opened.

Stein has staged little comedy: the tone of his *Falstaff* was dark, cynical and
cruel. In turn, in his production Miller avoided slapstick just as carefully as
Stein, but nevertheless managed to combine the opera's humour and melancholy into one harmonious vision. Norman Platt, Artistic Director of the late
Kent Opera, recalls:

Miller handled the penultimate scene, where Falstaff comes out of the river, quite
beautifully. Falstaff came on through a fence at the side – it was superbly lit by Nick
Chelton towards evening, and gradually grew darker as the scene went on – and as he
tried to get his boots off and put his feet in a bowl of water, people came on behind the
fence and stood watching him. He called for a drink, and the chap who brought it just
stood there staring at him – what on earth was he doing, sitting there absolutely
soaked with his feet in a bowl of water? It was entirely wordless, achieved purely by
expression. Jonathan managed to make that short scene simultaneously deeply touching and irresistibly funny. (*personal communication*)

Stein's *Falstaff* did display one of the great strengths which he has in
common with Miller – an acknowledgement of the past, and a firm belief in

its value. The galleried timber set – like an Elizabethan theatre (the underlying motif, in fact, for the set of Miller's *Otello*, companion piece to *Falstaff*)
– of Stein's *Falstaff* recognised the opera's Shakespearian origin; his *Phedra* –
like Miller's *Andromache* – struck a balance between the worlds of Greek
myth and seventeenth-century France; and in his *Otello* the de Chirico
perspectives of Lucio Fanti's sets combined with Moidele Bickel's Italian
Renaissance costumes to create a modern view of the past.

While Miller sees theatre as essentially improvised and 'raffish', Peter
Stein has often shown a fondness for pictorial spectacle that harkens back to
nineteenth-century naturalism. The enormous, scrupulously realistic sets for
Stein's *Three Sisters* were so impressive that they tended to overshadow the
cast (while the austere sets for Miller's production were specifically designed
to focus all the attention on the cast); a forest of real birch trees had the same
effect in his *Summerfolk*, as did the real coal used to stoke the engine-room
boilers in his production of *The Hairy Ape*. But Stein's scenic spectacles are
so articulate that they can evoke a multi-layered social and cultural world
onstage – the sixteenth century in *Shakespeare's Memory* and *As You Like It*,
for instance, just as Miller did with the eighteenth century for *The Magic
Flute*. Like Miller, Stein achieves this effect through detailed research and
powerfully imaginative stagecraft. His remarkable work in this vein at the
Schaubühne in the 1970s and early 1980s established the theatre as precisely
the focal point of dramatic innovation that the Old Vic became under Miller's
artistic direction.

Connections can be found between the directorial work of Miller and
Giorgio Strehler and Luca Ronconi. Strehler – the co-founder (with Paolo
Grassi in 1947) and director of the Piccolo Teatro di Milano, as well as the
Artistic Director of the Theatre de l'Europe in Paris – is particularly
renowned for his work in the classics: a series of Goldoni and Mozart
revivals, a monumental *Simon Boccanegra*, and an epic conflation of Shakespeare's history cycle. Ronconi also relishes the challenge of epic theatre –
his work has ranged from *The Oresteia* to O'Neill's *Strange Interlude*, as well as
Orlando Furioso played in a vast arena with horses and carts hurtling through
the audience, a nine-hour production of Holz's *Ignorabimus*, and Purcell's
Fairy Queen staged as an open-air extravaganza in two acres of the Boboli
Gardens in Florence and involving oxen, swans, horses and dozens of
carriages. Strehler acknowledges the direct influence of the actor-directors
Louis Jouvet and Jacques Copeau, the mime artist Etienne Decroux and the
writer-director Bertolt Brecht. Strehler is a devout Brechtian, as his productions of *Galileo* and *The Threepenny Opera* testify; and Brecht has also
affected much of Ronconi's work, even in his production of Goldoni's *La
serva amorosa*, played on a virtually bare stage against a white traverse curtain.

Miller, however, has never subscribed to Brechtian dogma. Early on in his career he directed Alexander Goehr's opera *Arden Must Die*, and the composer recalled that 'he characterised it very differently from the original Hamburg production, which was very Brechtian in the tradition of Caspar Neher – Jonathan is not by nature Brechtian, and he moved away from all that'. When Miller tackled his only Brecht work, *Mahagonny*, for the Los Angeles Music Center, he avoided Brecht's didactic staging techniques and ideology, and his production stripped away the rigid trappings of signs, half-curtains and Marxist dialectic. Brecht and Weill intended the piece as a modern morality play portraying the greed and excess of Mahagonny, an imaginary American city of gold and pleasure where the only crime is an inability to pay the bill. The première of *Mahagonny* in Nazi Germany in 1930 caused a riot. Miller gave it added bite by setting it in the early days of Hollywood, bringing the action uncomfortably close to home for the Los Angeles audience.

Like Miller, both Strehler and Ronconi are highly responsive to the visual arts, and their work is rich in allusions to (principally Italian) painters (Bernardo Bellotto and Jacopo Marieschi for Strehler's *Don Giovanni*, Fra Galgario for his *Marriage of Figaro*) and architecture (the ornate onstage façade of the Teatro Olimpico at Vicenza served as the background for Ronconi's production of *The Bacchae* in Vienna, while towering Palladian colonnades framed Strehler's *Simon Boccanegra* and *Don Giovanni*). For all three directors, the lighting is just as important as the set – Miller, Strehler and Ronconi all make striking use of silhouette and chiaroscuro. Ronconi is particularly daring on a scenic level – the steep rakes and sharp angles of his production of *The Legend of Tsar Sultan* rivalled those of Miller's *Tosca* and *Andromache*. Inevitably, all three have been drawn to the great works of the classical repertory – the plays of Shakespeare and Aeschylus, the Chekhov quartet and the Mozart operas. Miller and Strehler both staged *King Lear* with striking, haunting simplicity, setting their productions in a dark, charred and bare space: a brutal, abstract world in an unspecified past. But while Miller drew on anthropology and social history to set his *Tempest* in the seventeenth-century context of Europe reaching out to the New World, Strehler staged it as a study in theatricality, with Prospero as a director-figure, Ariel soaring through the air on a deliberately unconcealed wire, and the scenery collapsing at the climax like the striking of a set at the end of a production, as Ariel ran out through the auditorium to freedom. There were many visual similarities between the two productions – in both, the opening storm at sea was evoked by billowing blue silk drapes, and followed by a sudden, magical transformation to a bare, sandy stage; Caliban was portrayed as a black slave rather than as a fish-like monster; and atmospheric lighting and baroque music were used throughout to exquisite effect.

Miller and Strehler both took care to set their Mozart productions in the eighteenth century, though Strehler left their Enlightenment aspects under-stated. While Miller's *Marriage of Figaro* was marked by its restrained humour and social realism, Strehler's production featured the broad comedy of *commedia dell'arte*. Likewise, Strehler's *Don Giovanni* had Leporello and the Don rolling about on the ground together, while Miller treated their relation-ship according to the eighteenth-century master–servant convention. Miller reflected the themes of *Don Giovanni* in his setting, choosing Goya's dark, late eighteenth-century Spanish Enlightenment world as the background to the action, whereas Strehler went to Italian art (chiefly the landscapes of Bernardo Bellotto) for a more pictorial effect. In addition, both directors have also made highly successful forays into the seventeenth-century French world of Corneille: just as Strehler visually acknowledged the baroque style of *The Theatrical Illusion* in the design scheme for his production, so Miller reflected the elaborately contrived style of *The Liar* in the false architectural frontages and undisguised wooden flats of Peter J. Davison's obviously artificial sets.

Ronconi's work is more idiosyncratic than Strehler's, with a daring use of stage design that parallels Miller's work with Richard Hudson and Philip Prowse. Miller's *Merchant of Venice* took place in the late nineteenth century, while Ronconi's production – a scenic spectacle in the Max Reinhardt tradition – unfolded against an Elizabethan financial background of safes, treasure and gold coins. Ronconi is also a skilled adapter – his *Revenger's Tragedy* was set in the Habsburg court at Vienna, his pre-Chéreau *Valkyrie* in Germany during the Industrial Revolution, and his *Phedra* in a late nine-teenth-century observatory. His production of Jommelli's *Fetonte* – like Miller's *Magic Flute* – took place not in the world of ancient myth, but in the eighteenth century, the period of its composition (it was played out on the various levels of a vast open-fronted palace, the rooms cluttered with huge astronomical instruments).

When faced with the challenge of staging ancient Greek tragedy in the twentieth century, Miller and Ronconi have responded in similar ways, updating the setting to the late Renaissance as a 'bridging point' between the present and the remote past. Ronconi's production of *The Bacchae* was set against the background of the Teatro Olimpico at Vicenza during the seventeenth century, complete with a baroque score. Miller's production of Aeschylus' *Prometheus Bound* (in an adaptation by Robert Lowell) for the Yale Repertory Theatre is here described by its founding director, Robert Brustein:

Our resident designer, Michael Annals, was responsible for the design – an awesome creation so huge we had to remove the entire stage floor. Miller had set the play in an undesignated country during the seventeenth century – probably Spain during the Inquisition, though he wanted this to remain vague. Annals provided statue-bearing niches and platforms of tortured, aging brick that went upward and downward as far as the eye could reach. 'It's supposed to suggest a structure far larger than you can see,' explained Miller in an interview, 'sort of a brick kiln, a Pharos or huge lighthouse on the Mediterranean going thousands of feet into the sea; no specific time, but some sort of decaying seventeenth-century culture that has gone bad. The characters are prisoners, they put on the play in this eternal imprisonment as a punishment' ... The result was a thoroughly modernized version of the ancient play, with contemporary resonances echoing all forms of tyranny ... but a version that nevertheless maintained a certain historical distance.[13]

Schooled in the principles of scientific philosophy, Miller has brought the intellectual rigour and clarity of Karl Popper's critical rationalism to the often vacuous and superficial world of the theatre. He is probably the only director to have written a book on Darwinism, and evolutionary theory is central to an understanding of Miller's work – it is a body of work, not separate items, based upon the variation and adaptation of an underlying aesthetic.

The evolution of Miller's work is visually exemplified by the set design (by Robert Israel) for his most recent production to date, *Don Giovanni* at the 1990 Maggio Musicale in Florence (part of Miller's ongoing Mozart cycle, itself an instance of his refinement and modification of previous work). The high, bricked-up windows evoked one of Miller's earliest productions, *Prometheus Bound*, while the creation of a shifting cityscape onstage was an expansion of one of his latest, *Mahagonny*. The oppressive grey walls poised at precarious angles, with allusions to neo-classicism set against touches of surrealism, emphasised elements from previous Miller productions ranging from *Measure for Measure*, *Tosca* and *The Emperor* to *Andromache*, *Bussy D'Ambois* and *La Traviata* – despite having different designers, all these productions displayed and developed the same aesthetic. Background scenes in the *Don Giovanni* were glimpsed through frontstage doors and archways – the Chardin-esque effect of rooms behind rooms, which Miller had employed over a decade earlier for *Figaro* and later adapted to a much larger scale for *King Lear* at the Old Vic.

Revelation is the operative word in Miller's work as a director: his revelations in casting are matched by his revelations in repertoire, unearthing long-neglected classics like *Bussy D'Ambois* and *The Liar* and showing familiar works – *Rigoletto* and *The Mikado*, *King Lear* and *The School for Scandal* – in a fresh light, the light of 'renovatio', reappraisal, redefinition, and renewal.

[13] Robert Brustein, *Making Scenes* (New York: Limelight Editions, 1984), p. 32.

II

WORK IN PROGRESS:
A DIALOGUE WITH
JONATHAN MILLER

Past performances

BEGINNINGS 1934–1970

Michael Romain   Do you remember your first impressions of the theatre as a child?

Jonathan Miller   The first thing I ever saw in the theatre was the garish brilliance of war-time pantomime – *Jack and the Beanstalk*. Lots of little girls in character shoes and bright orange make-up, and that brilliant phosphorescent light of old-fashioned English pantomime. I remember the loudness of the voices, the artificiality of the singing, and falling hopelessly in love with the Principal Girl. I was absolutely unaware of the tacky unconvincingness of the scenery – as soon as the curtain went up, it disclosed a world of such wonderful, artificial, fantastic brilliance, that it seemed to me to be the acme of desirability.

MR   Were you taken to the theatre often by your parents?

JM   I started going to the theatre with them after the war, and that was a different sort of experience altogether – I was much older, already in my early teens. I was taken to the Old Vic to see *Bartholomew Fair*, and *Henry V* with people like Alec Clunes in the title role, Roger Livesey as the Chorus and Paul Rogers as the Dauphin.

MR   Paul Rogers was later to appear in your production of *The Freeway* and play Gloucester in your *King Lear* – both at the Old Vic again.

JM   That's right – it's been very strange to make contact with actors whom I had seen and admired in my youth, and who were simply creatures of the stage. They had as much relation to me as brilliantly illuminated fish seen through the glass of an aquarium. I could no more inhabit their medium than they could ever come into mine. The experience of actually working with people whom I had previously seen on the stage was extraordinary. It wasn't so much that I could scarcely believe my luck at being able to work with people I had so admired in the past – it was a much more complicated experience. I could not relate the person who I knew – with all his pauses, his imperfection, his age and his clothes – to the person who seemed to have no texture to his clothes or face, just this brilliant aquarium presence that he had on the other side of the footlights (when indeed there *were* still footlights).

MR   What else did you see?

JM   I remember a suite of plays done under the direction of Hugh Hunt at the New Theatre with Yvonne Mitchell, George Benson and Michael Redgrave, including *Love's Labour's Lost* and *She Stoops to Conquer*, with Redgrave as Marlowe.

MR   Had you already developed a preference for the classics?

JM   Those were the only type of plays that I ever saw. At that time I had absolutely no feeling that I would ever enter that world. It wasn't that it seemed infinitely remote – it was simply a different type of experience. It was very similar in some ways to the experience of plunging into the darkness under the Mappin Terraces to the Zoo's aquarium – there was this other world behind the invisible transparency of glass, a brilliantly illuminated cube in which things were weightlessly suspended in their vivid magnificence.

MR   Were you interested in the idea of the 'fourth wall' at this point?

JM   No, I didn't think of anything of that sort – I was simply enchanted by the transparency of the fourth wall. I didn't know the term and I was unaware of the idea of a fourth wall – I was enchanted by what the fourth wall, in all its wonderful transparency, disclosed. It disclosed a world illuminated by a light which never escaped into the world in which I sat in the darkness. What enchanted me about both the theatre and the aquarium was the annihilating darkness in which one sat as a member of the audience, scarcely aware of oneself, only raptly attentive to this brilliantly illuminated world which lay beyond the transparency, which was instantly disclosed as soon as that wonderfully, suggestively illuminated curtain rose.

MR You've often used curtains in the designs for your productions – *Bussy D'Ambois*, *La Traviata* and *The Liar*, for example. Is this a result of your early experiences as a theatregoer?

JM I don't think so. As I say, I cannot in any way connect my subsequent work in the theatre with my experiences as a child in the audience. It seems to be a different world. To have penetrated into that aquarium, to be a participant in it, to be a director in it – I cannot in any way relate that to what it was like to be a witness of it. I never had any desire to penetrate into it, or to manage or direct it, at all – it was simply something which I found enchanting at every visit.

MR How did it feel to be the Artistic Director of the theatre which you visited so often as a child?

JM I cannot put the two together. They are such different modes of experience that I cannot relate one to the other. As I stand on the stage sometimes during rehearsals and look out into the darkness where I once sat, I cannot in any sense identify myself with that darkened, childish spectator who once looked into the world in which I now stand as a director. Nor can I, as I stand on that stage, feel my actors to be in any sense like the way they looked from the position that I watched them from. They are two absolutely different modes of existence – it's really rather like *Alice*. I've always been fascinated by penetrable interfaces. What is enchanting about *Alice Through the Looking Glass*, and what has always intrigued me about it, is the thought of this mercury surface through which she frictionlessly passes. I have always been fascinated by the room that lies on the other side of the transparency of the mirror.

MR Rather like passing through a proscenium arch?

JM Yes, it is. Or rather, put it the other way – going through a proscenium, going through a mirror, going through the glass of an aquarium, penetrating into the spherical glass of those little paperweights in which a snowstorm is to be seen, is something which has always fascinated me. Some people would say, 'Oh, that's because you're interested in a fantasy world.' It's not that what goes on in that world is more luminous and interesting than what goes on in my own life, but that I've always been fascinated by the idea that, if one could only find the right entrance, one could slip through the mercury surface of the mirror – wonderfully and frictionlessly penetrable as it is for Alice in *The Looking Glass*, or as in the aquarium where you can't even see the glass (there isn't even a proscenium arch), or like the other side of a silver screen surrounded by darkness in a cinema. What interests me is the co-existence of the world in which one exists as a spectator and the brilliantly illuminated world in which a 'spectated action' goes on. I can't stress too strongly that it's nothing to do with the fact that the action seen seems more glamorous or more interesting than the action in which one participates as a perfectly ordinary person in the real world. It's the idea that there are two worlds that run parallel to one another.

MR   How did you feel in this respect when you entered that world of the stage as a performer?

JM   When I had my first experience of performing on the stage, I did have the feeling of penetrating into this brilliant world – I always looked forward to those enchanted occasions once a year when I did school revues, when somehow all school rules were alleviated. One was allowed to be a performer in this brilliant box – one was in the aquarium for the first time. I sometimes feel that, even now, when I stand in the darkened wings and look onto the stage at people acting with one another, disregarding one's own managerial gaze – it isn't any longer the gaze of the spectator looking at it from the viewpoint designed for the audience by the director, but a gaze looking sidelong at it through the slips of scenery and ropes in which the action is somehow going on for the benefit of spectators that you, as a person standing in the wings, can't see. I never get tired of standing in the wings watching it, because you're much closer up to the action than you would be as a member of the audience. You see the imperfections, and that wonderful moment when the actors plunge offstage with their brilliant artificial smiles which are meant for one another in their role as protagon-ists of the play – you see the smile disappear or transform itself into a smile intended for the stage-manager or for you the director standing there in the wings, as the actors come out of the swimming-bath of the action, shaking themselves like spaniels, and go backstage.

MR   Your comic forte revealed itself as soon as you began performing in the school revues.

JM   I never acted at school – I just did revue sketches. At Cambridge I was Sir Politic Would-Be in the Marlowe Society's production of *Volpone*, and in *Bartholomew Fair* I played the madman – coming nowhere near the enchanted, sprite-like madman played by Paul Rogers in the Old Vic production.

MR   You were often compared at the time to Danny Kaye.

JM   For some reason, as a 14-year-old boy I became completely intoxicated with the image of Danny Kaye. I just wanted to be as much like him as I could possibly be – I was star-struck. I also loved Betty Grable when I was a small boy – I liked her legs and her blonde hair. It was the same sort of infatuation that I had for the radiantly virtuous, wonderfully attractive and textureless girl who I saw in pantomime.

MR   *Beyond the Fringe*, which you co-wrote and performed in between 1960 and 1964 in the West End and on Broadway, was your most sustained work as a performer.

JM   Yes – I was not simply a performer in that, but was a participant with Alan, Peter and Dudley in writing it and hacking it together, and suddenly finding that we had created a theatrical novel.

MR   Did you expect its success?

JM   I think we did – it sounds arrogant to say it, but I think we knew that it was funnier than anything we had ever seen. It wasn't because it was satirical. It was inadvertently satirical – because, in fact, we didn't come from the straightforward theatrical tradition, there was a broader range of topics and we naturally strayed into all sorts of things which seemed silly and foolish at the time. We were creatures of the post-war generation, and that was the point at which English society was undergoing a great deal of introspection and change. We coincided with the things that happened – perhaps in some ways more significantly – in other areas of theatre, like *Look Back in Anger*. Things were on the move, and we simply expressed the mood of the time – we were creatures of that time.

MR   To what extent did *Beyond the Fringe* contribute to your subsequent performance as a director?

JM   In a purely practical sense it gave me an entrée, as we all became famous through being part of a very, very successful show. And it gave me a much greater understanding of performers because I had actually stood up onstage and withstood the difficulties of an audience night after night. It was obviously a highly restricted type of performance, but nevertheless to go out there and battle with an audience gave me a deep understanding of what was involved. Also, I became tremendously familiar with timing, as indeed the four of us did, and we became really very accomplished technicians of comedy. We learned to experiment and refine it – I think I'm quite skilled at that now, and can give very good advice to actors.

MR   What do you think made George Devine ask you to direct *Under Plain Cover* at the Royal Court in 1962: your debut as a director?

JM   Desperation! Here was this John Osborne play which I gather no one else wanted to do. John Dexter had probably been invited to direct both plays in the double bill, and I think that with an unerring eye for the fashionable he chose to do the first one, *The Blood of the Bambergs*, because it was about Princess Margaret's wedding and he knew that it would create a fascinating scandal. Oddly enough, it turned out to be the least interesting of the two; and this rather modest, idiosyncratic and cranky little number – which I did because no one else, I think, would touch it – was my introduction to directing. Devine asked me out of desperation, and that was an example of my being shoehorned into the theatre by the reputation which I had from *Beyond the Fringe*.

MR   What were your feelings at this point about medicine?

JM   Well, I thought I was going to go back to it – I really did. I think I was in some state of disillusion, not with medicine but certainly with the social life that went with medicine – the unconscionably long hours. The young junior hospital doctors complain, quite rightly, about the hours they work now, but those are nothing compared to the hours that we worked – and there was no body that spoke up for us in those days.

MR   Was the theatre a temporary respite for you then?

JM   Yes, it was in some ways. I suppose the reason why I didn't go back to medicine was that by comparison with the liberty of the theatre – the fact, for instance, that you could choose your own times of the day to rehearse – the life of a young doctor was a terrible constraint. At that time the ladder was very long and very narrow, with a lot of rotten rungs on it, and if you put a foot wrong you could wait until you were 40 to become a consultant. That meant long hours of very uncongenial residential work in hospitals where residencies were appalling, food was dreadful, the hours were very bad and the prospects were very poor. Also, I was married by that time and I knew how many people crucified their families on the unremitting demands of junior medicine. So I was therefore very vulnerable and susceptible to the appeals of the theatre, but it wasn't because the theatre was glamorous. I never really found it as glamorous as it was when I sat, this darkened and invisible spectator, watching the illuminated aquarium. I didn't feel, as I went into the theatre, 'At last, I'm in the aquarium!' I could not marry the image that I had of it with the image that I now have of being in it – simply another place to work.

MR   *Under Plain Cover* was your very first production – do you think that your direction was largely instinctive?

JM   Well it seemed very instinctive, yes. I was obviously anxious and had misgivings – I knew nothing about it. But I found that as long as one was prepared to say, 'I don't know what I ought to do here – tell me what I ought to do', then there was always someone to give me advice.

MR   George Devine?

JM   George Devine was admirable. I had great difficulties in the first technical rehearsal with the moving of the scenery – the set was a house which opened up like a shell – and there were all sorts of problems which I just didn't know how to handle. Devine, in a masterly way, came down and solved the problems with and for me. As far as directing the actors was concerned, I think that they appreciated a fresh eye and another way of thinking about how to perform. I don't think at any time I've ever had any really bad experiences with actors which I could put down to my not having been technically trained as a director. The same goes for my first opera as well – I never really felt any shortcoming by virtue of the fact that I wasn't trained. I slipped fairly effortlessly into both of those modes of direction: I could do it, and I think that is probably the only qualification you have to have. You need to feel, 'I think I know how to do this.'

MR   Your next production was *The Old Glory*, which launched the American Place Theatre in New York in 1964 – did that also come your way by chance?

JM   Yes, I knew Robert Lowell, the author, independently – I was living in New York at the time doing *Beyond the Fringe* and Lowell was a friend of my brother-in-law, so we were very well acquainted socially. I moved in that circle associated with the *New York Review of Books*. Lowell, again, had been having difficulty finding a director for *The Old Glory* – it was originally commissioned, I think, by some sort of grant given to him by the Ford Foundation to work in opera, with a view to it being a libretto of some sort.

It turned out to be a very large production – there was a lot of technical stuff and a great deal of management of vast numbers of people, like all the black slaves who had to be moved around and choreographed. There was a lot of surrealism too, particularly in the first part, *My Kinsman, Major Molineux*. But it all seemed to come easily to me – possibly because theatre has a lot in common with what one does as a child, which is making up games and themes.

MR You've always managed to retain a sense of the improvised in your work.

JM Well, yes, it's also to do with being a child. After all, most of what children do is, in fact, to pretend that things are something other than what they actually are. A child will get great pleasure out of putting its head down on a table and pushing a little wooden block around – by going 'Brrrrrr', it *is* a car.

MR So there's really no need for literal representation in the theatre.

JM No. It's all about pretence, and as long as you are, as it were, in touch with your childhood, I think you are probably a good director. A lot of what directing consists of is to do with being in touch with your childhood.

MR *The Old Glory* proved to be an enormous success with critics and audiences alike – did you consider pursuing a career as a director at that point?

JM No, I didn't really think about directing then either. As soon as I finished that production, I knew that I had to come back to London and seriously consider whether I was going back into medicine or not. I think that Pandora's Box had probably been opened by that time and I'd experienced the delights of liberty – the fact that at the end of a production I could take a few days off, or a month off, think about something else and not go to work. If you're working professionally in anything – law, medicine, accountancy or whatever – you finish one piece of work and the next morning you're back on another piece of work at 9.30 a.m., and you don't knock off until you've finished. What I liked about the theatre is what anyone in the arts enjoys, apart from the substantive work of the theatre – the bohemian openness of it all. It's very, very loosely textured, not tightly woven.

MR Was this what attracted you to the TV arts documentary series *Monitor* in 1964, with the flexible programming schedule that it offered?

JM I had no idea that I would get involved with anything like that. I went to see Huw Wheldon at the BBC and asked him whether I could learn how to make films, which seemed to be another medium that I would enjoy. He offered me the editorship of *Monitor*, which I rashly accepted and then immediately entered a dark tunnel of fruitless labour in which I really came in for a great deal of rejection and criticism. It was the first time since I'd been in the theatre and away from medicine that I encountered harsh, consistent public attacks.

MR   Why were you attacked? Looking at your ideas for the series, they seem very similar to those featured today on *The Late Show*.

JM   I think they were – many of the things that did happen later were the result of initiatives that I think I was the first to introduce. It was much more informal than anything that had been done before, and it was much less committed to the idea of there being a *beaux arts* – the whole of the *Monitor* series under Wheldon and his immediate successors was committed to the idea that there was this world of excellence and great artists whom you pursued like game-hunters. I was much more interested, first of all, in the process of art – what goes into doing it. I also wanted to lever open a gap to make room for things which perhaps in the early 1960s were not considered respectable – all sorts of things like Pop Art, Happenings, and the crude, unfinished business of rehearsal where you see the creative process actually happening.

That didn't happen very much in the early *Monitor* – respectable big OMs and CHs were visited. I introduced people like Susan Sontag, which instantly produced a fall-out that has scarcely ceased. It was at the point when she was first beginning to think about 'camp' – before she wrote the essay – and she spoke about the appeal of kitsch and rubbish. That, of course, appalled people, who actually thought that rubbish was what it was – rubbish. Kitsch and bad taste clearly marked a boundary between the clean and the dirty. In a sense, what I was doing was the equivalent of what Mary Douglas wrote about later on in *Purity and Danger* – I was violating clear-cut categories, and therefore making people very anxious. In very many areas of human activity, security and confidence are given by the existence of very clear-cut divisions, boundaries and frames – none more so than in the arts, where there are clear-cut distinctions between high art, low art, popular art and official art, the notion of the Academy, the Salon, the official performance of classical music.

Now, of course, all that is being broken down, and I think that I was fairly early on in the field of trying to break those barriers and break down the distinctions. When you do that, of course, it causes a great deal of unhappiness. The reaction caused unhappiness to me, because some people just thought that I was a trendy monster floundering around. I achieved my aims with great calculation and deliberation, because I've always been interested in making the frontiers visible. Most of the time when people operate on the assumption that there are frontiers, they do it without having any vision of the frontiers at all – therefore when you start to get near the borders, the border guards get very, very anxious and are quite eager to shoot people jumping across. Now, you see, in a way the fall of the Berlin Wall is the culmination of a long process of wall-destructions which have been going on since the 1960s.

MR   *The Drinking Party*, your 1965 film version of Plato's *Symposium*, was another example of your ability to break down barriers.

JM   Yes, it was a demystification of the Greeks as these marmoreal figures.

MR   And also of the popular view of philosophy as dramatically inert.

JM   That's right. I messed it around a little bit – I put the characters into the present, with the same sentiments expressed in modern clothes. It became an old school reunion for a group of Classics scholars, and actually proved very successful – after the long year of contempt and mockery, I suddenly burst through into another period of sunlight, briefly. I recall one woman who pursued me with a great deal of venomous hatred for doing those things in *Monitor* – a journalist on the *Guardian*, who attacked every single one of my *Monitor* programmes because, again, she was an upholder of the mandarin approach to the arts.

     Now I've begun to meditate retrospectively, I can recognise all sorts of things – which I didn't think of at the time as belonging to a class of activities – as being a consistent return to an underlying theme: that is, surfaces, interfaces, frames, divisions, proscenium arches, the distinction between a representing world and a represented world, the idea of things which are transformed by geometrical perspective, things that are transformed by virtue of the fact that they go through a projector.

MR   This is almost Chomsky territory.

JM   It's partly Chomsky – that's why I'm interested in him, because he himself is interested in the notion of transformation. How do you preserve constant meanings under the surface of change?

MR   The idea of generative grammar?

1 Scene from *The Drinking Party*, from Plato's *Symposium*, with Alan Bennett (centre) and Leo McKern (head of table), BBC TV 1965

JM   It's got a relationship to that. While I am not a very good mathematician, there are certain issues in mathematics which deeply interest me. One of these is the notion of set theory and what is called 'mapping' – the idea that there is a set x and a set y, and the various items in set x can be mapped in a one-to-one relationship to the items in set y. That, after all, is what representation is. It's what graphs are about, what equations are about, and what the notion of functions is about. That again, I think, is a subset of a much larger range of concerns that I have: the fact that as a small child I should have been so intrigued by the idea of there being a world beyond the wall of the theatre, a world on the other side of the aquarium glass.

MR   Your next production, a TV film of *Alice in Wonderland* in 1966, gave you the chance to explore all of these themes on screen.

JM   Yes, it was all about dreaming. Dreaming is an internal world which bears a reference to a world that you live in and replays it in all sorts of dishevelled versions.

MR   You made remarkable use, in the film, of isolated images – the scene, for instance, where Alice passes a man in a large bath as she runs through the woods.

JM   That was my concern with the incidents that occur in dreams, which pass unnoticed at the time and only in retrospect seem odd. They seem odd because after the dream you are like the spectator on the other side of the aquarium glass, able to look at the contents of the aquarium and see it as exotic. When you are in the aquarium, in the dream, the events, being the natural denizens of that world, seem to be perfectly natural.

MR   You got away from the traditional fish heads and frog masks, too.

JM   There were several reasons why I did that. One was a negative reason – I knew that there was no way in which you could reproduce literally in realistic photography the effect that you can get so effortlessly in an engraving that lies on a page. There is no sense there that the characters are wearing masks – they are simply engraved figures that happen to have fishes' or frogs' heads. Whereas when you have real people you have to put them in a mask, and it is quite visibly a shaky mask or else a rather accomplished mask. Whichever way you care to look at it, whether it's a bad mask or a good mask, it's visibly a mask. On the page it is simply a frog footman – I had John Bird play the role with no mask or make-up at all.
   Those are the negative reasons. I realised that you could not use the

characters in the same way as they were used on the page, because the characters as represented on the page faded off imperceptibly into the grey grid of the text. That's partly because of that particular vignetting which is used on the page of Victorian illustrations, where you don't have a sharply cut-off edge – it just fades into the text. There's no clear-cut division between text and illustration – the illustrations just smoke out of the text. I knew that there was no way in which that could be done on film.

The positive reason for doing it was that I knew that in some sense the work was a *roman à clef*, that Dodgson was actually talking about people that the little girl, Liddell, would have known, that it was about the childhood of an Oxford girl who had grown up in the gardens and cloisters of Christ Church, Oxford. I wanted to reproduce the world of the Victorian child, with all that implies – the allusions, the ambiguities and so on. I knew that it wasn't simply a story for a child – it was also, we can see at this distance, a story about childhood, about growing up.

MR Was it this break with tradition that caused the controversy after the film was screened?

JM It caused a controversy simply because it did not do what was previously done.

MR You mean the Disney style?

JM Either the Disney style, or more probably the fact that it simply broke away from Tenniel. A lot of the time, you see, people work very automatically – precedent seems to be the only guide to subsequent performance. If this were the case, then all evolution would come to a standstill. You simply have to allow for the fact that what Darwin calls 'variation' is built into the very nature of reproduction. Things which have to be reproduced in order to exist quite unavoidably start to vary from the prototype – they start to depart from the prototype. In biology the reason for that is that the genetic material is unstable – it has a built-in tendency to generate mistakes. Now some of those mistakes are fatal, and cause the death of the organism at a very early stage before it even appears on the scene as a competitor. But the fact of such instability is the raw material of change and adaptation to new circumstances. I think something comparable happens in the arts, particularly the reproductive arts. For something to have to be reproduced means that there is the unavoidable possibility of it departing and drifting away from the prototype. It's an extremely interesting business.

33

MR   You developed these themes in your idea of the 'after-life' of a work of art in your book, *Subsequent Performances*.

JM   It extends to the after-life of anything. After all, the whole of evolution is the story of life's after-life. We are the after-life of trilobites. The passage of time in living nature – as opposed to inorganic nature, which merely wears away – introduces emergent, unprecedented novelties, and I've always been committed to the idea that novelty and invention are built into the enterprise. In the case of nature, the novelties are introduced without deliberate foresight; and even in the reproductive arts where there's no specific intention to introduce novelty, novelty will occur whether you like it or not, so you might as well be master of the process rather than victim of it.

   This is partly because of the nature of copying. Now if you have a mechanical copying process, such as printing, the change is merely a process of what one would call degradation. Second, third, fourth and ultimately hundredth generation prints taken off a copper plate simply get blurred – the basic format doesn't change, the resolution suffers and it simply degrades with each successive copy. But when copying is brought about not by a mechanical machine, but by the intervention of a human operator who undertakes to copy, the copying is not just a process of degradation, if it is that at all. It's a process of innovation, because, even if you don't want to, you can't copy faithfully. Even a genius like Mozart was quite incapable of copying his own performance of one of his own sonatas – he would irresistibly introduce variations.

   You can see this in a very simple way in an area which has nothing whatever to do with the arts. If you get people to stand in a row in front of you, make a series of gestures and ask the people to copy them, then although they will all see the same thing they will all copy it differently. That's not simply because their limbs are less capable – they are people who can vie with one another for the sensitivity and accuracy with which they take a full cup from the table to the sink, or pour sugar without spilling it, so it can't be a mechanical failure. It's because what they see, and think is being exemplified by what they see, differs from one person to the other. So the intervention of a human copier means that you have variation built into the system. So once again, one might as well be the master of the process – insofar as you can't be complete master, because many, many things creep in merely by virtue of the fact that the copying process is fraught with error.

   I'm thinking here of fundamental deep problems of the whole business of the reproductive arts. They are genetically unstable. In a way, it's not an accidental similarity. Some people might say, 'Oh, this is simply a tendentious analogy you're drawing between biological reproduction and artistic reproduction.' It's not at all tendentious – they are comparable situations in that they involve the idea of second, third and fourth generations of something which purports to be the same thing. Rabbits of the nth generation are recognised by a breeder as being instances of rabbits, but nevertheless they are quite clearly not in fact faithful reproductions of the parents of the first generation. Simply to go through that series of genetic cascades from one generation to another is to introduce variation – thank God, otherwise we would never have become anything other than trilobites.

MR *Prometheus Bound*, which you directed at Yale in 1967, is an instance of this – Aeschylus through Robert Lowell, the adapter, through you, the director.

JM Once again, there was a whole series of refractions. There, of course, the processes were quite deliberate. Even if Lowell had set himself the task of a so-called faithful translation of Aeschylus, the problem would have been almost insuperable merely because going from Greek into English is something which introduces variation and drifts the thing off course. Even to do it again in Greek, two thousand years later, would have meant that the genetic apparatus would have expressed itself in a different way.

I'm very interested in this whole idea of double domains. Johannson, the great early twentieth-century geneticist, introduced the distinction between genotypes and phenotypes. The genotype is the set of as yet unexpressed genetic instructions contained in the fertilised ovum; the phenotype is the final performance of that genetic script. As any literate biologist understands, the genotype does not guarantee identical performances – it depends where the script is going to be performed. If you perform the genotype of a Japanese in the environment of California, he will necessarily be six inches larger than his Japanese counterpart. The genetic instructions are the same, but under different circumstances that genotype has a different phenotypic expression.

MR Your decision to give *Prometheus Bound* a seventeenth-century setting was an example of the deliberate process, then.

JM That's right – I was trying to be master of the change rather than merely the inadvertent victim of it by saying, 'Let's try to actually self-consciously control the otherwise insuperable problem of taking a play from remote antiquity, which has undergone very little in the way of subsequent performance, and see what happens if it is refracted through a Renaissance period in which, in fact, these works were beginning to be rediscovered and "renovatio" was going on, added to which there is also the vision of the twentieth century.' These are complex superimpositions which you have to be self-consciously aware of, rather than thinking you're doing the thing faithfully and deluding yourself because, in fact, as you think you are doing something faithfully these inadvertent drifts away from the prototype will occur whether you think you are doing it or not.

MR   In 1968 you directed a TV film version of M. R. James' ghost story *Oh Whistle and I'll Come to You* – what was your attitude towards its super-natural theme?

JM   I've always been interested in the supernatural – partly because I don't believe in it and at the same time am very frightened of it. People often say, 'Surely that's hypocritical?' No, it is possible with one's rational mind to dismiss the possibility of a life after death, or of there being supernatural things in the world, and at the same time to be deeply scared – because there are parts of one's nervous system to which one doesn't have access. The uncanny is capable of grabbing even the most rational.

MR   How did you see James' story?

JM   Well, the Professor, this strange crusty bachelor who had denied so much of his emotional life, was caught out by it, as so often happens – one's emotions, feelings and impulses, which one denies and represses, lie in wait and can sometimes ambush one. This was the story of an ambush.

MR   Your direction and camera-work were extremely effective – the cross-cutting, panning and long-shot, the use of silence.

JM   I wanted to create an air of foreboding, silence, and the intimation that things were hovering beneath the surface. I suppose that my interest in the supernatural is again part of this interest that I have in there being two domains – that beyond the world of what is visible lies the possibility that there might be something else, if only one could get the right entrance. It's not because I believe that this is the case, but simply that I'm preoccupied with the relationship between worlds which lie very close together, separated by an absolutely impenetrable barrier which every now and then, magically, is perhaps opened, its impenetrability relieved to let something come through the opening.

MR   Which happens at the climax of your film . . .

JM   Yes – something escapes from the other world. Now, other worlds for me are not necessarily supernatural worlds – supernatural worlds are just a very good way of expressing the notion of there being another world. I suppose the film that most influenced me as a child – although when I saw it again I found it absurdly sentimental – was the Powell and Pressburger film *A Matter of Life and Death*. Again, I was enchanted by the idea that somehow, up there in the constellations, there was this other world of people after death.

MR   Like your *Alice in Wonderland, Oh Whistle and I'll Come to You* was a startlingly original piece of film-making – were you particularly attracted to film at this point?

JM   I enjoyed doing it, chiefly because of all the possibilities that the medium had. I had always enjoyed projectors and magic lanterns when I was a child – again, the idea of there being a transformation, something travelled along, the phosphorescent beam, this fluted cone of light which invisibly conveyed an image to a screen, which did not in fact reconstitute itself as an image until it landed on the screen. I was always fascinated by that – the idea that no matter where in the beam a screen was lowered, wherever it intersected the beam an image would constitute itself.

MR   What went wrong with your first feature film, *Take a Girl like You* for Columbia Pictures in 1970?

JM   Every now and then you make terrible mistakes about the genre or your own motives for doing the film. I wanted to make a commercial movie. I thought, 'Well, here are people making money out of films, I've made no money out of any of the things that I've done, so I might as well try and do it.' It was a horror. It caught up with me the other day, late at night in California – I was having a sleepless night, and quite suddenly this appalling thing came back at me on late, late television at about 4.00 a.m. I had another shemozzle later on with *Tristan and Isolde* – it was an unfortunate circumstance, something I shouldn't have done. I was flattered by the invitation to do it, flattered by the idea of co-operating with an artist like David Hockney, and thought it would be a wonderful thing – of course, you misunderstand your own motives and the possibility that is inherent in a project. There were no possibilities inherent in that project.

MR   You returned to the theatre immediately after *Take a Girl like You* to direct a series of plays – *Twelfth Night, Julius Caesar* and *Hamlet* – for the Oxford and Cambridge Shakespeare Company, working on a very small scale – do you prefer to work in that way?

JM   Practically all the things I've done on a small scale have been the things I've really enjoyed. They're congenial small groups – you don't have a gala audience in wait, you don't get ambushed by them. I would put together as my happiest times in the theatre – and in most respects my most achieved productions – the plays with the Oxford and Cambridge Shakespeare Company, my work with Kent Opera, the tiny little 'roundabout' production of *Measure for Measure* that I did for Olivier, and *The Emperor* which I did for the Theatre Upstairs at the Royal Court. In all of those circumstances you sacrifice money and do it with unself-consciousness, not with any sense of self-congratulation or virtue. In the case of *The Emperor*, I gave my fee to pay for the set. Those have been the great occasions, and I think that in the dark hours of the depressed early morning you recognise that sometimes you have betrayed your own best interests by allowing yourself to be seduced into working on a big scale for glamorous institutions – almost all of them have got some sort of Midas curse attached to them.

MR   You've done that very rarely, though.

JM   Well, yes, only a couple of times. That doesn't mean, of course, that I haven't had successful encounters with the large.

MR   *Tosca* at the Maggio Musicale in Florence, *Rigoletto* at the London Coliseum, *The Mikado* at the Los Angeles Music Center and the Houston Grand Opera ...

JM   I've had successful, and indeed happy, encounters with the large, yes, but the deeply satisfying sense of community – in that Ivan Illich sense of convivial communities – has almost invariably been associated with very small groups.

MR   How did you approach your first production for the Oxford and Cambridge Shakespeare Company, *Twelfth Night*?

JM   It was a Tudor *Twelfth Night*. We had a tremendous amount of Monteverdi in it, because I felt that there were all sorts of passions contained in some of the Monteverdi madrigals that just kept the thing aloft with a sense of repressed, stoical intensity. I'd quite like to do that play again.

MR   Your *Julius Caesar*, based very much on the painting of Giorgio de Chirico, was the first time that you put your idea of historical parallax to use on stage.

JM I struck a balance between the idea of an antiquity that is nominally referred to (I say nominally because the fact that it's mentioned doesn't mean that it's being *used* in that way), the nominal Republican Rome, the actual Tudor artefact and the twentieth century – with all the subsequent theatrical developments which lie between them. Unless you take note of the three planes which co-exist and of this notion of historical parallax – the idea that if you move your head slightly, these planes separate out – you don't confront the problem. People think that what you do is straightforward – 'It's about Rome, so you do it in Rome.' This makes the fatal confusion which philosophers point out – but, again, theatre people seem completely unaware of the distinction – between 'use' and 'mention'. The fact that something is *mentioned* doesn't mean that it's being *used* in the way that you might think by virtue of the mention.

To mention Republican Rome does not mean that Shakespeare is using it in that way – he's using it metaphorically to deal with his own time. You can't even take that literally now, because things have moved on such a long way. De Chirico was an Italian painter who made allusions in his work to both classical Rome and the Renaissance in which Shakespeare lived, but who was also talking about the twentieth century and the world of fascist Italy. So without having to be plonkingly modernised, making a direct allusion to fascist Rome – there was nothing fascist in my production – and without having to be scrupulously and idiotically faithful to an archaeological Rome, I achieved something which was actually a new object, which had allusions – and nothing more – to all three periods.

MR 'Renovatio' again.

JM 'Renovatio' is what you do all the time – you renew.

MR Not all directors, do that, though.

JM It's commonly thought that you only renew if you just pick up a work, whole, from the period in which it's supposed to be and plonk it down, whole, in the period in which you now live. The process of transformation is actually much more subtle than that.

MR When you staged *Hamlet* as your final production for the company, what prompted you to cut the opening scene?

JM It's something that I wouldn't dream of doing now, and in fact I didn't do it in either of my two subsequent performances. It was a youthful *jeu d'esprit* – I wanted to cut straight to the brilliance of the court. You lose a magical moment of watchfulness and ominousness, the sense that things are wrong; but you gain a tremendous sense of shock and surprise. I quite liked doing what I did. Of course, people were appalled by it as if one had violated something or committed an act of vandalism – you can only vandalise an evening, you can't vandalise a play. The play is always there to have its scene put back on again – it's a seamless act of sewing it back on.

MR   How did that *Hamlet* compare to your two subsequent productions of the play?

JM   I think the first one was the best. It had an urgency and directness, with an austere Tudor setting. It was played in a bare box based, in some senses, on Frances Yates' 'memory theatre' – I scrupulously copied the engraving that was in Frances' book. I had this eager young man, Hugh Thomas, still at Oxford, who simply *was* Hamlet – he was a university student. Everyone who plays it older than that is doomed to failure.

THE NATIONAL THEATRE 1970–1974 (ASSOCIATE DIRECTOR 1973–1975)

MR   What brought you to the National Theatre?

JM   I don't know exactly who was responsible for the early moves in my direction – I suspect that it was Tynan, Larry and Joan between them. I would imagine that Tynan might have initially suggested it.

MR   Are you nostalgic for those days when Olivier was running the National at the Old Vic?

JM   We all are, I think, about that period. Larry was enormously generous and encouraging to the younger actors, and indeed to the directors that he chose. I look back on the National under Larry with nothing but pleasure. It was a family. It was a very small outfit, and we lived in those bomber-command shacks in that yard behind Aquinas Street. Larry had a very unglamorous office, and he was always in and out of the canteen – he was accessible, and just very nice to be with. Tynan was very much a part of it, and he took a very active role in rehearsals, script-editing and things of that sort. It was a very convivial outfit. It may be that one romanticises it too much in hindsight, but I think I'm accurate about it. The fact that so many people look back on it with affection and nostalgia means that there must have been something there – these things do come from the top.

MR You've kept that atmosphere at the Old Vic now that you're Artistic Director there yourself.

JM I've kept something like it – obviously I haven't got the sort of charisma that Larry had. But I've done everything to undermine any sort of recognisable authority, so that while there is in a sense a 'top' from which things come, things can flow very readily and easily to the top and the gradient from top to bottom is extremely shallow. There isn't a steep cliff, there is no carefully calculated inaccessibility, nothing to emphasise authority. I did learn that from Larry. It's also a natural temperament – I don't like bossing people around.

MR You made your debut at the National with *The Merchant of Venice* in 1970 – what was it like to direct Olivier as Shylock?

JM It was easy. There are two reasons for that ease. One is that I knew what I wanted, and Larry recognised that what I wanted was good – he had an eye for the main chance, and the chances that I offered were very good. Secondly, a lot of what made it easy came from his enormously generous good manners. He didn't throw his weight around – having made himself a member of my cast, he behaved as if he was simply one amongst a number of professionals collaborating on an enterprise that we all had to further. I can still remember long, difficult rehearsals when I was quite ill at ease about something – the scene where Shylock is tormented by the Christians, for instance. I did it many times, in many different ways, and Larry allowed himself to be pushed around and allowed me to be uncertain, hesitant and experimental without ever saying, 'Look, you're wasting my time – I'm a distinguished actor and I know how to do this.' If he had a better way to do it, he certainly didn't pull rank and say, 'Look, this is what we're going to do – you obviously don't know what to do.' Eventually I found a way of doing it, as one always does in rehearsals. But he never became impatient, and a lot of what made it easy was the generosity that he extended to me.

MR How did he feel about the late nineteenth-century setting of your production?

JM He liked it immediately. If fact, he had all sorts of crazy ideas which had been encouraged by Tynan – he wanted Bassanio to play all three of the suitors in disguise, as if that would guarantee his success. That was an idea which Tynan had got from Orson Welles, and it seemed to me to be a rather trivial, silly trick. But I managed to talk him out of it in the very early stages of discussion long before we began rehearsing.

I knew all along that I wanted the late nineteenth-century setting, because I had seen those Primoli photographs and I had been reading Svevo's novels – it seemed to me to be a way of escaping from the pantomime Renaissance. I suspect that if I were to do the play again I would return to the Renaissance, because I'm much more interested now in the idea of the representation of Jew and Christian in a Renaissance setting.

MR How did you treat the anti-Semitic elements in the play?

JM It seemed to me to be just that awful snobbish anti-Semitism of businessmen. I didn't treat it as racial anti-Semitism, although that had come to the fore in Europe by the nineteenth century.

MR You presented Lorenzo in a comic light, which was quite a departure from the norm.

JM Yes, I was very much attacked for that because people have always seen him as a straightforward romantic hero. I just wanted him to be rather a dolt, really – a pipe-smoking, nice young country squire, who's rather woodenly romantic.

MR Presumably the success of *The Merchant of Venice* led to your next production for the National, *Danton's Death*, in 1971?

JM Larry was so pleased with *The Merchant* that he said to me, 'Look, I've always wanted to do *Danton's Death*. It's in my gift – I will give it to you.' The production had a dream-like quality, based around all the interest that German Romanticism had in anatomy and medicine – Büchner, in fact, was a young Romantic biologist. Again, no one saw that. Unfortunately, I knew something which most of the audience didn't, which was the curious cultural intersection of the early nineteenth century in Germany where Romanticism and what was called *Natur-philosophie* came together. That was what was going on – all the German Romantics were involved in biology. But you can't expect any of the critics to know that – they don't know anything.

MR Unlike many recent revivals, yours didn't over-stress the political content and degenerate into agitprop.

JM It wasn't agitprop – it was actually a rather pessimistic piece about the Revolution. Büchner thought that the Revolution would devour its own children. By that time, Europe was extremely sceptical about revolution. It was several decades before the Marxist formulation of the European situation, and most European intellectuals were deeply pessimistic about the prospects of the Revolution. The Revolution turned out to be something which issued in outrage and atrocity, and ultimately resulted in a dull bourgeois restoration.

MR   It would be interesting to see you do the play again in the current political climate, particularly in view of the change sweeping through Eastern Europe.

JM   Yes. When I did it at the National, Tynan, with his rather fashionable radicalism, felt that it ought to be Marxist, which seemed foolish to me. There's nothing Marxist about it. Büchner is extremely pessimistic about the real revolutionaries – he portrays Robespierre and Saint-Just as these monsters, which indeed they were.

MR   How did you come to re-stage your 1968 Nottingham Playhouse production of *The School for Scandal* for the National at the Old Vic in 1972?

JM   Tynan and Olivier had seen it at Nottingham and wanted it for the National. Simple as that.

MR   It was probably the first time that they had seen the play stripped of affectation and given a down-to-earth treatment.

JM   That's right – I don't know of any director who had done it before. It wasn't that I wanted to make it squalid, though I felt that the servants should be grubby and the maid pregnant. I looked at Hogarth and based it on *Marriage à la Mode* – it wasn't *Gin Lane*, nor, on the other hand, was it *Chatsworth*. It isn't white wigs and beauty spots – it's the world of the minor gentry.

MR   You also dispensed with the traditional style of heavily affected diction.

JM   There had to be great accuracy because it's beautifully poised prose, but it could be spoken with dispatch, address and naturalism – that's what I tried to achieve.

MR   You've described it as a play of moral elegance.

JM   It is – it's a play which is filled with all sorts of moral ironies. I see it as continuous in some respects with the fiction of Jane Austen, which is also about the minor gentry.

MR   *Mansfield Park*, for instance.

JM   That's right – there are no dukes. This is the Tory squirearchy, the people who upheld the Protestant succession.

MR   You returned to the Nottingham Playhouse in 1973 to direct *The Malcontent* – how did you respond to the lurid imagery of the text?

JM   The English view of the Italian world of usurping, stabbing and poisoning is a sort of early seventeenth-century surrealism. So I had these figures with white faces, black lipstick and giant ruffs moving like insects through a dark world. I brought out the bizarre and nightmarish atmosphere of the play very strongly.

MR   You also brought out its comic elements with great exuberance.

JM   It was a sort of *Goon Show* – frightfully funny. Derek Godfrey was magnificent in the title role. But again, there was a sort of epicene shriek from certain critics.

GREENWICH THEATRE 1974–1975

MR   When you resigned from the National Theatre in February 1975, after Peter Hall took over, did Greenwich Theatre provide you with an alternative base?

JM   It was my leap out into freedom – Greenwich provided me with a place to do things which I couldn't do anywhere else.

MR   What inspired you to stage *Hamlet, Ghosts* and *The Seagull* all together in one season under the overall title of 'Family Romances' at Greenwich in 1974?

JM   I had been invited to direct a play at Greenwich. Shortly before that I had directed *The Seagull*, at Chichester, and I was very struck during the rehearsals by the fact that it had the same internal structure as *Hamlet* and *Ghosts*. So I said to Greenwich, 'Rather than just doing one play, why don't we do a season of three plays closely related to one another, in which we would rehearse them all at once and then open them one after another? The superimposition would reveal the similarities.' They loved the idea, and we put together a cast with all the same people going through the season in the analogous parts, which created a genuine ensemble company.

MR   This was one of the first instances of a director using structuralism not only to build a repertory but also to anatomise a play – looking back on it now, do you feel that the season came ahead of its time?

JM Certainly the critics were unaware of structuralism – they simply had no idea of its existence. They didn't see what the season was – when I called it 'Family Romances', they just thought this was some sort of sentimental name for something. They were quite unaware that it was a specific reference to an essay by Freud. It struck me that there was something of Freud's essay in each of those plays, the idea of a boy having a fantasy after his father has disappeared. It seemed loosely a good name to call it, but the critics assumed it was a sentimental umbrella title to get the punters in. They didn't even see any particular reason why the three plays were being done together.

MR Contrary to tradition, you brought out the wit and humour latent in the text of *Ghosts*.

JM Yes, it was much funnier than usual. Irene Worth played Mrs Alving with great wit, and Robert Stephens as Pastor Manders was much less like a dry pastor and much more like an ordinary man. Robert and Irene both surpassed themselves in *Ghosts* and *The Seagull*.

MR There was a remarkable moment when Irene Worth's Mrs Alving suddenly became helpless with laughter as the Orphanage burned down.

JM That's right – the total Dadaist absurdity of the whole situation suddenly strikes her.

MR What was your approach to the final scene of the play?

JM It was based on a psychoanalytic idea expressed in an essay by Karl Abraham about a young man who developed hysterical blindness in the face of a memory of his father, who was a philandering paragon of sexual power. I drew on this Abraham essay because I don't believe that people go blind from syphilis in thirty seconds. When hysterical afflictions occur, they don't produce terror but tend to produce what is described by Déjerine as *la belle indifférence*. I played the ending rather like that. Oswald's mother was alarmed, but not him. And I left the ending open – I just had her counting out the pills as if she was really trying to decide how much you need to kill someone. 'Yes, yes . . . no, no that's too many . . . yes, that's it . . . no, no' and so on.

MR When you moved on to *The Seagull*, you explored the previously overlooked scientific themes in the play which preoccupied Chekhov – how did you view those?

JM   Young intellectuals at the end of the nineteenth century were interested in themes associated with what used to be known as 'Vitalism' – what is it that makes life into life? – and that's explicitly discussed in the play. It might just be a matter of organisation rather than something sporadic, for instance, and a young writer such as Konstantin would have concerned himself with these things.

There were those who were real dyed-in-the-wool Vitalists, who believed that living matter was matter to which the vital principle had been added; and then there were the Materialists, who felt that life was nothing more than the physical organisation of matter, which is what Medviedenko actually says in the play. Konstantin's own play, in fact, is a Romantic view of evolution.

There is even a sort of Darwinism in the ending, in that Konstantin is weak and, in a sense, degenerate in the way that nineteenth-century theorists often stressed the idea of degeneracy. But Nina, in some curious way, plucky little defeated thing that she is, she actually somehow survives and goes off into the outside world, although she is defeated, whereas Konstantin actually dies.

MR   It was an ideal piece for the ensemble company that you had built up.

JM   It's a play about an ensemble, it's a play about a class and a household. There aren't any main parts in Chekhov.

MR   What made you have Arkadina go back to baby-talk as she tended her son's injured head?

JM   At that moment she's a mother taking great pleasure in having a helpless child. It's easy for her to be affectionate to a son who is in fact in a completely subservient, abject state of helplessness.

MR   How did you see the conflict between Konstantin and Trigorin?

JM   I felt that the contrast between the two men was, in a sense, Chekhov's own view of himself. He was divided between the two characters: Trigorin is in fact the writer that Chekhov became, that he was somehow slightly ashamed of being; while Konstantin is the young experimental writer that Chekhov might have been, but ceased to be when he went public – at least he was experimental with his play, foolish and failing though it was.

MR   How did you build up to the climax?

JM   There was a long, long pause after Dorn comes back and says, 'Just as I thought – one of my ether bottles has exploded.' He tries to spin out the time as long as he can before he actually has to impart the news to Trigorin. He walks around the room, looks at the table, and notices little details like the writing desk filled with torn-up papers and the glass placed carefully back on the carafe, a doctor's eye applied to the post-mortem details. Then, as surreptitiously as he can, he murmurs 'The fact is, Konstantin has shot himself.' The people around the table gradually become aware of this, and Arkadina is the last one to look up.

MR Your next production at Greenwich was *The Importance of Being Earnest* in 1975 – how did you arrive at the German characterisation of Lady Bracknell?

JM I cast Irene Handl as Lady Bracknell because I wanted to have the role played not as an aristocrat, but – as so many Edwardian aristocrats were – as a Gaiety Girl who had married above her station to some stage-door Johnny aristocrat, and who had learned a certain amount of cut-glass gentility in the process, which would have made all that stuff about the address in Grosvenor Square much more amusing. I knew that Irene Handl would be marvellous for that air of slightly genteel coarseness.

Unfortunately, though, she forgot her lines all the time. So in desperation at the last run-through, when the actors were getting absolutely frantic because she never fed them her cues, I said, 'Look, all of you do it in accents for the run-through – it'll help you relax.' So the boys came on and did it in American, and Irene said, 'I'll do it in German, because I'm half German myself.' She sailed through it as this German aristocrat – 'A hendbeg?' – and proved absolutely wonderful.

At the end, I said to her, 'You've got to do it like that for the performances.' She replied, 'Oh I can't dear, I couldn't possibly do that. He would never have allowed it.' I told her that Wilde would have been much more upset by the fact that she couldn't remember a single word, and would certainly have preferred a few words in German rather than no words at all in English. So she did it, and of course it caused an absolute outrage. Some critics instantly said, 'It's brilliant – it's there in the text', not realising in the slightest that it was an act of total despair – I would never have done it otherwise. It's amazing the way that the strain to make sense will extend to giving you credit for something which in fact was probably motivated by total panic, as this was.

MR How did you treat the rest of the characterisation?

JM I made Algernon and John a little more thoughtful than usual, but also brought out the fact that they were really Hoorays. Gwendolen was played by Angela Down as a frosty, icy creature, and Benjamin Whitrow was absolutely dazzling as Canon Chasuble. Miss Prism is usually played as this timid little creature, but Joan Sanderson played her quite brilliantly as this enormous battleaxe – when she crumbles in the face of Lady Bracknell's 'Prism!', she virtually melts down her own collar.

MR   You'd previously suggested doing *The Importance* at the National with an all-male cast.

JM   That was a sort of wild fantasy – I thought of doing it with Peter Bull or Leo McKern as Lady Bracknell. So much was made of it by people who said it was 'typical Jonathan Miller' – it was just a *jeu d'esprit*, which one has every now and then. People said 'That's not what Wilde meant.' Of course it's not what he meant – the notion of meaning is much more negotiable. I still think that Peter Bull would have been wonderful in the role.

MR   What prompted you to give the name 'Bed Tricks' to your 1975 season of *Measure for Measure* and *All's Well that Ends Well* at Greenwich?

JM   'Bed Tricks' is a name given by English scholars to plays which involve a switch of girls in the darkness – Isabella and Mariana in *Measure* and Helena and Diana in *All's Well*. So I called the season 'Bed Tricks' because both plays involved the bed-swap. And the critics, of course, never having heard of the term, assumed that it was another Raymond's Revue Bar title.

MR   You cast much younger actors that usual as Bertram and Parolles in the *All's Well*.

JM   That way they were just two giggling schoolboys. Parolles was rather marvellous like that, instead of the usual older man – he became that awful schoolboy one brings home for the holidays, and who turns out to be the sort of chap that makes one's parents say 'I do wish you wouldn't mix with him – he's the wrong type.' Bertram is a very unsympathetic character, and he was played as an evasive, rather awful cad. Helena is a rather interesting, sad creature, this ambiguous figure of a girl who is a doctor's daughter, credited with his powers and therefore highly suspect, almost a witch, and middle-class enough to horrify an aristocrat like Bertram.

MR   To what extent was the *Measure For Measure* a development on your previous production for the National Theatre in 1974?

JM   It was much the same thing and used exactly the same set (when I did it for the third time in Italy more than ten years later, I took it much more into the world of the painter George Grosz). It was absolutely Kafka-esque,

48

with the stage lined with all these doors – I was basing it very much on things like Kafka's novel *The Trial*. I took Shakespeare's setting of Vienna and said 'All right, let's see what happens if it is the Vienna – or middle-Europe – of that clerkly 1920s world.' It worked very well, and we referred to the photographs of August Sander as well as, to a lesser degree, the work of George Grosz.

MR You also returned to another Shakespeare play in 1975 when you directed a BBC TV production of *King Lear*, which you had previously staged at the Nottingham Playhouse in 1969 – how was the television version a development on the original stage production?

JM I think I went further, in the television *King Lear*, towards the idea of Edgar seeing himself as Christ in the way that those mendicant madmen did – that was very much based on Norman Cohn's book *The Pursuit of the Millennium* (though obviously I didn't want Edgar to be seen *as* Christ). There was a sort of Miltonic feeling about it – I think that there is a partnership between Edgar and Edmund which is very much like Christ and Lucifer. I'm not saying that they *are* them, but that they are metaphorical references, allusions to them. There is also a partnership between Lear and the Fool – I've never varied that at all. The sisters were accurate portraits of women exasperated by the demands of a silly old man – they're driven as mad by him as he is by them. I used the etchings of Jacques Callot for the Nottingham *Lear* because I wanted to evoke the Thirty Years War; but for the television production I took the lighting and the tone from Caravaggio. I also used the paintings of Georges de la Tour for television, simply to get the lighting of certain intimate scenes – the scene in the hovel, and things like that. I've drawn on de la Tour again and again – it's such wonderfully dramatic stage lighting.

KENT OPERA 1975–1982

MR In 1974 you directed your first opera, Alexander Goehr's *Arden Must Die* at Sadler's Wells – did you have a conscious desire to move into opera at that point?

JM It simply happened that I was asked – most of the things that have happened to me have been the result of people inviting me to do things. Someone said, 'Would you like to do an opera?' and I replied, 'I'm not sure I know how to – I don't read music.' They said, 'Well, have a go.' So I agreed, and rather enjoyed it. *Arden Must Die* had been a big success in

Germany, but the English are hopeless at recognising new things. My production was very surreal – very much the sort of thing that Richard Jones is doing now – and filled with big, crazy things: the dead body was lowered from the flies at the end with stab wounds in it, and the tribunal was a completely insane toy-town tribunal with these policemen rising up and down, licking their pencils and writing things down in their notebooks. It was rather funny, really.

MR   The following year you directed *The Cunning Little Vixen* at Glynde-bourne, and that turned out to be the hit of the season there.

JM   It was actually an extremely difficult thing to do, and I often felt at the beginning that I didn't have the measure of it. And then suddenly, about a week into rehearsals, I found that I knew how it worked. I realised that it was this wonderful, heartwarming pantheistic work, and immediately it all came together. The Robertsons' sets and costumes were absolutely magnificent, and we had a good time working it all out. I couldn't come back to revive it the following year because I was tied up with *The Body in Question*.

MR   As in your film of *Alice in Wonderland*, you avoided literal representation of the animals in the opera.

JM   There is no way in which you can reproduce animals on a stage, other than by some sort of awful, coy frisking. It's said that the great performance of the opera was Felsenstein's production, where he had done exactly that. It may well be that it worked at that time, but the time has passed for that sort of literalism – again, it's the difference between use and mention. I went down to what was being metaphorically referred to. I felt that the animal world represented a sort of *ancien régime* of nature, in the same way that peasants with their ancient costumes represent an old world which was gradually being replaced by that mundane world of people who no longer dressed up in their peasant uniform. So it seemed that we could portray the animals as a peasant world – so much peasant costume, in fact, is based on animal forms.

MR   Between 1975 and 1982 you were a regular director for Kent Opera – how do you look back on your time with the company?

JM   In many respects it was the happiest time of my life as a director, because I was working on a simple, small scale, and generally that's the kind of opera I like best of all. Accordingly, it was some of the best work I've ever done. During my time with Kent, though, we had to suffer that extraordinary condescension from the big opera houses and the critics, who regarded us as 'plucky little Kent, who are doing amazing work, considering'.

MR   You worked with the same conductor and designer for all seven productions for Kent Opera.

JM   The team of Roger Norrington, Bernard Culshaw and myself came together just like that. Bernard and I had worked together before with the Oxford and Cambridge Shakespeare Company, where we had learned to work on a small scale. Roger was the first conductor I had come across who had this strong commitment to the past – but a modern approach to it – and at the same time a deep sense of the dramatic onstage. It was a strong triumvirate, and we worked well together.

MR   Your first production for the company was *Così fan tutte* in 1975 – like all of your subsequent Mozart productions, it was rooted very firmly in the late eighteenth century.

JM   The *Così* was visually based entirely on a book that Robert Rosenblum wrote, called *Transformations in Late Eighteenth Century Art*, in which he talks about the fact that as you get towards the neo-classical period, from 1770 onwards, the picture plane becomes flattened. So we played the opera on a very shallow platform no more than about 6 feet deep, backed by a plain terracotta wall in the neo-classical style, with the stage bare except for a Récamier couch centrally placed between the two entrances. It was based very much on the early David pictures, and in some ways I think it was probably the best *Così* out of the three I've done so far.

MR   You set *Rigoletto*, your next production for Kent Opera, in the period of its composition, the mid-nineteenth century. Did you have Dickensian themes in mind, such as the father–daughter relationship?

JM   Yes, it was rather Dickensian in several ways, but it was also to do with the Risorgimento – Sparafucile, for example, was dressed in a Garibaldi shirt, so there was a sense that he was not just an assassin and ruffian, but somebody who had in fact taken part in revolutionary events as a soldier of fortune. For his first entrance, I placed a great big light in one corner so that he was initially seen as a vast shadow – it was a very striking moment. It's been very interesting doing *Rigoletto* in two quasi-anachronistic ways, ways of avoiding that awful Zeffirelli-esque pantomime. I wanted to get away from all that operatic grandeur.

MR   You drew on the paintings of Poussin for your production of *Orfeo* in 1976 – another case of historical parallax?

JM   It struck me that I was dealing with an opera written in the seventeenth century about classical antiquity, and written by someone who himself had some sort of commitment to Stoical values, so I wanted to find some image which was a counterpart to that. As Poussin was painting classical pastorals in Rome in the seventeenth century, it seemed almost inevitable to draw on his work. *Orfeo* is not a naturalistic piece – the genre is poised, with extremely controlled expression of feeling, which is visually matched by the style of Poussin. This was a development of my idea of historical parallax, and in relation to Poussin for *Orfeo* I saw three periods – our own period, his period, and the period that he referred to – and I tried to achieve something that would align these three.

MR   The poised, controlled style of movement that you took from the Poussin paintings was tremendously effective onstage, particularly for Charon the Ferryman.

JM   Charon just used his oar and his body to cross to Hades. We rehearsed that for days, trying to get the singer to feel the extraordinary sense of a strong muddy current moving against a pole, with that V-shape of ripples that spreads around and that tremendous feeling of having to pull. He just moved the whole time, very slowly, and it actually created the sense of a boat without him ever being on a boat at all. At the same time, Orfeo circled him in slow motion to quite hypnotic effect.

MR   One of the most innovative features of your *Eugene Onegin* in 1977 was your complete reappraisal of the character of Lensky – how did you arrive at that?

JM   If Lensky is portrayed simply as a passionate young man, it becomes rather uninteresting – I like it when people have defects of some sort, some unexpected failing. I felt that Lensky was so often played as this romantic, duelling Lermontovian hero, whereas I saw him as a plump gig-lamped figure who can't quite see, rather like Schubert – a lot of Schubert's songs, like 'Die Winterreise', are rather like Lensky's aria. I was struck by the romantic sadness of those Schubert songs, and it's rather touching when romantic feelings are housed in someone who looks so unpromising.

   Lensky is not a romantic hero, just a person who has romantic and heroic visions of himself and gets involved in this duel. We portrayed him as myopic – perhaps he misinterpreted what was going on because he couldn't quite see. When he got shot his spectacles fell off, and he died scrambling around for them on the ground. At the end of the scene, on the very last chord, Onegin stood wistfully looking down at his dead friend, picked up his spectacles and just held them up, as if thinking 'Good heavens, is that what the world looked like to my friend?' It was a very moving moment.

MR Your treatment of the final scene of the opera was reminiscent of the end of *The Cherry Orchard*.

JM I set the last scene in the Gremins' house, covered in dust sheets and wrapped in gauze, as I assumed that Tatyana had been so frightened by the re-emergence of Onegin – and also by the re-emergence of her own strong feelings – that she had said to her husband Gremin 'We must pack and leave immediately.' Therefore when Onegin comes in he is intruding on a house which has already been packed up for the winter. I gave the scene a wintry feeling of all emotion having been frozen, rather like *The Cherry Orchard* indeed.

MR Your *La Traviata* for Kent Opera in 1979 was sharply focussed and pared down compared to the Grand Opera style of production that the piece normally receives.

JM Yes, it usually gets swamped under crinolines and chandeliers. I thought a lot about Flaubert's *Sentimental Education* when I directed it – I've always seen *La Traviata* as a bourgeois tragedy about two provincial figures who get destroyed by this world of Parisian desire and sophistication. I set it in the demi-monde, which was a world in which the aristocracy could let their hair down, where people could meet in an atmosphere of relaxed conviviality. I had figures like Baudelaire and Delacroix very much in mind for this. We based all the characters on Nadar's photographs of 1850 – the costumes were all made out of black and white material, and then slightly dyed to give them a tinted look.

MR You staged the key moments in the opera with remarkable stillness – for the first encounter between Violetta and Germont, for instance, the singers simply sat facing each other for almost the entire scene.

JM That's the way in which you intensify things onstage, but there are always some directors who feel that things aren't happening unless there is a lot of locomotor activity, which shows a complete misunderstanding of relationships. Very often, the most intense things happen with people very still, and there is no need to move them around – people may feel a vague restlessness, but they don't rush about. I never had Violetta rush around at the end, either – she never even left her bed.

MR   When you explored that scene in a television workshop, you came up with the idea of having Alfredo embrace his father on the death of Violetta.

JM   I suddenly realised that you have here a young boy who is very dependent on his father, and is moved by his father being moved – finally, when the girl dies, he and his father have only each other to cling to, both having lost someone.

MR   What drew you to Bruegel when you directed *Falstaff* for the company in 1980?

JM   I wanted to bring the humour of the piece closer to that of *The Merry Wives of Windsor*, but at the same time I wanted to set the production very accurately in the world of Bruegel. We had beekeepers moving hives around in the background of the garden scene – it was the world of *Haymaking*. In the final scene we used a great blasted oak tree with a red blanket thrown over it, as you get in the Bruegel pictures. When the fairies came on we referred to the surrealist paintings, and had them wearing funnels and kitchen colanders on their heads, which is exactly what they would have done – they had to improvise their dress, after all, and it became a rather festive *Walpurgisnacht*.

MR   The comedy in your production was much more subtle than in most revivals of the opera.

JM   I can't bear all that mugged comedy you usually get – it just has to be like the comedy of real life. It's a rather Chekhovian story, really. I used lots of comic details for the characterisation. I gave Bardolph, for example, a slight twitch, so we got a wonderful pay-off gag at the end when he came on disguised as the bride – the audience could tell who it was as soon as they saw this familiar twitching going on. I love those Tati-esque behavioural details.

MR   What made you refer to Goya for *Fidelio*, your last production for Kent Opera in 1982?

JM   Goya and Beethoven are almost indistinguishable figures – they have these great romantic figures extolling Enlightenment and liberty. That's why I had tricolour banners brought on at the end – it's a world of revolutionary liberty. Under Roger Norrington's influence, I've come to see *Fidelio* and *The Magic Flute* as the two great masonic operas, along with Haydn's *Creation*.

   We referred to those wonderful pictures by Goya of prisons and lunatic asylums for the production. We went as far as to dip the stage gauzes in a tea-coloured dye and then spatter them with sepia to give them that aquatint texture. The costumes were made from undyed linen and then painted brown to achieve the same aquatint effect.

Background detail like that matters enormously to me – I spent a lot of time on the first entrance of the Prisoners' Chorus, getting them to drift in and circle round a downblast of light in the centre of the stage. It doesn't work for all operas, though – pieces like *Orfeo* are highly artificial without any background detail of real life. They are just totally stylised instead, full of things like romantic nymphs which you can't naturalise in any way. But detail does work for *Fidelio* – most people in Germany call it a 'Biedermeier piece of bourgeois naturalism'.

MR How did you deal with the problem of the dialogue and the music in *Fidelio?*

JM You have to make the dialogue as natural as possible, and we re-wrote some of it and eventually got the singers to speak the lines as if they were in a play. The music arose quite naturally from the words without any sharp bridges – there must always be a cadence on the last line which leads into the music, so it doesn't sound as if there is an abrupt cessation of speech and an abrupt onset of music. It must be as if the feeling of the characters is beginning to suffuse the speech so that song is the inevitable next expression.

FREELANCE 1976–1979

MR How do you explain the remarkable success of your production of *The Three Sisters* in the West End in 1976?

JM It worked simply because I understood what the play was about. By that time I had thoroughly grasped this notion of conversational naturalism, and knew that there was a way of making Chekhov's dialogue sound real rather than like that well-mannered 'Virginia Water' type of production. It was all incredibly normal. That was partly because I saw that Masha is not the most important character, that it's actually a play in which there are no important characters – the character is the community. Therefore it was necessary to create a world in which you understood that these were three perfectly ordinary, rather commonplace, provincial sisters, who were really quite pretentious about themselves.

MR   Again, you were demystifying the received view of Chekhov, something you also did with the received view of the body when you performed the first autopsy to be seen on television in your 1977 BBC TV series *The Body in Question*.

JM   There is this idea of the boundary between the visible and the invisible – there are things which must not be seen and things which might be seen. That boundary has since been pushed back – we now see very badly mutilated bodies on news programmes. It wasn't that I wanted to be sensational – I simply said, look, here is a dignified thing, the body is taken apart after death in order to find out what the cause of death was. There's nothing dreadful about it.

MR   What was your overall aim in *The Body in Question*?

JM   I wanted to do a history of medicine and show that it was a history of civilisation. One of the things that had disappointed me about Kenneth Clark's *Civilisation* was that, again, it was this great mandarin thing claiming from the pre-*Monitor* world that civilisation was the fine things of life – the great paintings of Masaccio, beautiful silver, great cathedrals – as if in fact there was no contribution made by the person who invented the automatic governor to the machine, or by Newton, or by the great engineers. It seems to me that these things hang together – cultural historians call it *zusammenhängen*. The growth of knowledge of the body came from changes in self-consciousness about the nature of man and therefore about the nature of the world.

MR   The series displayed a very literate view of science.

JM   And a scientific view of literacy as well.

MR   You returned to Greenwich Theatre in 1979 to direct *She Would if She Could*, a play you had been thinking about for several years.

JM   Yes, I originally planned to do it at the National. At Greenwich we set it in a beautiful inlaid cabinet which opened up in all sorts of ways like a magic box. It was very elegant and formal, one of Bernard Culshaw's most inventive and interesting sets. The production too had a very formal atmosphere – it wasn't a squalid, naturalistic world because it is such a highly stylised piece. It depended on a sort of mechanical, clockwork feeling, which is why we had this magic box which opened up in all sorts of symmetrical ways. There were wonderful performances by the two young men, David Horovitch and David Firth.

MR Who had also played Bertram and Parolles for you on the same stage.

JM That's right – I stick with the same actors again and again like that.

MR You went to Frankfurt next to direct *The Flying Dutchman* at the Opera House – were the paintings of Caspar David Friedrich your main reference for the production?

JM Yes. It seemed to me that the opera came before the great mythic world of *The Ring* – it was a sort of naturalistic German Romantic fairy-story, coming much more from the world of something like *Der Freischütz*. So I had to think of the visual sensibility which corresponded to that. The strange, romantic, metaphysical infinity of Caspar David Friedrich's paintings seem to me to be appropriate to it.

MR You avoided the Wagner tradition of static staging in your production.

JM Yes, it was much more involved and naturalistic. The scene in the *Spinnstube* was much more like a natural group of fishermen's wives waiting for their husbands to come back, that social world which was obviously observed in those fishing villages. As for the idea of the painting, I wanted to get that strange, mystical E.T.A. Hoffmann world of the magical and the supernatural. So in the *Spinnstube*, instead of having the picture hanging on the wall, I had Senta painting the picture. You never see it – you saw her painting all the time while she was in the trance, and then, at the moment at the end when the Dutchman comes in, a brilliant shaft of light falls behind her as he walks through the door, and suddenly you know from the way that he looks at the picture that she has in some strange way anticipated his arrival by painting him. Some of her earlier pictures were propped up around the room, and they were pictures of the scene we had previously witnessed, as if somehow in some strange prophetic way she had foreseen the event.

MR You crossed over to Austria next, to direct *A Midsummer Night's Dream* at the Vienna Burgtheater.

JM That was a bit of a shemozzle, because it was just much too big.

MR How did you approach the play?

JM I wanted to get the natural world as well as the supernatural – again, *A Midsummer Night's Dream* is another play about passing across a strange membrane which separates the night world of fantasy and dreams from the day world of ordinary social relationships. That's wonderfully shown in Bruegel, whose work I drew on for the production.

MR   Did you use Hieronymus Bosch's paintings, too?

JM   Yes – it was actually much more Bosch than Bruegel. Certainly when we got to the night scene, the fairies and so forth were all based on those monsters that came out of the Bosch world. It was very surreal indeed in the forest.

THE BBC TV SHAKESPEARE 1980–1982
(PRODUCER/DIRECTOR)

MR   What was your aim when you became the producer and director of the BBC TV Shakespeare series in 1980?

JM   I began to develop aims once I'd started working on it, because I had no plans to do the Shakespeares until I was suddenly asked to take over the series. They were already two years into what by that time was quite clearly a collision course with disaster and literalism. I, of course, would have liked to have done the thing with all the possibilities which in one direction pointed towards my *Measure for Measure* and in another direction towards my de Chirico *Julius Caesar*. But by that time the series was contracted to the Americans who had forbidden any sort of 'monkey tricks', as they called it. But at least I was able to say, 'Well, whatever it is, I will not have cardboard sets and it's not going to have that literal, open-air theatre look. There will be no white trellis-work, gazebos or anything like that.' I managed to secure an agreement that the Roman and Greek plays were not to be represented in the costume of the period mentioned – my *Timon of Athens*, for example, was done in Elizabethan dress.

MR   How did you respond to the problems of directing Shakespeare for television?

JM   It was very difficult, because the space for which these plays are destined is actually a bare board. You get pushed towards a sort of naturalism on TV which is not altogether friendly to the text of Shake-speare. But I'm quite proud of what we achieved, and people I commissioned, like Elijah Moshinsky, were very successful – he did some nice things like *Love's Labour's Lost* and *All's Well that Ends Well*. I think I was responsible for bringing in some interesting people. I tried to get other directors, like Bergman and Brook, to come in but none of them were able to do it, partly because they didn't agree to abide by the guidelines that had been laid down by the BBC.

MR   The first production that you directed in the series was *The Taming of the Shrew*, which you had previously staged at Chichester in 1972 – was there perhaps more emphasis on Puritanism in the Chichester production?

JM   A little bit more, yes. But the interesting thing about the television production was the casting of John Cleese; and also the set, which was made entirely out of used BBC scenic plywood. It was modelled on Serlio's designs for an Italian comedy.

MR   What inspired you to cast Cleese as Petruchio?

MR   Partly his tyrannical anger as Basil Fawlty in *Fawlty Towers*, and partly because I recognised that there was also a sort of brooding tenderness inside the man as well. It came off very well.

MR   What was your approach to *Antony and Cleopatra*, your next production in the series?

JM   I wanted to take that sort of 'Distinguished Evening in the Theatre', H. M. Tennant-type romance out of it. The thing about Antony is that he is a ruffian, as he's described by Octavius Caesar, and Cleopatra is a Greek slut, not a serpent of the Nile. The production looked very rich and had some of the quality of the Veronese paintings which I referred to.

MR   Your use of long-shots in that production achieved a tableau effect very evocative of the great Veronese canvases.

JM   I like using long-shots and grouping people in deep shots so that you don't have to widen out, nor do you have to have single shots cutting backwards and forwards between close-ups.

MR   You stayed with the Italian Renaissance setting when you directed *Timon of Athens* in 1981.

JM   Again, there was simply a wooden set with no pretence at scenic-wall reality. It was actually surprisingly beautiful and adapted well for those rough, mad scenes in the desert. I saw it quite clearly as a play about money and greed, and I'd like to do it again now in some sort of modern version.

MR   The revelation of your *Othello* was Bob Hoskins' performance as Iago – that was a very inventive piece of casting.

JM   Yes, he was wonderful in the role – and that was long before he became a big star. Anthony Hopkins was a little bit operatic as Othello, and I had problems with people saying that I ought to have cast a black actor instead.

I think it was the last moment in the history of the British theatre when one could cast a white actor in the role without having really terrible trouble. Again, I set it in a Renaissance world – it was based on one particular Italian palace which I knew, which had these splendid inlaid doors.

MR   You got away from the interpretation of the play which sees it simply as a study in jealousy.

JM   It's not a play about jealousy – it's a play about envy exploiting jealousy in order to get its satisfaction. Jealousy is one of the furnishings of the play, but the propulsive power of the play is Iago's envy. 'He hath a daily beauty in his life / That makes me ugly,' he says of Cassio – that's what the whole play is about.

MR   You followed that with a production of *Troilus and Cressida* set against an intricately conceived visual background expressing, again, your idea of historical parallax.

JM   I wanted to get something that would reconcile the antiquity which is mentioned with the Renaissance period in which it was written, with references to eternal war – with which we are only too familiar. So you have three periods vying for expression, and I wanted to find something which would reconcile that. I knew perfectly well, as so few critics seemed to know, that the Gothic Middle Ages were the ones that made the most consistent references to the story of Cressida – Chaucer and Henryson, for example. Most of the great early Renaissance and late Gothic tapestries show a Gothic world of the Greek stories – there's a great sequence of such tapestries in the Norton Simon Museum. So I wanted to find a painter – though, obviously, not to simply copy him literally – who would give me some sort of reconciling image which would refer to the past but also refer to the Renaissance, without being quite in either, and Cranach's world of the early German Renaissance seemed to be perfect for that. But, at the same time, I didn't want it to be just a literal re-creation of that – I wanted to quote it, ironically. Therefore the characters were all put into that costume, but the costumes were turned slightly khaki and they all had their name-tags in Gothic on them, so that it looked a little bit like *M*A*S*H* – there were references to *M*A*S*H* without reproducing it. The Greek encampment was this canvas world of ammunition boxes and pin-ups of Cranach's Eve – there were several jokes in it like that.

MR   Most of your work operates in that way – through allusion and metaphor.

JM   Complicated allusions in all directions, yes.

MR   For your final production in the series you returned to *King Lear* for the third time – as in your previous production, you achieved a Caravaggio-like chiaroscuro effect on screen.

JM   Yes, but it wasn't a reproduction of Caravaggio. I wanted to get away from that literal frontal lighting of television – I wanted to use light sparingly, to sneak it in from the sides rather than flood it in, and Caravaggio is a good starting-point for that.

MR   And you had Michael Hordern and Frank Middlemass playing Lear and the Fool – for the third time, in fact.

JM   I've never got away from the idea of an old Fool – in my fourth production I still had an old Fool, though Peter Bayliss played him this time. That sort of ironic, impatient wisdom that the Fool has is something that you can't quite credit a young person with. This romantic idea of the defective juvenile who is a prophet is just twaddle.

MR   I felt that Michael Hordern's portrayal of Lear's madness was much more startling and uninhibited than anything I'd seen before – did you draw on your clinical experience for that?

JM   Yes – I think I helped him to do that properly. He was very mad indeed. I did the same with Eric Porter at the Old Vic – he was constantly playing with himself and almost revealing his genitals, which is what old mad people do. It's a very ugly thing, madness – there's nothing pretty or prophetic about it.

THE ENGLISH NATIONAL OPERA 1978–1987
(ASSOCIATE DIRECTOR)

MR   *The Marriage of Figaro* began your long association with the ENO at the London Coliseum, and continued your progress through the Mozart operas – you've always, in fact, displayed a very strong affinity with Mozart in your work.

JM   I've enjoyed Mozart more than any other composer, partly because I think that he's perhaps the best musical dramatist that we have. That's slightly unfair in the sense that Verdi is also a master dramatist, but there is a style, a restraint and a formality about Mozart's drama which I find very attractive, over and above the fact that it is just an endless delight listening to his music.

I like his rich humanism, too – that's the world of the European Enlightenment, which I take great pleasure in. I like that subtle tension that exists between the passions and reason. The idea that the passions are best expressed and controlled when regulated by reason, and that reason is only tolerable if in fact it is constantly nourished by the passions. It's a beautifully balanced eighteenth-century tension.

One of the things which I enjoy as a director is the reconstitution of the *mentalité* of a particular period, and I think that Mozart gives one the opportunity for re-creating the *mentalité* of late eighteenth-century Europe, hovering on the edge of the Revolution.

MR   There's an increasing trend now towards updating Mozart into the twentieth century, as Peter Sellars is doing with his Mozart/da Ponte series at the Pepsico Summerfare in New York.

JM   I feel that there is a great overvaluing of our own time, a demand that if works are taken from the past they should be forced to address themselves to the present. Whereas I feel that with Shakespeare and particularly with Mozart, somehow the greatness of these works is partly related to the fact that they express something of a past which is recognisably different from our own while still, at the same time, giving some sort of evidence of the way things are now. There is a reluctance today to come to terms with the past or acknowledge it, or a feeling somehow that it's boringly traditional to re-create something in the costumes of the past as if your theatrical imagination is stifled by seeing people look as they once looked. I find that very regrettable.

Obviously there's no way in which you can avoid being modern. Simply to do a classic in the twentieth century is automatically to bring all sorts of ideas to bear which could not have been known by the period in question. So, for example, a Peter Stein version of *Otello* or *Falstaff* makes no effort to bring it into modern times, but brings a modern theatrical technique and sensibility to bear on something which is in the past. That is the best approach.

MR   Were you exposed to much Mozart as a child?

JM   I knew all of his symphonies, piano concertos and much of his orchestral music when I was young, but I didn't really know his operas in depth until I began working on them. But I've always had a strong sense of sympathy and affection for him as a person and for his work.

MR   That sympathy and affection comes out in your Mozart productions – you're one of the few directors who treats his recitative seriously as dramatic diction.

JM   Recitative seems to me to be the only part of a Mozart opera which proceeds in real time. It is, in fact, very nearly like ordinary talk, and should be treated as such, like the prose passages in Shakespeare. Obviously in Shakespeare there are long artificial passages of verse, and those are the equivalent in some respects of the arias in Mozart; but I think that wherever it is quite clear that the action is being carried on in ordinary dramatic real time, then the properties of ordinary talk should be observed.

MR   Did you find the recitative a challenge when you directed your first Mozart opera, *Così fan tutte*, for Kent Opera in 1975?

JM   I recognised very early on when I began working on it with Roger Norrington that recitative was something which had to have variations in pace, just as ordinary talk does. You can't let it simply plonk on in some sort of metronomic regularity. So many of the recordings and performances that one hears simply carry it on musically, with a pause between the end of the recitative and the onset of the aria – I think that they have got to be much more closely integrated than that. Norrington had a great deal of influence on me as I thought about this – he made me realise that there was a way of reconciling the musical demands of recitative with its quite self-evident demands to be the expression of talk.

MR   *The Marriage of Figaro* marked your debut at the Coliseum in 1978 – like the *Così*, it was firmly rooted in the world of the eighteenth century.

JM   Once again, I felt no temptation to bring the opera into the twentieth century. What makes it intelligible is the social world of the eighteenth century, of the household of a minor rural aristocrat. Not only is there the *droit de seigneur*, which is simply the most prominent and famous issue in the opera; but the social relationships are defined by eighteenth-century conditions and really have no meaning outside that – the whole thing would just fall to bits.

MR   How do you see *Figaro* in relation to the other major Mozart operas?

JM   As Starobinski points out, they are all representations of a social order which is about to undergo quite radical reappraisal in the light of thought which was already current in Europe by the 1760s. It isn't that they foresee the Revolution – they are part and parcel of the sensibility which culminated in the Revolution.

MR   What distinguished your production from all the other *Figaro*s that I've seen was your complete avoidance of the clumsy humour with which directors normally swamp the piece.

JM   So often *Figaro* is associated with certain sterotypes of opera comedy, cardboard cut-out characters, and filled with all sorts of traditional opera business. That seemed to me outdated and repulsive. There is this awful idea of the twinkling jolly fellow Figaro, the twinkling soubrette Susanna and the pompous blundering Bartolo – they can all be dealt with just as humorously, but without resort to those terrible clichés. You simply make it socially real.

MR   You achieved a very sensitive level of social realism in a number of ways – bringing on the Countess with her two small children at the start of Act 2, for instance.

JM   I wanted to create a real household, and it seemed to me improbable, to say the least, that someone who has been courted with such passion in *The Barber of Seville*, and who is capable of having a child by Cherubino in *La Mère coupable*, would not have produced children for Almaviva. They are conspicuous by their absence, and although they are not specifically mentioned it seemed to me that the pathos of the Countess's situation would be more poignantly expressed if we could see briefly that she has in fact borne children for this man.

MR   Your next production at the Coliseum was *The Turn of the Screw* in 1979 – an appropriate choice in view of your film *Oh Whistle and I'll Come to You*.

JM   *The Turn of the Screw* was a wonderful moment, certainly one of the happiest times I ever had at the ENO. I had deeply enjoyed the *Figaro*. I thought it was one of the most beautiful things I'd ever done – I got the social scene right, I understood the play and then went to the opera really knowing what that eighteenth-century world was like, and I was able to re-create it with great subtlety. *The Turn of the Screw* was an even more satisfying episode. It was a small unit of people, very concentrated, and I was able to produce a hallucinatory world of the supernatural. It tied up indeed with my *Whistle and I'll Come to You* – I've always been interested in examining just what it is that brings the hair up on the back of your spine. The production was deeply affected by the fact that I really took very great care with the Jamesian idea that the events had happened forty or fifty years earlier than the chorus, which took it into the world of Laycock Abbey and the Fox Talbot photographs.

MR How did you respond to the Freudian elements of the piece?

JM Not directly – only in so much as I acknowledged the idea of the unacknowledged sexual impulses that would bubble up to the surface in all sorts of ways in a child's imagination. But you can't avoid that – if you're a literate creature of the twentieth century, Freud implicitly determines your choices without you thinking 'I'm being Freudian.' Anyway, being Freudian for most people simply means phallic symbols and things like that – it's just sickening the way that Freud is misinterpreted today.

MR You're one of the few directors to have gone straight from Shakespeare's *Othello* to Verdi's *Otello* – how did your *Othello* for the BBC TV Shakespeare series in 1981 inform your production of Verdi's opera at the Coliseum only a few weeks afterwards?

JM In many ways it kept bumping up my disappointment with the opera, which grossly over-simplifies motives – particularly those of Iago, who turns into a sort of cardboard villain. But it's still a wonderful opera, so I had a good time.

MR You then staged one of your most famous productions, the 'Mafia' *Rigoletto* at the Coliseum in 1982 – has that, in a sense, proved a problem in that some people now regard you primarily as an updater?

JM Yes, unfortunately – 'Where are you going to put it now?' they ask each time I do an opera.

MR The production played to sell-out houses, and was subsequently televised, regularly revived at the Coliseum and taken on a tour of the United States which culminated in a season at the Metropolitan Opera House in New York – did you expect its success?

JM No, not really, though I knew it was going to be quite interesting. It was a really innovative piece of work without in fact being just a glib piece of modernisation.

MR What was the origin of your 1986 production of *Tosca* at the Maggio Musicale in Florence, which you later re-staged for the ENO in London?

JM Zubin Mehta had seen my *Rigoletto* and when we were talking one day in New York he said 'You know, I've always wanted to do *Tosca*.' We simultaneously said that it really ought to be set in fascist Italy, which I'd always wanted to do. I wanted to set it in the world of Rossellini's *Rome, Open City* – a grey, gritty, Anna Magnani movie world.

MR Many members of the audience in Florence must have lived through the events which formed the background to your production – what was their reaction?

JM It was fantastic, overwhelming – I'd never known anything like it. The production touched a raw nerve of Italian historical guilt, grief and nostalgia. An old woman came up to me afterwards and put a piece of paper in my pocket with the names written on it of people who had been tortured by the fascists, saying 'Thank you for remembering our dead.'

MR Your next production for the ENO was *The Mikado* in 1986 – how do you account for its phenomenal success in London, Los Angeles and Houston?

JM It's just extremely funny and beautiful to look at, and it has verve, energy, an absolutely unrestrained sense of fun and great inventiveness. The piece had been completely embalmed up till then in this literal Japaneserie – again, it's a failure to distinguish between use and mention.

MR When you directed *The Barber of Seville* for the ENO in 1987, you broke away from the tradition of taking the title literally by returning to its Goldoni-esque origins.

JM Yes, with those wonderful dolls, but without being a literal re-creation of *commedia dell'arte*.

MR Bartolo looked as if he'd stepped out of the surgery of Hogarth's *Quack Doctor*.

JM Bartolo the anatomist. It was based on something I'd seen in Bologna – a doctor who was in fact famous as a maker of wax anatomical models.

FREELANCE 1982–1989

MR When you were going from project to project as a freelance director in the early 1980s, did you ever feel the need for a base?

JM I think I've always felt that it would be nice to have a small place in which to work. It turned out to be slightly larger than I'd imagined when I was offered the Old Vic in 1987.

MR You directed your third production of *Hamlet* at the Donmar Warehouse in 1982 – were you attracted to that theatre by the potential of a small space?

JM   I like the idea of a small space, and it proved very pleasant. (I didn't like the fact that we got forced into a much larger theatre, the Piccadilly, later on just in order to pay the mortgage on it.) It was a very clear *Hamlet*, with nothing romantic about it. There were all sorts of psychological motives which were very clearly delineated in it.

MR   How did you approach the madness in the play?

JM   I tried to get Ophelia's madness to look much less feyly romantic – it usually becomes a sort of Laura Ashley scene. I had her really hallucinating, listening to voices, as well as attempting to force her fingers down her throat. I don't think Hamlet is mad – he feigns madness, he feigns eccentricity and tangential thought, that's all. Anton Lesser was wonderful in the role – agonised, like a student, vulnerable and intelligent, fastidious and pained. I wanted to make Claudius slightly sympathetic. Here was a man who was a victim not necessarily of lust but perhaps of overpowering love, which actually might have made him want to murder his competitor. I'm very interested in the idea of people whose motives are complicated rather than simple and stereotyped. The idea that villainy is a pure, unstructured motive is simple-minded. The idea that this is a lustful monster makes him just uninteresting. I love the idea of people who in fact do dreadful things in the name of quite commendable feelings. Perhaps he loved her. Hamlet is the one who thinks dirty thoughts about them – he keeps on talking about 'incestuous sheets', and making love over the nasty sty and all that horrible imagery of love.

MR   For your next project, the BBC TV series *States of Mind*, you acted almost as an impresario, bringing together a variety of psychologists who complemented each other in different ways, as, in fact, you had done a decade earlier for your book on Freud.

JM   I was following my own line of curiosity – at that time I was beginning to develop a major interest in modern cognitive psychology. The great revolution that took place in psychology in the late 1950s was acknowledged in the series. The episodes weren't all about that, but it was perhaps a larger representation than there had been previously in any public medium of those people who represented what was called cognitivism and functionalism – Dennett, Fodor, Mandler and George Miller, they all represented the great forefront of the cognitive revolution.

MR   Your work in the theatre has always been uniquely informed on a psychological level.

JM It has always been informed by moral psychology, the psychology of motive, dynamic psychology, or loosely speaking, psychoanalytic psychology. I had always kept that rather separate from my neurologically-determined experimental, scientific psychology. But over the last ten years my interest has swung very heavily in the direction of cognitivism, so-called functionalism, and the experimental psychology of memory, perception and so forth – information-processing.

MR When did you begin to develop an interest in speech act theory?

JM When I was studying linguistics, which was to do with my long exposure to philosophy. Ever since I was at Cambridge I've been interested in the philosophy of science, and I was deeply influenced there by people who I suppose you would loosely say belonged to the Karl Popper, Peter Medawar anti-inductivist school.

MR Very anti-Freudian.

JM I didn't take on board their anti-Freudianism; what I was influenced by was their interest in hypothetico-deductive systems – the role taken in hypothesis as opposed to induction. The classical Baconian theory of scientific theory-making was that you gathered a heap of data and then generalised. But, of course, people like Popper, Russell Hanson and Richard Gregory – and even Gombrich in his theories about art – put much more emphasis not on what were called the data-driven ideas but on hypothesis-driven ideas – that is, what you often do is to arrive at a hypothesis which goes far beyond the information given, and then you check to see. I was deeply influenced by that sort of Popperian science and by my teacher at Cambridge, Russell Hanson.

   I continued way into the seventies when a lot of that was modified under the auspices of Thomas Kuhn in his *Structure of the Scientific Revolutions*, where he talked much more about the role of the scientific community on the acceptance and the acceptability of scientific theory. I came under the influence of that, and I also became very influenced by the work of John Austin in the late fifties after the posthumous publication of his William James lectures *How To Do Things with Words* – what were called 'performative utterances' – and the development of that by John Searle in speech act theory. Speech act theory has influenced my work in the theatre not in the sense that it's determined my choices on stage, but in the sense that it's retrospectively encouraged me to take the initiative that I would have taken for other reasons because it seemed to corroborate speech act theory. Cognitive psychology and experimental psychology are much more concerned with events which occur quite far down in the psychological process and don't really impinge on choices which occur in the theatre – they're to do with information-processing, the perception of objects, recognition, memory and that really has no effect on the theatre at all.

MR   You gathered together a rich cast for your next production, *The Beggar's Opera* for BBC TV in 1984.

JM   That's right – Roger Daltrey, Peter Bayliss, Bob Hoskins, Rosie Ashe and Graham Crowden, among others. Daltrey's Macheath got well away from that 'Gentleman Jack' stereotype – he was a crook, a rough Cockney crook. Daltrey had this extraordinary sexual energy on screen – he gave Macheath this anarchic Cockney energy so that he became an East End gangster.

MR   Like *McVicar* [a crime thriller starring Roger Daltrey]?

JM   Yes – seeing the *McVicar* film, in fact, was what made me cast Roger.

MR   You returned to Mozart in 1985 when you directed a film version of *Così fan tutte* for BBC TV – how was that a development on your previous productions of the opera for Kent Opera and St Louis Opera, Missouri?

JM   They all changed, but it was a variation on a theme of the eighteenth-century concerns with the conflict between nature and reason. I was always concerned to maintain its very strict, symmetrical eighteenth-century structure, and not to haul it into the twentieth century. I was very struck by the paintings of Joseph Wright of Derby and based the first scene on them – I wanted young men hanging over the illuminated table of an eighteenth-century *philosophe*, who was concerned to demonstrate the fact that human nature was not what these young men in their sentimental delusions thought it to be.

MR   When you directed *Long Day's Journey into Night* in 1986 – first on Broadway, then in London's West End and finally as a BBC TV film – your approach to the text was partly determined by your interest in the dynamics of conversation, as in your *Three Sisters* – was this particular case related to the research work you had just done at Sussex University?

JM   Yes – I was very, very interested there in the organisation of talk, the rhythms of conversation. It was the sort of work which had been investigated and examined very carefully not only by Erving Goffman but also by a very interesting man called Emanuel Schegloff at UCLA.

MR   You were dealing with a sacred cow when you directed the play first of all in America.

JM   Again there were rigid canons of how it ought to be done – that it should move slowly with great mythical dignity, that these contemporary figures were casting large mythical shadows which would remind one of the *Agamemnon*. I think that's balderdash. What makes it attractive is that it's about ordinary people living out a rather mean, squashed little life, being dishonest with each other and with themselves, and that's enough to be going on with, thank you very much. You don't need to mythologise that in order to make it important and interesting.

MR   Instead of taking the traditional approach to the play and mythologising it, you naturalised it.

JM   Totally. I managed to take an hour and ten minutes off the running time because I got them speaking at the right speed and overlapping their lines a little bit. Everyone talked about it as 'the overlapping production' – it's just that there was some overlapping in it, as there is in normal conversation. People don't necessarily hear other people out to the end. The cast were excellent, particularly the two boys, who were just dazzling.

MR   What inspired you to cast Jack Lemmon as James Tyrone?

JM   A producer said to me, 'I've got the rights to the play – who would you cast as James Tyrone if you were going to do it?' I replied that I would quite like to see what would happen if you had someone like Jack Lemmon, who could play him as a shmuck. You mustn't take a character at his own evaluation of himself, or indeed even at the author's evaluation. There's no indication that James Tyrone was a great actor at all – he was a sentimental old ham. He may have been a barnstormer at one time, but he was a foolish, mean person who just lived in theatrical digs too much.

MR   The following year you returned to the Royal Court – for the first time in twenty-five years – to direct your adaptation (with Michael Hastings) of Kapúscínski's *The Emperor* at the Theatre Upstairs.

JM   *The Emperor* is something of which I'm very proud indeed. It was pure and clear, and Michael Hastings and I worked well on the adaptation – we slimmed it down and produced a clear version. In rehearsal with these really wonderful black actors, and particularly with Nabil Shaban, something very peculiar emerged which somehow was larger than the sum of its parts and brought something to it that the text didn't have in its own right.

I'm not saying it got better than the text, but it brought something to it which the mere reading of the text didn't have.

MR   The surrealism of your production was extraordinary – like Maya-kovsky or Kafka.

JM   It was very Kafka-esque, yes, and indeed Kapúscínski saw himself in that tradition. It wasn't really about Ethiopia – as he said, it was about Poland and language.

MR   The production was a huge success – after a sell-out run in the Theatre Upstairs it transferred to the main house, before being filmed for television and toured to Poland.

JM   The transfer from the studio space of the Theatre Upstairs to the main stage of the Royal Court was not so favourable to the production. There's a certain correct proportion for a thing of that sort, just as there was with the *Hamlet,* and you get an explosive decompression when you put it into a large chamber for which it's not intended – it gets denatured, and if you suddenly, explosively reduce the pressure the stuff just flies apart. The production later went to Warsaw and was enormously successful there – Kapúscínski was very, very pleased with it and really enjoyed our version.

MR   Then came your bad experience with *Tristan and Isolde* at the Los Angeles Music Center ...

JM   It was one of those things where you make a wrong choice – it was the wrong place, for a start. It turned out to be 'An Occasion', for the display of a David Hockney set – I was nothing more than an estate agent showing people around the premises.

MR   You went to Stratford next to make your debut with the Royal Shake-speare Company, directing *The Taming of the Shrew.*

JM   I was suddenly invited to do it out of the blue by Terry Hands. I think by that time he recognised that he had to have new blood in the place – not that I'm that new blood, but I certainly was for the RSC. The production was honest to the past – which, again, is very unfashionable today – and it re-created a Tudor world of marriage. It demonstrated the idea that the role of the husband and father in the Tudor household, particularly in the Puritan household, was very much based on authority, not in order to flatter some demand of men but because there was a theological idea derived from St Paul, and indeed from the Old Testament, which placed the husband and the father as a magistrate acting on behalf of God in a fallen world. The idea of original sin there was not that everyone is sinful, but that since we are the inheritors of this original sin of Adam's the world can only be kept in order by the exercise of some authority who acted as God's deputy on earth. I simply followed that through, and added to it the idea that Kate's behaviour is that of an unloved child. Anyone who has children should know that.

MR   I remember Kate's first entrance, snipping off locks of her hair.

JM   That's uglification – if you are thought to be unattractive and un-pleasant, you start to mutilate yourself to confirm other people's diagnosis.

MR   To what extent was the production a development on your two pre-vious versions?

JM   It went a long way beyond them in that respect, emphasising the uglification. The sixteenth-century world is, as the social historian Peter Laslett said in those great works that he did in the sixties, a particular structure of social life that one doesn't look back to with any nostalgia. We can't look back to it with nostalgia because we didn't experience it, but there is not even any vicarious nostalgia – we don't want to go back to it. But nevertheless it seems to be something which we ought to visit. We have some sort of commitment, I believe – as the Annales historians like Braudel, Bloch and Febvre point out – to reconstruct and understand the *mentalité* of a given period, not to reconstruct it according to our own standards.

MR   You displayed that commitment in your television production of Michael Ignatieff's *Dialogue in the Dark* in 1989, a Schama-esque evo-cation and examination of the eighteenth-century world of the Enlightenment.

JM   Yes – it was an attempt to create a sense of what it was like to live in that world of the Enlightenment, still darkened by fears of the after-life.

MR   You had directed philosophical dialogues for television before that – *The Drinking Party* from Plato's *Symposium*, and *The Death of Socrates*, for instance.

JM   I've always liked the idea of the philosophical dialogue. It seems to me that ideas are dramatic, but there's a philistine notion today – particularly in the press – that ideas can't be dramatic, that the only things that can be dramatic are powerful emotions which issue in strong and dramatic actions. But I think that there are inner actions of the mind, and conflicts of ideas, which are also dramatic. People say, 'Oh, you let your head rule your heart' – it seems to me that the heart and the head are both provinces of dramatic action. I'm interested in Hume and Boswell, the participants in the dialogue – as I am in Johnson – because I'm interested in eighteenth-century thought.

THE OLD VIC 1988–1990 (ARTISTIC DIRECTOR)

MR How did you become Artistic Director of the Old Vic?

JM I was asked. It was completely fortuitous, like so many of the events in my life – unsolicited invitations come my way and I say, 'Yes, I don't mind if I do.' The Mirvishes, I think, had become disappointed with the outcome of the previous regime at the Vic, when it wasn't going anywhere, and they realised that it really ought to have someone with an idea. So they came to me and said, 'Have you got a way of doing it?' I replied 'I think I do – if we can restore it to its classical function.' It had acquired its reputation under the auspices of Lilian Baylis, who regarded it as a place in which the classics should be seen. Then we had to renew that idea and also bring it into some sort of relationship with the modern European theatre.

MR Was that your aim for the Old Vic?

JM Yes – I wanted to have a classical theatre which would go back to what I had enjoyed as a child, and add to it features of the European repertoire which were very conspicuous by their absence from much of the traditional planning.

MR You developed a very innovative production style straight away in your work with Richard Hudson.

JM I was determined to have a clean sweep visually.

MR You opened your first season at the Old Vic with a production of Racine's *Andromache* – how did you face the problem of translating a playwright whose works are often described as unplayable in English?

JM I was first drawn to the play by reading Richard Wilbur's translation, which seemed to jog along in a rather monotonous way from one rhyming couplet to the next and seemed inappropriate to tragedy (although it worked very beautifully in comedy for *The Liar*). So I then had to consider someone else – I wanted to have a muscular, rather modern translation which would honour the peculiar austerity of Racine and at the same time bring it into the twentieth century. I naturally went to a poet first of all, and asked Craig Raine to do it. He turned in a very peculiar transformation which went far beyond what I could possibly do in my inaugural production, though it did have tremendously salient virtues – it was very energetic indeed. But it was so far out, such a radical transformation of time, place and character, that I think it would have been suicidal to have opened with it. So I reluctantly had to turn it down. Finally, in an emergency, I went to my friend Eric Korn, who had always been a witty writer, a good translator and a poet at school. He turned in a rather energetic and interesting translation, but some people hated it – it drew an endless series of condescending remarks from people who suddenly became the greatest French experts in the world. I still think it's a wonderful translation.

MR   Your production was as concentrated on a dramatic level as Racine's text is on a literary level.

JM   It was concentrated, austere, ruined, despairing and bleak. It brought out all sorts of references to the past and to the present in this strange, suffocating limbo.

2 Set design by Richard Hudson for *Andromache*, Old Vic 1988

MR The movement had a baroque, poised quality.

JM Yes, but at the same without being static or studiously reproductive. The set, in fact, was based on the façade of the Coronet Cinema in Notting Hill Gate, and then we simply stacked the various storeys on it. It was a marvellous creation of Richard Hudson's.

MR Its tilted, toppling angles were stunning – nothing like it had been seen before in the London theatre.

JM Yes, but some people still said, 'I can't understand why it has to be at that angle.'

MR You followed it with a revival of N. F. Simpson's *One Way Pendulum* – did you have a soft spot for the play, having appeared in the film version yourself in 1964?

JM Yes I did, but unfortunately it turned out to be a bad choice. It was admirably acted by a first-rate cast – Peter Bayliss, Graham Crowden, John Bird and John Fortune, among others – but the play itself was caught in a sort of time-warp, I'm afraid. It was not the right time to do it, even though it was a good production and beautifully performed.

MR Your next production, Chapman's *Bussy D'Ambois*, proved to be a revelation, as the play had lain unperformed ever since its première in 1604.

JM In a way, it's the thing I'm almost more proud of than anything else in the season, really. It was a highly original, interesting thing to do, staged clearly and with imagination. I gave it an edge of surrealism, which is there in Chapman anyway. It honoured the period and made references to other times. Quite predictably – and typically – the critics wondered why it was being done at all.

MR What drew you to it?

JM It just seemed to me to be so interesting. Its dense, pessimistic atheism was one of the things that I liked so much. It's filled with the most wonderful scenes – the adulterous scenes between Tamyra and Bussy, the formal insulting scene between Monsieur and Bussy, and the court scenes. There are also those electrifyingly peculiar ghosts. It's a marvellous play.

MR You then directed *The Tempest*, a play which you had previously staged at the Mermaid Theatre in 1970.

JM   The Old Vic *Tempest* had several things in common with the production
that I had done at the Mermaid, where Graham Crowden played Prospero.
I was very proud of Max von Sydow's Prospero at the Vic – he was sober,
restrained and noble.

MR   The Old Vic production seemed to embody the idea of sixteenth-
century Europe reaching out to the New World.

JM   It was that, and the idea of a certain people being recognisably 'other'.
I became very fascinated by that.

MR   You also broke away from stereotypes like the campy, sprite-like
Ariel.

JM   I can't bear all that. I was deeply influenced in my approach to the play
by *Prospero and Caliban*, a work of psychoanalytic anthropology by
Mannoni, and by the idea of what happens to a character when in fact
someone submits to the role of infant – the infantilising of people, and the
resentment which underlies infantile subjection.

MR   That came out strongly in your treatment of Miranda.

JM   Yes, indeed – they're all children. She achieves her womanhood only at
the moment when she escapes from this paternal control of her father. The
same applies to Ariel and Caliban – they're all infants, looking towards
adulthood of some sort.

MR   Your final production in your first Old Vic season was a musical,
Leonard Bernstein's *Candide* – were you attracted to it because of the
Enlightenment themes of Voltaire's novel?

JM   Yes I was, even though those themes are not so conspicuously present
in the musical as they are in the original novel. The music had done
something very different to it, particularly in its previous incarnations. We
had a devil of a time restructuring and making a new organism out of a
thing which had actually always been in bits and pieces – we had a real job
of surgical reconstruction. I rather wanted to put together a musical. It was
Broadway, and at the same time it did make very imaginative visual
references to the past. Richard Hudson's work on that was simply
masterly.

MR   You opened your second season at the Old Vic in 1989 with your
fourth production of *King Lear* – how did it compare to its predecessors?

JM   It was the one which departed most from the others. Each one of the
previous three had really been very closely clustered around the inaugural

3 Paul Rogers (silhouetted) as Gloucester, *King Lear*, Old Vic 1989

production. I broke much further away in that I deliberately chose much older sons and daughters for Gloucester and Lear. It seemed to me to be middle-aged children becoming impatient with elderly parents. I suppose that's the result of having grown to that age myself – I wanted to see what would happen if you really had the daughters in their fifties. The appearance of the production was partly based on *Ivan the Terrible*, with references to the Russian court.

MR In the summer, you directed *La Traviata* for Glimmerglass Opera in New York State – I remember you referring to a catalogue from a Paris costume show during rehearsals.

JM I used that for the setting. I wanted a bare space, which nevertheless allowed me to make unconfusing references to where it was set. I didn't want to set it in a limbo – it is a socially realistic world, like that of Flaubert's novels – but I didn't want to have it just heavily and literally upholstered like a traditional production. I had long lusted after that set of whitewashed boards which had been used for a costume exhibition at the Musée des Arts Décoratifs in Paris. Bernard Culshaw and I worked on that together – it was virtually a co-design. In fact, I painted half the set myself. I love mucking in like that.

MR   Unlike most *Traviata*s, it never descended into the stock responses and exaggerated gestures of Grand Opera.

JM   It was an intimate piece of realistic drama. The costumes were very much based on the appearance of those Nadar photographs of 1850.

MR   Like your previous production for Kent Opera, there were many moments of total stillness – the encounters between Violetta and Germont, for instance, or Germont and Alfredo.

JM   As I say, I believe that stillness is very eloquent. There are a lot of directors who believe that they're not showing their hand unless things are moving. I've been justified in my choices in that respect by Sherrington, the neurologist, who showed that just as much energy goes into inaction as excitation – you can actually create an enormously energetic effect by abstaining from action. Often, by action, you disperse much of the energy contained in a scene.

MR   There was plenty of action in your next production, though: *Mahagonny* at the Los Angeles Music Center.

JM   Yes there was – it's a huge great anarchic farce. I based it on the world of the painter George Grosz and – much more, really – Hollywood movies, particularly those of the Keystone Cops and Mack Sennett. It's a difficult piece, and at this particular time in history its Marxism and its exemplary, formulary economic cynicism is extremely threadbare – I simply said, 'Let's make it into a slightly cynical romance', which is the most that it is. To lend oneself to that elementary, didactic Brechtianism is simply to be out of touch with modern times. I refuse – at a time when Berlin is breaking down the Wall – to actually do a production based on what was going on behind the Wall at its worst. Brecht was a fraudulent Marxist, a quisling.

MR   You also avoided the ritual Brechtiana of banners, signs etc.

JM   I can't bear all that self-conscious street-demo promotion.

MR   You returned to the Old Vic at the end of the 1989 season to direct

Corneille's comedy *The Liar*, a play never seen before in Britain – what attracted you to it?

JM   What attracted me to it was the arrival of an unsolicited manuscript from Ranjit Bolt. Quite suddenly this rather masterly translation, with its brilliant, fizzing *joie de vivre*, arrived on my desk and I just said, 'Well, this must be done.' I was originally going to do it a year later, but when we had to cancel our scheduled production of *Lulu* because of the illness of Peter Zadek I had to move very quickly, and here was this thing standing by and ready to go. It was a very risky thing to do – it's so light and frothy that it's like a soufflé, and when you take it out of the oven it could very easily collapse. But we managed to cook it at just the right temperature and just the right rate, so that when it came out of the oven it was wonderfully light and meringue-like.

MR   One of the highlights of your production was the double-act of Alex Jennings and Desmond Barrit as the eponymous liar and his servant.

JM   I had worked with Alex Jennings before when he was in my *Taming of the Shrew* at the RSC, and I'd already had him at the Old Vic in Richard Jones' production of *Too Clever by Half*. So I knew his work well – the two of them just seemed ideal together.

MR   Peter J. Davison's set designs further developed the visual theme of unconcealed artifice that you had used in your recent *Traviata* and *Mahagonny*.

JM   Yes, except it was much more directly making allusions to pretence and lying, and to the theatrical illusion itself. Some of the set was turned back to front in order to make a reference to the idea that what you see on the surface is not what in fact is behind.

FUTURE PLANS 1990 . . .

MR   You've directed all four major Mozart operas (*Così* no less than three times), and you're now about to embark on a new Mozart cycle with Zubin Mehta at the Maggio Musicale in Florence. How much will it be a development on your original productions?

JM   Obviously I will reconsider the operas, but I'll also borrow bits and pieces from my earlier work. It's impossible to go completely against one's own previous ideas – there are very few of my productions which I would want to change altogether. And because I've got the same team for all four there will undoubtedly be a unity of approach, though they will inevitably be very different productions because they are very different operas. *Cosi*, for example, is much more artificial and mechanical than the others. Still, I feel that they are eighteenth-century works and are much more interesting if they are dealt with in that light.

MR   How about the other Mozart operas?

JM   I'd like to do *La Clemenza*. That, too, probably doesn't make much sense outside the world of the eighteenth century – it has nothing to do with Ancient Rome, nor is it to do with modern times. It is simply to do with a late eighteenth-century view of the clemency and mercy of an enlightened despot. I'd like to do *Die Entführung* too, but that's a much more artificial piece. Still, there are ways of getting away from all that 'Turkish Delight'.

MR   Your Mozart cycle begins in 1990 with *Don Giovanni* – how will that depart from your ENO production?

JM   Much of my work is in the nature of Midrash, a commentary on previous work. As with variations played by Mozart, I will take my old work and do it again, and almost invariably do a complicated and often – to me – unforseeable variation upon it.

MR   Will you refer to Goya, as you did at the Coliseum?

JM   No, I think it will make much more reference to the earlier eighteenth century. The peasant costumes are all based upon a North Italian painter of the eighteenth century called Cherutti. There will be no landscape in this, just great shards of architecture leaning against one another. This time I've got another tomb for the Commendatore – when I did the opera with Philip Prowse at the ENO, I'd seen a tomb in Strasburg by Pigalle. Now I've found another tomb by Pigalle, this time in Notre Dame, where the figure is leaning out of his coffin looking like Marat in his bath.

MR   You're also preparing a television series on language at the same time.

JM   It's an introduction to linguistics, seen in four different modes – the child's acquisition of language, the stroke patient's loss of language, the alternative language if you haven't got hearing, and then talk.

MR   Your other television project for 1991 is an epic undertaking, a history of lunacy entitled *Museums of Madness* – will that be in the tradition of *The Body In Question*?

JM   The same sort of thing, but slightly different because it's rather an unmanageable subject. It looks at the history of the idea to see how unstable and strangely undetermined this notion of lunacy is.

MR   You have a whole series of operas lined up for 1991, beginning with *The Girl of the Golden West* at La Scala, Milan.

JM   It's an odd piece. I think the production will look back to the early movies of the Wild West, and also at the mining photographs of the 1850s and 1860s.

MR   After that you'll return to Janáček, when you direct *Katya Kabanova* at the Metropolitan Opera House, New York.

JM   That will be very simple and focussed, so you can see things happening to the human relationships. I'm somewhat apprehensive, though, about working in big houses like the Met and La Scala – I don't think my best work is necessarily in those places. It's a very risky thing to do – like trying to walk the tightrope stretched between the twin towers of the World Trade Center in New York.

MR   Then it's back to Florence for the continuation of your Mozart cycle at the Maggio Musicale.

JM   Constantly refining my Mozart productions is very interesting. Midrash, again.

MR   The opera that year will be *Così fan tutte* – what are you aiming for in your fourth production of the opera?

JM   I want to draw on the work of Thomas Jones, a wonderful painter who simply just looks at rooftops in Naples. That would be a major development on my previous productions. I hope we can pull it off – it may only work in painting, so I'll have to really think about it very hard.

MR   You'll follow that with another Mozart, *The Magic Flute*, at the Mann Auditorium in Tel Aviv.

JM   That will be based on clockwork figures – I'm interested in those mechanical toys of the eighteenth century.

MR   In your *Magic Flute* for ENO and Scottish Opera, you based Papageno's appearance on a Meissenware bird-catcher.

JM   Yes indeed. The traditional way is to dress him in feathers, but I can't understand why *he* has to be like a bird – he catches birds, he doesn't have to look like one.

MR   In the summer of 1991, you'll return to Glimmerglass Opera in New York State – what attracts you to the company?

JM   It's a small outfit, and it's like a holiday with opera. I love it there.

MR   You have several operas planned for Glimmerglass, including *Fidelio* in 1991 and *The Makropulos Case* in 1992 – what do you have in mind for these at this early stage?

JM   I'd quite like to reproduce what I did with Bernard Culshaw in my Kent Opera *Fidelio* – it was very simple and abstract. I'm looking forward to *The Makropulos Case* enormously because I like Janáček very much – he's the greatest musical dramatist of the twentieth century.

Ideas and definitions of theatre

MR   How do you see the role of the director? You've compared it, for instance, to that of a museum curator.

JM   I think that's one of the things that a director is – in a sense, by default he's bound to be that. If, like me, you work almost exclusively with plays which come from the distant past, at least one of your functions is custodial. You have these artefacts which have been lying around in the basement of the building – often undisplayed, or perhaps too frequently displayed – so that therefore you've got a sort of custodial task of what you do with these ancient artefacts. So at least one aspect of a director's job, if he happens to involve himself with works from the distant past, is like that of a museum curator – you have to decide what is the purpose of displaying them, what sort of restoration work has to be done on them, with what other things they should be displayed, and what their genre is. In other words, all the sort of questions which arise in the mind of anyone who has the task of reviving, restoring and redisplaying works which have outlived their makers, which have got their own natural history and their own after-life.

   That's only one of the things a director is – that in a way is a necessary condition, you are unavoidably that if you deal with works from the past. The question is what you are in addition to that by virtue of simply being someone who has the task of putting stuff on the stage whether it comes from the past or not. In one sense you are a benevolent (I hope) paterfamilias – you run a small family of people who have assigned you the task of taking decisions.

MR Your own direction is very unself-conscious – you have no pretensions to being a guru.

JM I don't believe in being a source of wisdom, though I think I'm sometimes a source of information. One of the responsibilities of a director is to have read a lot, meditated a lot, seen many things, and to have had as full an education as he can achieve. But I don't believe that he's a figure of authority. I think that your cast defers to you necessarily – not because you have got this authoritarian role, but simply because there is an agreement which assigns to one person, who is not actually performing, the task of making some sort of decision about how everyone is to perform. In that sense it's a position of being a constitutional monarch.

MR You don't dictate to your actors, though.

JM I think I'm very undictatorial. I talk quite a lot, but I never insist or dictate. I prefer to suggest and stimulate. It's like being the benevolent father of a family in that you are a source of information and in some sense you have wider experience in reading than some of the actors have – therefore you can tell good stories. Much of the function of the director is to be a source of amusing, instructive stories, parables and proverbs. By putting all this together, you inspire the positive work of the actor. I don't think of the actor as a passive marionette who is manipulated by the director's hands – that would be a disaster. There are people, though, who do think of it like that.

I do have a strong idea about what the production ought to be like. That brings me to the third function of the director as I see it, which is to act like a critic – a literary critic, not a newspaper critic (God forbid one should be like that). There's a hermeneutic, interpretive function – you try to penetrate meanings of the text (not *the* meaning – I don't think there are univocal meanings). I think that this interpretive function is one of the main functions of a director, certainly one who deals with works from the past where the texts are becoming dark and in some sense impenetrable.

MR One of the distinguishing features of your work as a director is your ability to see a play or an opera in the light of the culture which produced it.

JM   It's very important to emphasise that the task of interpretation is not one of tying something in with other things – the question is, 'What do you bring to the act of interpretation?' You bring circumstantial evidence to bear, and the cultural circumstances are the other features of the *mentalité* of a given period which are found, seen and expressed in painting, law, rites and rituals, philosophy, beliefs and so forth. Therefore you simply have to acquaint yourself with what it was like to be *them* – one of the ways you do this is by looking at the stuff they've left behind them. Art is some of the stuff that gets preserved because it is valued at the time. Lots of other stuff which is less valued at the time doesn't get left behind, and therefore there are lots and lots of pieces of domestic equipment which don't survive. It's often those which would be much more valuable in helping you to make these acts of interpretation. The act of interpretation has to be armed and equipped. There's a very great danger if you think of it in terms of art history or 'cultivation' – there's an air of simply mandarin decoration. You have to acquaint yourself with what there is to be known about a given period. If you're doing research on a topic – whether it's in the theatre or not – you simply have to be familiar with the resources of a library. You have to know how to use it, how to cross-file and cross-reference.

MR   As in your reconstruction of the eighteenth-century world of the Enlightenment in your production of *The Magic Flute*?

JM   Perhaps it was more visibly bringing those things to bear, because of Ledoux, Boullée and the masonic ideas. In that particular case I was trying to get away from the traditional modern notion of masonry. Unfortunately most people, when representing freemasonry on the English stage for *The Magic Flute*, do so in terms of modern freemasonry – that is so fundamentally different from freemasonry as it was conceived in the eighteenth century, when it still had its Rosicrucian roots, as well as its horizontal connections with other occultist movements in Europe and notions of the ancient wisdom and theology. I simply had to retrieve what it meant for people at the time.

MR   How has your direction benefited from your background in science?

JM   I think the most important point is that I came into the theatre later and wasn't trained in the theatre. With people who start their professional life very early on in the theatre, the theatre is where they get their education rather than the place in which they apply their education. They educate themselves from production to production and do what is called their 'homework' – it's as if the production was an exercise which required homework to get the exercise done properly.

MR   Do you feel that the theatre is generally an insular area of activity?

JM   An awful lot of activities are cut off – science itself, for example. Very hard-core professional science makes it difficult for someone to acquire another education while doing it. One of the advantages of the theatre is that you don't have to work so hard that you can't spend a large amount of spare time reading other things. What happens in the theatre is that people tend to read with respect to the production they've got in hand and then not read in between or else read for entertainment. I've never read for entertainment in my life. Or, to put it another way, all my instruction is entertainment – I read all the time, and not with a view to a production. I hope that by the time I come to a production, the reason why I want to do it is that I'm already equipped to understand it and that's why I'm drawn to it, rather than having a project assigned to me and then having to read it up. I usually get drawn to the topic because what I've been reading over the last fifteen years has come to a head.

MR   You constantly move back and forth between theatre and opera – how do you see the relationship between them?

JM   The reason why I can move readily from one to the other is that they are simply different forms of address and talking. Once you've grasped the fact that song is a highly specialised form of talk, rather than an exclusive thing called music, that music on the voice is talk carried on by other methods, then there's no difficulty at all. In that sense they are one and the same. In another interesting way they are also complementary. There are certain things that you learn in the straight theatre *vis-à-vis* real, unmusical talk which can be applied very usefully to the acting which is involved in singing. You can nourish the opera with the sort of straightforward acting skills which are necessarily much more prominent in the speaking theatre – there's no way of disguising bad acting with beautiful singing. But conversely there are all sorts of aspects of rhythm, tone and musicality which I find wash backwards into the theatre as well. After a long period doing operas, going back to the dry secco of talk makes you begin to think in musical terms about it. So that as you go backwards and forwards, the music is vernacularised, and conversely the talk is melodised and harmonised by your experience with opera, so that the two are reciprocal.

MR   How about the simultaneous address in opera – sextets, quartets, and so on?

JM   One of the reasons why I actually did what I did in *Long Day's Journey into Night*, and indeed in other productions where I have introduced overlapping, is that I've always thought of it in musical terms rather than simply a mechanical talking-at-the-same-time. Obviously, one of the reasons why I allow and encourage people to talk simultaneously is that I think that talk as such – regardless of any musical evidence – is like that. You can't do it much in Shakespeare, but you can with ordinary plays.

MR   You did it with the courtiers in *The Tempest*.

JM   Yes, because they speak prose rather than verse. Also, I thought of the scene in *The Tempest* as a rather musical one, therefore I was much more encouraged to do that not merely by the fact that ordinary talk is like that, but also by the fact that in operas there often are scenes with four or five people singing at the same time, overlapping and often singing different stuff. In that sense my experience of opera encourages me to do lots of things in plays that I wouldn't otherwise do, and conversely my experience with organising talk on the stage encourages me to encourage singers to make their diction realistic as well as musically orthodox.

MR   Has your film work carried into the theatre? I'm thinking of the cinematic style of *Mahagonny*, for instance.

JM   I don't think that the cinema has really influenced me very much in making fluid movements and transitions on the stage. Even with my film of *Alice in Wonderland*, the fluidity came from the fluidity of mental imagery rather than the fluidity of the cinema. If I've been encouraged to make things move fluidly from one scene to another, it's not been because of the cinema – that's simply how I visualise it.

MR   You've described the late Colin Blakely as the epitome of everything you admire in an actor – what is that, exactly?

JM   What I liked about Colin Blakely is what I look for and admire in most of the actors that I like, and that is that you couldn't tell that he was an actor off the stage. He wasn't pretty, he had no actor's vanity, he hadn't got an actor's voice – there was nothing trained or beautiful about his voice, but he spoke beautifully if he had need to – and there was an air of unvarnished authenticity about him. This apart from the fact that I loved him personally – he was a person of great generosity and simplicity of heart.

MR   He would have been an ideal King Lear for you.

JM Oh, how wonderful that would have been. I think that he would have been marvellous. There are many things that I would have liked to have worked with him on. I had a marvellous time doing *Antony and Cleopatra* with him.

MR Did you see him play Astrov to Scofield's Vanya at the Royal Court in 1970?

JM Yes, that was the first time that I really noticed what it was that I liked about acting. There was such a sharp, distinct difference between the yodelling, Shaftesbury Avenue artificiality of the well-known actor as opposed to the straightforward, authentic realism of the less well-known actor. Eric Porter and Ronald Pickup are like that too – they just play themselves, as Colin Blakely did.

MR You've never subscribed to Method acting.

JM I don't believe in there being a special method, let alone one which somehow has a connection with psychoanalysis. Acting is mainly to do with pretending, as Olivier once said.

MR And acknowledging that pretence?

JM That's right. You have to be a very, very skilful pretender, and there may be all sorts of tricks you have to bring to the act of pretence which help you to forget yourself and to successfully pretend to be something other than who you are. But I don't think that it's done by closely identifying with the emotions or experiences that you are supposedly projecting. That may be one of the methods you have to use, but the idea of there being A Method, The Method, is just a dogma. It's a dogma which is to do with American public notions of authenticity, a personal authenticity not just cultural authenticity – the idea that to project yourself you must penetrate down to the deep personal self. It's useless for any play, really. I'm not saying that you ought not to be very real when you're in a play which demands active, energetic reality. But I don't believe that's done by really closely identifying with the experience of the person. You may have to study very carefully the sort of person you're trying to represent, and there may be some sort of way in which you can give meaning to the idea of 'getting into the skin' of the person. I don't know what that really means – probably it means understanding the sort of life that person has, studying them.

MR Style is surely also essential to an actor – I'm thinking, for instance, of the brilliant comic timing of Frances de la Tour's throwaway asides as Regan in your Old Vic *King Lear*.

JM Yes – that was not done by her consulting some memory of what it was like to be with her parents, or even any analogous experience. The act of pretence is a very mysterious business – what state of mind you have to be in in order to pretend to do something other than represent your own actual state of mind. One of the things which I find reassuring about actors that I admire is that they are unself-conscious and unpretentious about the pretendingness of what they do.

MR Was Olivier like that?

JM Yes. Olivier studied very carefully. He looked at the sort of person he was trying to represent and took pleasure in annotating and recording their foibles and idiosyncrasies, filtering and editing them so that the ones that he did in fact finally reproduce by a process of synecdoche came to stand for the whole. That's exactly what a very skilful draughtsman does.

MR How have you chosen your designers?

JM I worked for a long time with one team of designers, Pat Robertson and Rosemary Vercoe. We had a very long, happy and fruitful relationship, which I think lasted too long for the good of either party. Your habits become automatic, and you settle down into a comfortable domesticity which in the end works to the disadvantage of both the designer on the one hand and the director on the other (though the *Rigoletto*, which was one of the last things we did together, was very, very good indeed). What then happened was purely by default, not by any decision to split up the partnership. I had been asked to do *The Magic Flute* for Scottish Opera and, for reasons that I can't even remember, decided to commit adultery and asked Philip Prowse to design the production. I enjoyed the experience very much – it was a sort of aesthetic affair, with all the excitement associated with that sort of thing. I suddenly realised how comfortable and unquestioning I had become about the feel and structure of the theatre. Working with someone who had completely different ideas, and who had not been comfortably with me for fifteen years, suddenly pulled me up short – my style changed very abruptly and I began to think very differently.

I think it's very unlikely that in the future I will spend much time with any one designer. It's quite important now, for me at least, to have short, sharp and intense relations – sometimes perhaps extending over several productions with one designer, as I did for a year with Richard Hudson at the Old Vic. I'm sure that I will work with Richard again, but I think it would be disastrous for both of us if we were to become a partnership. It was a very fruitful partnership for the year that we worked together, and revealed many things to me. I was renovated and really enormously rejuvenated by working with a young designer who had all sorts of different assumptions about what the stage might look like. It isn't that there was any fault on the part of the Robertsons – there isn't any fault at all. It's just that a relationship between designer and director which goes on too long means that both parties don't question the fundamental principles of what they're doing. Your genre becomes too familiar, too unself-conscious and not self-critical enough. I like to think that I now come up against the astringency of a young designer and that they come up against a well-educated mind – therefore we both profit from it. Certainly, I know that in the future I will work with one, then another; short bouts of three or four productions with one and then go on to someone else – I think that now it's got to be serial monogamy. It may well be that I will settle down for a year with one designer as I did with Richard Hudson, but I certainly don't think a long second marriage is what I have in mind.

MR Another of the distinguishing features of your work is humour – even in Ibsen and Racine.

JM When you say it's a distinguishing feature – it's simply a distinguishing feature of me. It's just that I think the world is very funny, and it's often funniest at the moments when it's most tragic and destructive and horrible. I just think that life is extremely amusing – darkness is shot through with amusement, and amusement is shot through with tragedy. I see life as Samuel Johnson says Shakespeare did – as a world in which the reveller on the way to the bottle meets the mourner on the way to the grave, and the malice of one is undone by the frolic of another. It's a mixed world, and things don't segregate themselves neatly out of tragedy and comedy.

MR How about religion – has your attitude to that influenced your work?

JM Not noticeably, except that I have a sort of atheist pessimism about the world, which is why I think I identify closely with *King Lear*, which has a pessimistic view of the fact that we're the playthings of cosmic forces and don't really leave much more than a scratch on the surface of the universe. I sympathise greatly with *Bussy D'Ambois* because it makes that point explicit: Chapman actually thinks of nature as a random, blind agency heaping stuff together, and the stuff which nature heaps together sees further than nature herself – that's a wonderful act of intuition on Chapman's part, which anticipates Darwin by 400 years.

MR   Does the fact that you don't subscribe to any religious belief give you a certain irreverence?

JM   Yes it does, and it makes the institutions of religion very visible to me. Whereas if I subscribed to any one of them, I might not see all of them in the way that I do. Since most of the religious institutions with which we deal in plays are in fact ones in which one might otherwise believe – Judaism or Christianity – not subscribing to either of them does enable me to see both of them as leading to all sorts of absurdity. I treat them very much like an anthropologist.

MR   Has it been a conscious decision to work almost entirely in the classical repertory?

JM   It isn't that I'm not interested in the work of a current author, but that I think that the work of a current author is already 90 per cent directed. It's already got its intended meanings very near the surface, so that the function of the director is very much more reticent than I like to be. I like to be much more assertive than the director of a modern play can or should be. Because its meanings lie much nearer the surface, there's much less work for someone like myself to do. One of the jobs of directing that I enjoy is interpretive, and I don't think there's much of a job to be done interpreting modern texts, partly because we are co-extensive with the minds of their makers and therefore our assumptions are very close to being their assumptions. We might disagree with them, but nevertheless they take place in the same cultural context – they're what anthropologists would call 'commensurable'. Whereas the whole point about works which come from the distant past is that there is a very large degree of incommensurability, and it's in that space of incommensurability that I like to operate, where there's work for me to do. Some critics, or even playwrights, might sneeringly say, 'Well of course he does, because he prefers to work with dead authors who can't raise objections.' It's not that the liberty is given to me by the fact that the author's voice is muffled, but that the distance in time makes and creates a large interpretive gap, and therefore there's work to be done in that gap, interesting work. Whereas there's much less interesting work to be done in interpreting a play, or indeed any text, which is written at the same time as yourself, because there's a large degree of commensurability, or overlap of basic assumptions.

MR   You often refer in rehearsal to the work of sociologists Rom Harré and Erving Goffman – what attracts you to it?

JM   I've always been a close observer of human natural history. One of the reasons why I was a fairly good mimic as a child, and later on as a performer onstage, was that I had seen things – idiosyncrasies of behaviour. I enjoyed that very much indeed. When I was a doctor I enjoyed noticing little turns and quirks of behaviour which might have been neglected by my colleagues, or thought to be too trivial to be worth taking notice of. I've always seen and recognised that, more often than not, the trivial, negligible detail is often where the payload is. Freud proved this by identifying the importance of mistakes and slips of the tongue, or the supposed rubbish of dreamwork. So, in the same way, I've always paid attention to the negligible, the trivial, the circumstantial, and taken great pleasure in seeing it. Now you can't just observe in a vacuum – you need a theory in order to give you some way of gathering it all together and making sense of it. One of the things that draws me to Goffman and to people who are influenced by him – Rom Harré, Emanuel Schegloff, Harvey Sacks and many others – is that Goffman has a theory about behaviour in public, about interpersonal behaviour, about the way in which it is involved in maintaining self-esteem and shoring up the boundaries and walls of self. So I'm drawn to Goffman because he has what seems to me a plausible, far-reaching theory about interpersonal behaviour, and that after all is what one is representing on a stage – therefore I find him very interesting. He draws my attention to things that I have overlooked, in a way that I hope with my observations I have drawn other people's attention to things that they have overlooked. You're endlessly paying off debts if you live in a cultural world: you acknowledge the debt which you owe to people who have influenced you, and you pay that debt off not to them – except in the form of an explicit act of gratitude – but you pay off the debt by drawing the attention of other people to things that you have noticed which they might have overlooked.

MR   Has that also happened with Ernst Gombrich on a visual level?

JM   I was greatly influenced by Gombrich when I was younger, less now because other people have influenced me in the same field – Wölfflin, Panofsky, Schapiro and many other art historians, almost too many to mention. Gombrich influenced me not so much because of the art history, but because of the emphasis that he put upon the idea of the hypothesis preceding the gathering of evidence. I was influenced by Gombrich because of other people who also influenced me – with whom he has been closely associated on an intellectual level – who were also subscribers to the idea that the hypothesis often goes beyond the information given. That refers also to Karl Popper – it's anti-Baconian. The Baconian idea was that you heaped up lots of data and then made theories out of it, whereas of course we now know that it tends to go in the opposite direction – what you do is to make hypotheses often on the basis of very slender evidence and then you go looking for evidence which will corroborate or falsify what you have. I think this is a very useful way of thinking about art, perception and conduct in general. That cluster of people of whom Gombrich is a very important member – Gombrich, Medawar, Popper, Richard Gregory, and then of course associated thinkers like George Miller and Kenneth Craik – all put great emphasis on hypothesis-making, theory-testing and so forth. I've been very influenced by all of those, and Gombrich is simply one amongst a number of people.

MR You've also been influenced in your approach to works from the past by the Annales school of French historians.

JM Like many people who are interested in history I've been influenced by a number of historians, and the Annales historians have had a very, very powerful effect on my theatrical thinking. I like Auden's phrase 'breaking bread with the dead' – that's one of the reasons why we do these plays. But the Annales historians – Bloch, Febvre, Le Goff, Braudel – have had a great influence on me and made me think differently, as indeed have a number of historians of medicine who have also been influenced by the reaction against the Whig view of history. Roy Porter, for example, has influenced me, certainly in thinking about the history of medicine, and perhaps that's had an influence on the way I think about the theatre as well. In the history of medicine there's been a huge reaction against this progressionist idea that history is a slow story of a series of triumphant enlightenments – it's obviously not like that at all. We now think very differently about the history of medicine and science, and indeed the history of institutions and cultures.

MR How has your work as a director affected your personal life?

JM Directing abroad is a strain on family life. I go abroad perhaps too much, perhaps my children have suffered from my periodic absences. Yet they've not been as thick as all that – my absences have been thicker since my children grew up. There's nothing remotely 'showbiz' about my life – I simply happen to work in the theatre, and the rest of the time I have no connection with it at all. It doesn't impress me or amuse me until I'm actually on the floor working with the spanners and drills on the job.

MR How do you feel about the current state of the theatre?

JM I'm rather depressed by it. It's not thought to be interesting or exciting in the way that it once was. Audiences are much harder to draw into the theatre, unless they are drawn by hyperbolically complicated and glamorous musicals or famous names and very familiar plays. There is a morbid desire now to draw attention to the artwork, and a sort of punk surrealism which is part and parcel of the same sensibility that you find on *01 for London*, *Rapido* and pop videos. In a culture which is only 2 millimetres deep, the surrealism borrowed from the 1920s without acknowledgement to its roots is the prevailing form of stylish theatre. It hasn't got any thought behind it, though it often borrows the term 'Deconstructionism' to justify itself and have a fashionable name, but most of the people have never read anything deconstructionist at all – what they do is just borrow the name. I am rather against the idea of deconstructionism. I don't even credit the practitioners with an idea – I think that they are filled with fashionable nonsense. I'm heavily committed to a philosophical tradition of Anglo-American logical analysis and the anthropology of the late twentieth century – the balderdash that gets proffered in the name of deconstructionism and postmodernism is just advertising slogans.

MR Which directors do you admire today?

JM I like the continental directors – they seem to accomplish reconstruction and modernity without resort to shallow surrealist tricks, and their work is informed and nourished by some sort of relationship to the past and a willingness to take the past in its own terms (as far as one can identify what those terms are). In Britain, the Glasgow Citizens' Theatre is one for which I have great admiration.

MR You've been plagued by critics for much of your career – what are your feelings towards them?

JM I don't really think very much about critics – they are simply a chronic irritant. Some people say that I am too sensitive about them – most of the people who say it are usually critics themselves. They're one of the risks of the job. If you're a district officer who happens to work in Africa, you know that after a long time there you'll come back with hook-worm and bilharzia – I've got hook-worm and bilharzia.

MR Was Tynan a different case?

JM Yes – he was a practitioner, a presence in the theatre as well as a writer about it. He was accepted in the community, whereas none of the other

93

critics have been accepted – with the exception of Ronald Bryden, who worked as dramaturg for the Royal Shakespeare Company.

MR   Another fascination of yours is the idea of visualising literature, which formed the basis of the Clark Lectures that you gave at Cambridge in 1984 – is this a further development of your interest in the nature of representation?

JM   As I was saying earlier, I've always been interested in the notion of representation and in the logical principles that link two forms of representation which supposedly refer to the same thing. What is the relationship between a description of A and a depiction of A? Is the mere fact that they converge on the same reference enough to say that they are the same? I don't believe they are: I believe, in Frege's view of the matter, that reference does not necessarily mean that they have the same sense – things can have an identical reference without having the same sense. It is difficult to go from a description to a depiction, because descriptions are often so conspicuously lacking in the things which a depiction must have in order not to count as a depiction with holes in it. Conversely, there are many things in a description which simply cannot be put into a depiction – propositional attitudes and complicated subtleties of tense – so that there are sins of omission and sins of commission in a depiction which supposedly is a depiction of whatever it is that is described. Describing and depicting are not the same enterprise, even though they happen to have a common reference.

MR   How does this apply, for instance, to your film version of *Alice in Wonderland*?

JM   I didn't try to go from a description to a depiction – I made it quite clear that what I was doing was a travesty. It is not my depiction of what is described in Lewis Carroll, but is something altogether different.

MR   To what extent will a reader visualise a character in a novel?

JM   Visualising is not in fact picturing in the full sense of the word picturing. Making a picture outside the body with your hands – be it with a camera or with paint and canvas – is not the same business as making a picture inside your head. They don't differ from one another merely by virtue of their location. By being inside the head, wherever that is – and it's not quite clear what being inside the head is, or indeed where it is – but by virtue of being what we call 'inside the head', it isn't really a picture in the full sense of the word picture. That's really the essence of my argument.

III

CONVERSATIONS

Designers

RICHARD HUDSON

Richard Hudson designed *The Emperor* (Royal Court 1987), *Andromache, One Way Pendulum, Bussy D'Ambois, The Tempest, Candide* and *King Lear* (Old Vic 1988/9).

Michael Romain   How did you come to be Jonathan's resident designer for the whole of his first Old Vic season in 1988?

Richard Hudson   I was originally introduced to Jonathan by Richard Jones, who had worked as his assistant at Scottish Opera – he suggested that I go and see him while we were doing *Mignon* at Wexford.

When I got back to London, Jonathan just rang up one morning and said, 'Can you come over and see me now? Bring your portfolio.' He saw my portfolio, which just contained production designs and photographs of models, and immediately asked me to design the six plays that made up his first Old Vic season. Then the next day he phoned again and said, 'Oh, by the way, I'm also doing *The Emperor* at the Royal Court, so you'd better design that as well.'

I was absolutely amazed – although he had heard about my work, he'd never actually seen anything of mine on stage.

MR   Your first collaboration with Jonathan was on *The Emperor* at the Royal

Court in 1987 – how did you decide to realise Kapúscínski's novel on stage?

RH   We agreed right from the start that we wouldn't attempt to evoke a literal Ethiopia – we just wanted to create an atmosphere in which the events could unfold. There was never any attempt to make it look African, or to make anybody look like Haile Selassie's civil servants, or anything like that. Because we were staging it in the studio space of the Theatre Upstairs we were working on a very limited budget, so we just had to think of a very simple way of evoking a Kafka-esque atmosphere of mystery and intrigue.

We discussed several ideas for the set, and eventually Jonathan nudged me towards the idea of constructing it almost entirely from doors – it was only later that I learned that doors had also formed the background of his *Measure for Measure*.

MR   What was Jonathan's aim for the Old Vic when he became Artistic Director?

RH   He wanted to do something that was unlike anything in the other London theatres. Possibly that's why he picked me – I'd certainly designed very few plays before, and my work for him at the Old Vic to a large degree made that sort of audience aware for the first time of innovative theatre design. This had been around in opera houses for ages, of course, and it seems to me that only directors who have worked in opera as well as theatre are that visually aware and ready to take risks. Jonathan simply wouldn't be interested in doing something that didn't take risks.

MR   It was certainly a risk to open the Old Vic season with Racine's *Andromache* – how did the intensity of the play inform your designs?

RH   We approached it rather like *The Emperor* – it was a question of conjuring up the right atmosphere: an oppressive, prison-like feeling, as if the characters were trapped and unable to escape. I eventually came up with a ruined palace that hung over the actors' heads at such a steep angle that it looked as if it would collapse at any minute.

One of the main references for this set design was the Coronet Cinema in Notting Hill Gate, which was Jonathan's idea. At night the structure is lit from below with strange sulphurous yellow lights, so that the windows and all the Edwardian architecture look terribly gloomy and threatening. The set started off already raked, but each time Jonathan saw the model we pushed it a bit further up so that when the actors eventually went on it for the first time they found it very difficult to walk on. By tipping the floor forward so much that it was at right angles to the wall, we were able to make the walls look as if they were falling forward.

We gave the costumes an abstract seventeenth-century style – it took a very long time to find the right period, and we didn't finally decide until the play went into rehearsal. At one point we were thinking of doing it in modern dress, but the translation went through several versions, which was why we took so long to make up our minds.

The Eric Korn translation that we finally used was immensely powerful, and certainly didn't deserve the criticism that it got from reviewers – it was absolutely in the spirit of the piece. The performances were excellent; in particular Penelope Wilton was terribly moving in a role you would not immediately have associated her with – Jonathan is always good at bringing new things out of a performer. He'd worked with her many times before, as he had with most of the cast – Janet Suzman, Peter Eyre, John Barron. He's a director who likes to have familiar faces around him.

MR   How did you respond to the comic surrealism of your next play with Jonathan, *One Way Pendulum*?

RH   Through a mixture of Magritte and absolute naturalism. Once I'd designed the basic set I added lots of little surreal touches – china ducks flying off the living-room wall into a Magritte sky, for instance – as Jonathan wanted to get both a surrealist effect and the sense of a normal living-room. It has to be rooted in reality – if it takes place in a completely mad space, then you would miss the point and lose the humour. They have to be real people living in a real space, which is why I restricted the surrealism to the top of the set.

Having appeared in the film version, Jonathan loved the play, and gathered together a fantastic cast. The play itself turned out to be the problem, as it seemed rather dated and didn't really go down as well as we'd hoped.

MR   When you came to Chapman's *Bussy D'Ambois*, did you find it difficult tackling a play that had not been staged since 1604?

RH   It's a very difficult play to read, let alone to stage. We decided that we wouldn't do it in the obvious way, which would have been to have everybody encrusted with jewels, *Revenger's Tragedy* style, with black sets and gloomy corridors. What we did was simply wipe the slate clean and do it on a very clear, cool set with very crisp, sharp and simple costumes so that one could just get the words over. This approach worked, as we were able to tell the story very clearly. The way that Jonathan staged it meant that, despite the complex language, the audience could follow the action throughout.

The set was comprised of classical pilasters, which would change position to form corridors, chambers and so on. It was important with a play that long and complex not to get slowed down with elaborate scene changes – it was really a question of coming up with a simple solution that worked for the whole play.

At the top of the pilasters I put lots of little architectural markings. That was Jonathan's idea – he loves those anamorphic paintings and drawings that play about with perspective, and one of the references that he gave me for the set were the perspective drawings of Jan Vredeman de Vries, the seventeenth-century Dutchman, which gave me the markings for the top of the set.

For the opening scene of the play we needed something completely different, and Jonathan decided to use a huge old curtain. That first scene is like a front-cloth scene, and by using a curtain which could afterwards be swept up at the sides and suspended over the stage it was able to become part of the setting for the rest of the play

Most of the budget for *Bussy D'Ambois* was actually spent on the costumes, not only because there were so many of them but also because they were period dress which is always expensive. Jonathan suggested Moroni as a reference for the costume designs – they had hardly any decoration except little ruffs, and were incredibly simple with very strong shades and tones. Jonathan is constantly coming up with all kinds of artistic references, which is always stimulating but sometimes rather overwhelming as it takes such a long time to sift through them all.

Originally he was going to use pseudo-seventeenth-century music, but I told him that it sounded like a TV 'Play for Today' so he decided to cut the music and go instead for some sort of atmospheric sound-effect. At the very last minute he came up with this amplified whispering, which proved tremendously effective in the background.

MR   Your next collaboration came with *The Tempest* – how did you solve one of the play's chief staging problems, the transformation at the beginning from the shipwreck at sea to Prospero's island?

RH   I designed a very simple set – just a raked floor with a texture of sand on it, and a blue cyclorama in the background with two large boxes in front of it – so that we could stage the opening sequence as simply as possible.

We covered the stage with a vast blue silk stage-cloth – 18 square metres of silk – and positioned lots of electric fans underneath it all over the stage, as well as at the sides. Also hidden under this stage-cloth was the actor playing Ariel. When the play started we switched on the fans and and Ariel began leaping up and down, so that the blue stage-cloth billowed up and down like a stormy sea, and this, combined with the boxes at the back rocking hydraulically with the sailors perched on top, and all the appropriate sound and lighting effects, conjured up the effect of a real tempest.

When the storm subsided and the fans stopped, the cloth was simply pulled down through a large hole in the centre of the stage by Ariel, who seemed to make it disappear himself. It was a conjuring trick, really, and like all the best tricks it was incredibly simple. Jonathan was initially rather worried about the safety of the sailors up on top of the boxes, but he loved it once he saw it work on stage. It was a bit of a risk in performance, but the effect was absolutely thrilling.

MR   Jonathan portrayed the inhabitants of the island as natives rather than spirits – how did you fit the native dress into the seventeenth-century world of the production?

RH   The costume references came from New Guinea and the Nuba tribe, and I arranged them in such a way that they had seventeenth-century shapes. The women's skirts, for instance, were like panniers, decorated with grass, beads and shells. I was born in Africa, so I loved researching for the designs.

MR   When you designed Jonathan's production of *Candide* – first for Scottish Opera, then at the Old Vic – you were faced with a rambling, convoluted plot structure – was your giant toy-box an immediate solution?

RH   No, not at all – we spent ages trying all sorts of ideas to give the piece continuity and a strong narrative thread. I found it very difficult, perhaps the most demanding show of the season. But once we hit upon the toy-box, everything fell into place – it provided a marvellous way to tell this complex story very clearly and simply, with the box gradually filling up with various objects from Candide's progress around the world. Bernstein himself loved it when he saw the show, and thought that we had made it work for the first time.

MR   Did you adapt the costumes to match the toy-box?

RH   None of the costumes were straight eighteenth-century – they were mostly big and bold, like toys and puppets. They were made of scenic canvas that had been dyed, so that they all had that stiff, toy-like quality. I chose particularly thick fabrics so that the characters would look like those dolls where the fabric of their clothes is always too thick in scale for the size of their bodies. Most of the costumes had references – for the Venice scenes, for instance, Jonathan pointed me in the direction of Pietro Longhi.

I originally designed all the masks myself, but then I saw the Messer-schmidt exhibition at the Institute of Contemporary Arts and immediately realised that they were much better than anything that I could do. So we just copied them and used them in the show.

MR   What inspired your progressively receding sets for *King Lear?*

RH   Jonathan remembered that ages ago I'd shown him some photographs I'd taken of a house on the Isle of Wight, an eighteenth-century building that had burned down and been preserved as a shell by English Heritage. I took a lot of photos of the brick walls – which you could see had been destroyed by fire – and of details of the doorways and window-frames. They had obviously made an impression on Jonathan, and we used them as a starting-point for the set.

The basic idea was to pare the set down to its simplest form. At the beginning of the play it was very oppressive, with the action pushed forward and played on the apron stage before a heavy brick wall, with the stage boxes at the front of the stalls taken out and bricked up. As each scene progressed, the walls would fly up so that the stage space went back a bit further and a bit further, gradually getting bigger and bigger, but no less oppressive. Because we had started the play so far forward on the stage we gained much more depth, so that when we reached the end of the play the stage went back an amazingly long way, right to the back wall of the theatre when it was all opened up.

The storm on the heath was based on the storm scene in *The Tempest*, but done upside down. We used an even bigger sheet of black silk – 25 square metres – which was suspended from the flies and taken right back into the scene dock, with electric fans on the floor and up in the flies to create the effect of billowing storm clouds by blowing the silk back and forth. The heath itself was basically just a bare stage with a brick floor.

It was beautifully lit by Paul Pyant, although it was actually a very difficult set to light because it just led off into the wings through a lot of black masking. But there was a wonderful chiaroscuro effect in the lighting, with lots of Caravaggio-style shadow – both Jonathan and I are very keen on side-lighting, and the actors often had half of their faces in darkness which made it much more atmospheric. This was highly effective

4 Set design by Richard Hudson for the storm scene, *King Lear*, Old Vic 1989

in the scene in the hovel, which Jonathan filled with sleeping figures like the ones you see just down the road from the Old Vic under Waterloo Bridge.

It took ages, though, to find the right period for the costumes for *King Lear*. I wanted to do it in twentieth-century dress and that was always the idea, but Eric Porter (who played Lear) was very unhappy with that and asked us to use some sort of period costume. We were originally thinking of setting it in the 1930s, with all the men in suits and the women looking like incredibly glamorous film stars, which would have worked very well, particularly when you got the contrast with the down-and-outs in the hovel.

I think Jonathan was a bit disappointed that we couldn't use that – we then played around with all sorts of things and finally came up with these pseudo-Afghan robes, which actually worked very well. If I'd had more time, I would have broken all the costumes down a lot more – they should have been shabbier.

Once we had settled on these robes, I watched Eisenstein's *Ivan the Terrible* and used that as a reference for some of the costumes – Regan and Goneril, for instance. A lot of the courtiers wore tunics shaped like Russian coats, with Russian-style dhoti trousers underneath. In *Ivan the*

Terrible all the robes are encrusted with gold, jewels and embroidery – I took all that decoration away so we were just left with the shapes.

The *King Lear* turned out to be the most successful show we did at the Old Vic, and proved immensely popular with audiences – I know a lot of people who regard it as the best *Lear* they have ever seen.

ROBERT ISRAEL

Robert Israel designed *Mahagonny* (Los Angeles Music Center Opera 1989), *Don Giovanni* (Maggio Musicale, Florence 1990) and *Katya Kabanova* (Metropolitan Opera, New York 1991).

Michael Romain   When you first met Jonathan in 1987 – while he was directing *The Mikado* in Los Angeles – did you find that you both shared the same visual aesthetic?

Robert Israel   Yes, exactly that. There was also a verbal shorthand that we both had in common, and because of that it was clear that we would be critical of things – whether we did them or other people did them – in the same way.

MR   You designed Jonathan's production of *Mahagonny* for the Los Angeles Music Centre Opera in 1989 – what ideas did he initially throw at you?

RI   The first thing that Jonathan talked about was America, and then we looked at lots of pictures from films like *The Gold Rush*. We soon got on to talking about sound stages and Hollywood, and things coalesced into the idea of that kind of America of Great Hope. Not what you think of today as being America, but the America of Great Hope that you had at the turn of the century or in the 1890s.

Then we started thinking about the golden age of Southern California, the age of Chaplin, Keaton and Langdon. We had to do a kind of dance – with Jonathan and me it was not an apprehensive dance at this point, but a dance of trying to figure out what it was we wanted to do, where the consistencies and inconsistencies lay, and which ideas to follow through and which to abandon.

We gradually developed a strategy, an armature that allowed us to hang ideas on it, so we could know, within some kind of subjective frame of reference, where things were worthwhile continuing and codifying and where they were not. With *Katya Kabanova*, which Jonathan and I are working on at the moment, we've got that frame of reference and we know what the elements are – now it is by dealing with all those elements within that consistent frame of reference that we will find the look of the production. We have both moved very quickly on *Katya* in terms of our critical appreciation of what the problems could be.

MR   How did the Hollywood metaphor in your *Mahagonny* evolve?

RI   We were in Los Angeles! Brecht, like all of Europe at the time, was fascinated by movies. If there is an America paved with gold, it's the one seen through the lens of Hollywood. That lens is a bizarre make-believe that is sometimes truly wonderful and sometimes a façade. So Jonathan encouraged me to use flats with false backs for the scenery, like a studio back-lot.

MR   Where did Giotto come into the production?

RI   We had *The Rest on the Flight to Egypt* hanging over the stage at the beginning when the fugitives came on and their car broke down. But we finally decided against using *The Massacre of the Innocents* in the scene where Jimmy is executed (we used an electric chair instead of a gallows) – the death row chamber looked a lot grimmer without any decoration. The production came straight after the Chinese massacre in Tiananmen Square so, as *Mahagonny* is a vaguely communist piece, we toyed with the idea of removing the Giotto at the beginning and hanging a portrait of Chairman Mao upside down in its place. Jonathan drew a lot on the silent comedy films of Mack Sennett for the way the characters moved and behaved, and we used these for costume references too – they were stereotypical silent movie costume.

MR   What is the attraction for a designer of working with Jonathan?

RI   The way that Jonathan collaborates on the designs is what I consider the healthiest possible director–designer relationship. He has a real sense of visual consistency and sophistication.

Jonathan knows that a play is not just text – it's theatre, not literature. He is very aware that what happens on the stage is realised by the actors speaking their lines in an environment that stems from the play. Most directors – who are not very good – think of plays in purely literary terms, assuming that all the exposition is there in the text. It isn't, as Jonathan well knows.

Part of the reason that he is so visually aware is his vast knowledge of art and art history, which he is able to put to practical use on the stage. We talk not so much about the painting as the space that the painter creates in the painting. That gives you the texture and the atmosphere of the piece – on some level, it gives you a meeting-point between the stage and the visual arts.

Jonathan won't ever say to me 'This should look like Goya.' He will say, 'This should look like a collaboration between Robert Israel and Jonathan Miller which uses Goya as a common denominator to get somewhere else.' We talk about it, but ultimately what we're going to do is not verbal so we have to find metaphoric relationships that are not the thing that we're aiming at but somehow give us an oblique reference for where we want to get to.

MR How are you approaching your next collaboration, *Don Giovanni*, at the 1990 Maggio Musicale in Florence?

RI We've gone for a sombre, mysterious tone, with a certain icy humour within that. Jonathan wanted to evoke a sense of the streets that plays such a vital part in the action – streets and spaces that open up and contract. We'll use one basic set, which changes itself in the course of the opera – walls move, open up and pivot to expose large expanses and then close down on them to reduce them to small corners. There will be lots of shadows, made by both light and painting, so that the whole thing will take on a palpable ambiguity.

MR After that, you go to New York with Jonathan for *Katya Kabanova* at the Metropolitan Opera in 1991.

RI We have decided to use two sets, even though the opera has three acts. The first set is a little room in a house – not a complete house – set in a landscape. The back of the landscape rises, with some trees dotted about on it as well as some miniature Russian buildings – a church, another house. It's obliquely icon-like in its flatness on the deep stage. The room subsequently revolves to form a building, the sky is replaced by a new sky and the buildings move, so we see the same location from a different perspective. There's a further sense of flatness in the thinness of the walls and the tonality of the colours. In the third act we'll have a very flat ruined colonnade against this vast sky. And that's all – it's very simple.

There will be huge expanses around this little room on the empty stage, and the miniature buildings may each be on a different scale so that the church is a little bit smaller than the other house. We aim to have a lot of side-lighting coming through to give it a very dramatic effect.

MR How did you and Jonathan arrive at this design scheme?

RI   We never really talked about it until we got to it, and then when we had got to it we were very happy. Little things pointed us on the way – for instance, we'll have little icons in the colonnade from Orthodox churches in Yugoslavia, Romania, Russia and Czechoslovakia.

MR   What do you feel characterises Jonathan's work?

RI   One of his productions which impressed me the most was his film of *Alice in Wonderland*, which was very controversial when it was first shown. People wanted some kind of slavish reproduction of the traditional fairy-tale view of the book, but Jonathan came up with this marvellous dream version full of the most bizarre Victorian imagery. His *Alice in Wonderland* is an original work, and it doesn't turn Lewis Carroll into one of the Apostles. There is no reverence, which is why it works so well. No one has a rabbit mask or a mouse face, the men in livery don't have fish heads, and it's really wonderful for the freshness and originality that Jonathan brings to it.

BERNARD CULSHAW

Bernard Culshaw designed *Hamlet* and *Julius Caesar* (Oxford and Cambridge Shakespeare Company 1969/70), *Measure for Measure* (National Theatre at the Old Vic 1974 and Greenwich Theatre 1975), *Arden Must Die* (Sadler's Wells 1974) *Così fan tutte* and *Rigoletto* (Kent Opera 1975) *Orfeo* (Kent Opera 1976) *Eugene Onegin* (Kent Opera 1977), *She Would if She Could* (Greenwich Theatre 1979), *La Traviata* (Kent Opera 1979), *Falstaff* (Kent Opera 1980), *Fidelio* (Kent Opera 1982) and *La Traviata* (Glimmerglass Opera 1989).

Michael Romain   You first worked with Jonathan in 1969, when you designed his productions of *Hamlet* and *Julius Caesar* for the Oxford and Cambridge Shakespeare Company – what struck you about his approach to the look of a production?

Bernard Culshaw   The fact that he always seemed to have some kind of visual reference up his sleeve – he could point you towards painters and photo-graphers that you didn't even know existed, or whose relevance was not immediately apparent.

   The *Julius Caesar*, for example, was inspired by de Chirico – the stage was an orange ramp, backed by a bare sky. The women had basic classical garb on, Caesar wore an all-white costume – hat, frock-coat, etc. – and looked rather like a statue, and everyone else was dressed like tailors'

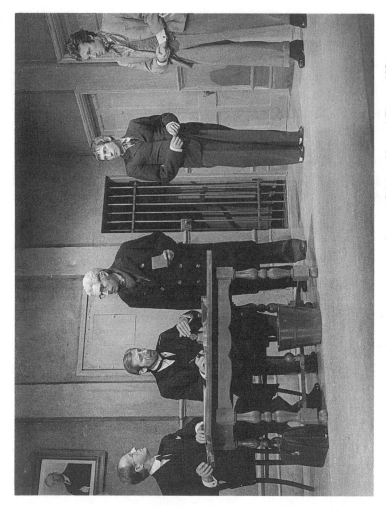

5 Scene from *Measure for Measure*, designed by Bernard Culshaw, National Theatre 1974

dummies. There were some wonderfully appropriate bizarre effects – during Mark Antony's speech in the Forum, the crowd didn't use real words but instead made strange buzzing noises like bees.

For *Hamlet*, Jonathan referred to Frances Yates' book on the 'theatre of memory', which was a study of Elizabethan theatre imagery based on ideas about the brain and the nature of memory. The set was inspired by Elizabethan etchings that illustrated this thesis.

MR When you designed Jonathan's *Measure for Measure* for the National Theatre in 1974, how did you evoke the world of Freud's Vienna which Jonathan envisaged for the production?

BC We referred to photographs from the 1920s and 1930s by August Sander, the Viennese photographer, which were an enormous help in terms of the designs and characterisation. Jonathan never intends his visual references to be slavishly re-created – he won't say, 'That is the set I want' but, 'That is the world I want', and you have to take that spirit and come up with your own set.

The set for *Measure* had, like the photographs, lots of corners in the background, which evoked this bureaucratic world. It was the Vienna of the 1920s and 1930s, before Hitler invaded. The production had an atmosphere of town-hall corruption, a Kafka-esque sense of a faceless bureaucracy. The set resembled the sort of grey box-like office that you might find in a DSS building or a town-hall. It gradually filled up with several doors, which each indicated different things – some doors were quite grand, some were rough like prison doors, and some were bland like the office. It was all done on a small scale because it was a mobile production, which had to be toured in a transit van on a very low budget.

MR Did Jonathan already have the Mafia community in mind when he staged his first *Rigoletto* in 1975?

BC We did initially talk about setting *Rigoletto* either in New York in the 1950s or Italy just before the First World War. Kent Opera wouldn't have it, though, so we set it in the age of composition, the 1850s, instead. The opera has a lot of very difficult scenes to stage – the abduction of Gilda, for instance, or the quartet in the last act – and we managed to get them right by staging them very simply. We had one big central truck which revolved to show first the palace, then Rigoletto's house, then the palace again with a slight variation, and finally the tavern.

Jonathan gave Rigoletto himself more of a limp than the usual full hunchback, and made him into quite a comic figure – we gave him a toy-like miniature violin to play, so he was obviously seen to be the local buffoon rather than the standard court jester.

MR   When you designed Jonathan's *Orfeo* for Kent Opera in 1976, he took the style of the production from the paintings of Poussin – how did you respond to that?

BC   The challenge for me was to get the costumes to look like the figures in those paintings, while for Jonathan it was to get the groupings and movements to look as though they had come from that baroque world. It was not a question, though, of taking a picture and saying 'And now we go into this pose' – it's more about knowing the material so that one can draw freely from it. It's not actually copying it. I've sometimes copied a costume from a painting or a photograph, but never a set. Most of the things that have excited Jonathan in his visual references have been to do with people, in situations portrayed by other people. It's never a question of 'Those are the sort of windows that we want.'

MR   Your next collaboration with Jonathan for Kent Opera, *Eugene Onegin* in 1977, seemed to be based more on invention than any one great source of reference.

BC   Yes, it was more of a direct response to the work than saying 'This fits into that artistic movement.' I found a book which had reproductions of early nineteenth-century Russian paintings and referred to those for the costumes, but the rest was pure invention – a very simple bare stage, with solid country furniture and a few props. We used a certain amount of naturalistic detail, and Jonathan did a lot of research into that side of it – into the way that the characters would have drunk lemonade, for example. What was the lemonade like? How was it served? What happens at a name-day party? How were duels fought? etc. etc.

   The staging was very sharply focussed and austere. Jonathan described me at the time as a master of the bare stage, and said that was why he liked working with me. I took that as a double-edged compliment and said that I'd quite like to design some scenery sometime.

MR   How did the photographs of Nadar influence your designs for Jonathan's *La Traviata* for Kent Opera in 1979?

BC   Jonathan wanted the *Traviata* to evoke Nadar's photographs of 1850, so we looked at the figures in these pictures and thought 'What kind of set could these people inhabit?' We decided to use plain canvas scenery, which was minimally formed into suggesting architectural or decorative shapes. As we were drawing our inspiration from photographs, we limited ourselves to the range of tones that you would find in them. So all the material was very pale, with the characters wearing dark costumes. There was nothing decorous about it – the stage was littered with empty bottles and dirty glasses for the party scenes. Violetta's illness was very real too – Jonathan coached her through all the right symptoms in her death scene.

When we did *La Traviata* again for Glimmerglass Opera in New York in 1989, we used a lot of the original Nadar costume designs. The set was totally different, though – it was simply a big, rather bleak white box, with lots of doors and gaps for the different exits and entrances throughout the action.

MR   How did you use Bruegel as a visual reference for Jonathan's *Falstaff* for Kent Opera in 1980?

BC   We didn't try to make the action look as if it was happening in the Netherlands – we used ideas from Bruegel's work for characterisation. In the garden scene, for example, we had beehives in the background tended by some bee-keepers – taken from Bruegel – wearing strange cowled costumes with woven meshes over their faces, quite surreal at first sight.

In the final scene the designs became more 'Bruegel' and bizarre, and we put in one of those lightning-struck trees that you get in the paintings, split in half with the odd branch or two sticking out or growing under the stage. There were lots of strange objects scattered around, like a tall pole with rags hanging off a cartwheel on top of it. The so-called fairies were actually the townspeople dressed up in bizarre costumes from Bruegel, with great big spoons sticking out over their heads or through their hats, things that they would have found in their own kitchens.

Although that scene took place at night, the lights were deliberately exposed at the sides of the stage. Early on Jonathan had said, 'I don't want any masking – I want to be able to see the chorus assembling in the wings.' So we just concentrated on the middle of the stage, and didn't worry what went on around that. It was almost a Brechtian idea, a kind of anti-Grand Opera way of thinking.

MR   What inspired the use of Goya for Jonathan's *Fidelio* for Kent Opera in 1982?

BC   Jonathan had just been to an exhibition of Goya prints at the British Museum, and he was struck by the parallels between these two artists of the Enlightenment, Goya and Beethoven. Nothing in the production was directly copied from a Goya print – we simply drew parallels, especially with Goya's etchings of prisoners shackled together.

Jonathan encouraged me to reproduce onstage some of the techniques that Goya used in his etchings, using aquatint, for example, then buffing some of it away. So I used a lot of gauzes, which had the kind of texture that you'd get in a print of aquatint, so that one could see people in different layers and qualities of light – some brightly lit, some in shadow, but all part of the same picture. We took a chiaroscuro effect directly from Goya, building levels of density within the light which could shift and change. It was one of the most successful productions I've done with Jonathan in terms of putting on stage the ideas that you get from the initial reference rather than just copying it.

Because it was a standing set, we could achieve the scene changes very quickly indeed just by lighting. For the quartet in the first scene, for instance, the characters just went into positions behind the gauzes in such a way that they were all occupying the same space but were made separate in their thoughts by the scenery and lighting.

MR   Your set for Jonathan's production of *She Would if She Could* at Greenwich in 1979 seemed to match the intricate artifice of the play very accurately.

BC   I devised a rather ingenious magic-box, based on an inlaid seventeenth-century Dutch cabinet – the characters made their exits and entrances through it, and when you opened the doors you didn't know what would be behind them. It used those strange tricks of perspective which Jonathan always likes; though, like any conjuring trick, it was technically very simple.

STEFANOS LAZARIDIS

Stefanos Lazaridis designed *Tosca* (Maggio Musicale, Florence 1986, English National Opera 1987 and Houston Grand Opera 1991), *The Mikado* (English National Opera 1986, Los Angeles Music Center Opera 1987 and Houston Grand Opera 1989), *The Taming of the Shrew* (Royal Shakespeare Company 1987 at Stratford-upon-Avon and the Barbican Theatre) and *La fanciulla del West* (*The Girl of the Golden West*) (La Scala, Milan and Teatro Regio, Turin 1991).

Michael Romain   How did you work with Jonathan when you designed his *Tosca* for the 1986 Maggio Musicale, Florence?

Stefanos Lazaridis   We hardly knew each other before Jonathan asked me out of the blue to design his *Tosca*. I asked him how he was going to stage it and he replied, *"Roma, città aperta"* – we'll draw our inspiration from the Rossellini film.' He explained that he was going to set it not in 1800 but in 1944, with the Allied armies advancing on Mussolini's Rome. I found this a very interesting concept indeed, and immediately realised that it would work tremendously well with the Italian audiences – they could relate very strongly to a *Tosca* set in an era that they or their families had lived through. Jonathan put it to me like this – 'We must find the right correspondence.'

Later on, we both went to Rome and saw all the places where these events had taken place, which I found a shattering experience – it was then that I understood that we were really doing something serious.

When the people at the Maggio asked to see some ideas on paper for the sets, I drew up some examples of what I thought Jonathan wanted to see and he was very happy with them. The Italians, though, went absolutely berserk and said that it was far too vast and detailed for the theatre. So I tried to find a summation of everything Jonathan had in mind, which produced this Expressionist set, half nightmarish and half realistic, on a very steeply raked stage.

It turned out to be a very powerful show in Italy, and the updating proved as effective as we had expected. Eva Marton was a superb Tosca, and I shall never forget the impact of the end of Act 1 with 30 children and a 100-strong chorus. The whole thing was an extraordinary event, and got a phenomenal ovation from the audience.

MR Did you work on the designs for Jonathan's ENO *Mikado* at the same time as you were doing *Tosca*?

SL That's right – while we were both in Florence waiting for them to construct the set, which took ages because it was such a complex operation. So I would meet up with Jonathan in the Anglo American Hotel and talk about *The Mikado*. He was quite clear that he wanted to get rid of the Japanese wrapping, because he believes that it was essentially an English piece. Because my upbringing had nothing to do with the world of Gilbert and Sullivan, I said to him 'Are you sure that you want me to do it?' 'Oh yes,' Jonathan said, 'just do it as a show.' So I approached it purely as a show, which is not the way I usually work.

Jonathan talked a lot then about the illogicality of the piece, and the almost surreal behaviour of the characters. I asked him what the equivalent of this was, and he said, 'Well, it's the Marx Brothers.' Suddenly it all became very clear. We watched lots of Marx Brothers movies, and never stopped laughing at the thought of doing *The Mikado* that way.

I tried all sorts of ideas for the designs with Busby Berkeley and big

Hollywood extravaganzas, and then I hit upon Syrie Maugham, the 1930s decorator *par excellence* who 'invented' white-upon-white-upon-white. When we were sitting in the Anglo American, Jonathan pointed out some sculptural details in the plasterwork and said 'Maybe we should explore the architecture in a rather bizarre way because of the illogicality of the piece.' Then we forgot about it while *Tosca* opened, and the designs happened almost effortlessly in a week once we got back to England.

MR   You set *The Mikado* in the foyer of a 1930s grand hotel – was this influenced by the time you spent in the Anglo American?

SL   Not directly – Jonathan wanted a space where people could come and go, a transitory location with nostalgic overtones. It's a bit like that hotel in Miami in *Some Like It Hot*, or the ones in the Marx Brothers films. It gave us the opportunity to create farcical situations with people going from one bedroom to another in a Feydeau-esque way.

It's such a bizarre piece that the Emperor of Japan and the English hotel came together quite effortlessly – the series of illogicalities upon illogicalities simply took off. We even put a view of Mount Fuji behind the window as an in-joke. It's a nonsense piece, and we reflected this with all sorts of things – decapitated heads, references to Margaret Dumont and Carol Channing, and so on. I enjoyed it all very much – it is a sizzling show, staged with great panache and bubbling spirits.

MR   When you designed Jonathan's *Taming of the Shrew* for the Royal Shakespeare Company in 1987, your approach was quite the reverse – the production was rooted very firmly in the world of the sixteenth century.

SL   Jonathan was very clear about that – he said at the beginning, 'We're not concerned about now – we're concerned about what all those values meant then. Therefore we must present it in that way – how things were then. Certain situations which are similar to ours today were dealt with in a totally different way then – we should be able to understand that in order to compare the two.' He was right, of course, and his production was very honest to the play – he looked at it in its social and historical context, and staged it on its own terms.

We looked through lots of books on Italian Renaissance art when we began discussing the set, and Jonathan came up with something on marquetry that he thought would work very well. I aimed simply to provide a space that could expand and contract to accommodate the various scenes, using sixteenth-century theatrical techniques.

PATRICK ROBERTSON AND ROSEMARY VERCOE

Patrick Robertson and Rosemary Vercoe designed *The School for Scandal*, *The Seagull*, and *King Lear* (Nottingham Playhouse 1968/9; *Danton's Death*, *The School for Scandal* and *The Marriage of Figaro* (National Theatre at The Old Vic 1971–4); *The Taming of the Shrew* and *The Seagull* (Chichester Festival Theatre 1972/3); *The Malcontent* (Nottingham Playhouse 1973); *The Seagull*, *Ghosts* and *Hamlet* (Greenwich Theatre 1974); *The Importance of Being Earnest*, and *All's Well that Ends Well* (Greenwich Theatre 1975); *The Cunning Little Vixen* (Glyndebourne 1975, Frankfurt Opera and Australian Opera 1977); *The Three Sisters* (Cambridge Theatre 1976); *The Marriage of Figaro* (1978); *The Flying Dutchman* (Frankfurt Opera 1979); *A Midsummer Night's Dream* (Vienna Burgtheater 1979); *The Turn of the Screw* (1979), *Arabella* (1980), *Otello* (1981) and *Rigoletto* (1982) all at English National Opera; and *The School for Scandal* (American Repertory Theatre 1982).

Michael Romain You were Jonathan's regular collaborators for fifteen years, designing the sets and costumes for twenty-four of his productions – how did you originally team up with him?

Patrick Robertson Rosemary and I happened to be working at the Nottingham Playhouse in 1968, when Stuart Burge invited Jonathan to come and direct *The School for Scandal* there. Our first encounter was over the telephone, when he gave us a brief for the play that was extremely detailed as to what he wanted in terms of mood and atmosphere – I'd never been given a brief as specific as that before.

MR Once you began working with Jonathan, was the design process a joint effort?

PR Jonathan would throw all sorts of artistic references at us – for *School for Scandal* they were Hogarth and Gillray – to give us the initial inspiration, which we would then use as a basis for the sets and costumes.

RV Jonathan had a strong visual interest in his productions, and was always very concerned about their look. I would always ask him right at the beginning if he had a particular line on the production. Sometimes he would have a very powerful line indeed with shows like *Rigoletto* and *The Malcontent*, and would shower us with pictures and photographs; on other occasions he would simply say, 'No, not particularly.' In the latter instance, we would present him with our ideas and come to some sort of agreement.

After a time we felt that we didn't need words any more, and were able to present him with designs that we knew he would go along with. We worked with him for so many years that we were able to build up a genuine shared understanding.

MR   What was Jonathan's original brief for *The School for Scandal*?

PR   He said that he didn't want any Haymarket gloss and frippery, so we took great pains to avoid that and gave it the dank, mildewy quality that he was after. He wanted a rough and gritty style, almost social realism, with snotty-nosed servants and draughty corridors. We went on to design two more productions of the play for him, but I think that the original Nottingham version was the best.

MR   Jonathan has always been interested in exploring the possibilities of perspective onstage – how did you achieve that extraordinary sense of depth in the background of his next production at Nottingham, *The Seagull*, in 1969?

PR   I worked on a principle which we would later return to for *The Cunning Little Vixen*, whereby we suspended a tent-like gauze structure over the stage and projected lots of foliage onto it from above and behind for the exterior scenes, with a view of the lake on the cyclorama at the back, so that we were able to create a totally three-dimensional effect.

 The interior scenes were played on a small truck downstage, with its walls made out of simulated lace wallpaper so that you could see through them to the garden behind. Jonathan encouraged the cast to use the garden background throughout the play – they would walk across the stage behind the gauze and look as if they were strolling way off in the distance, playing all sorts of tricks of perspective.

MR   Jonathan had Brechtian staging techniques in mind when he came to direct *King Lear* at Nottingham – did he intend using any scenery for that?

PR   No, he said that he didn't want to use a set at all, but in fact I eventually designed a sort of variable black box for the production. I simply suspended some screens of black gauze and heavy mesh on tracks over the stage, which could move and define area – this gave us different spaces within a black void as opposed to just a total black void. The screens were able to close off certain areas and open up others, but there were no scenic effects and everything was concentrated solely on the actors, under very atmospheric lighting.

MR   Your designs became much more stylised for Jonathan's next production, *Danton's Death*, for the National Theatre at the Old Vic in 1971.

PR   They were triggered off by an idea that Jonathan had come up with while visiting a museum in Bethnal Green. He showed us pictures of these costumed figures in glass cases, which I reproduced on stage without their heads, arranged on three tiers which could be illuminated from behind to silhouette their decapitated shapes. They were backed by classical statues at the start of the play, but as it progressed these gradually changed into brutish, muscular figures and finally disintegrated into virtual skeletons, reflecting the gradual break-up and decay of society.

There were several stylised sequences – I remember Jonathan saying to the cast at one point 'I want you to move as if you are ice-skaters.' All the gore and bloodshed of the guillotine was totally stylised – at the end of the play the cast just stood still and suddenly dropped their heads symbolically, while the screen at the back showed a silhouette of the guillotine descending.

MR   When Jonathan directed *The Cunning Little Vixen* at Glyndebourne in 1975, he was relatively new to opera – did this show in his direction?

PR   Not at all – he never seemed to be fazed by it. He was able to get the singers to act as well as sing, probably better than they would have done otherwise.

The only thing that he was initially slightly unsure about was the design scheme. He vacillated between one idea and another before deciding that he wanted the animals to be dressed in very fine and colourful costumes, and Rosemary hit upon the idea of using the ethnic costumes of Czecho-slovakia. At the last moment we nearly dropped all that in favour of a German Expressionist style, but eventually decided to stick to the original concept of the rather grey, drab humans and the colourfully attired animals. Apart from their make-up, the animals didn't actually look very animal-like – just rather beautiful and ethnic.

The production had a strong feeling of the countryside and the forest, and we were able to indicate the change of seasons on a vast cyclorama in the background. We used the same principle that we had originally devised for *The Seagull* at Nottingham – a tent-like gauze structure suspended over the stage – but with the added technical facilities at Glyndebourne we were able to use four powerful projectors to cross-fade from one scene to another and thus achieve a sense of continual movement. It all worked so well that the production was a big success, and subsequently transferred to opera houses in Frankfurt and Australia.

MR   When Jonathan directed *The Three Sisters* in the West End in 1976, he returned to a much more austere visual style.

PR He decided that there would be no scenery, just a variable platform which – with the appropriate furniture – would define each scene by itself. It was much the same idea that we had used at Greenwich – a small platform stage, very basic, made of planked wood patterned to give off different colours, lights and shades.

I think that the basic simplicity of the setting set the actors free to create the atmosphere themselves, rather than being encumbered by heavy wallpaper or portraits hanging on the walls. Jonathan was particularly happy with it because it was such a strong ensemble company, with people like Janet Suzman, Angela Down, Peter Bayliss and Nigel Davenport. They all made contributions to the production themselves, because they enjoyed the stimulus of Jonathan's direction and were keen to respond to it.

MR What inspired the production of *The Flying Dutchman* which Jonathan directed in Frankfurt in 1979?

RV The costumes – and the staging for the storm scenes – were based on the paintings of Caspar David Friedrich, which Jonathan felt were very appropriate to that sort of wandering wildness. There were lots of rampaging, drunken scenes for the sailors, but also several naturalistic moments – Senta, for example, was shown painting a portrait of the Dutchman before being distracted by the appearance of the ghostly figure himself.

MR You remained in Europe with Jonathan for his next production, *A Midsummer Night's Dream* at the Vienna Burgtheater.

PR We designed that as a sort of Hieronymus Bosch nightmare, very surreal for the scenes in the wood. The costumes were based on Bosch figures, with their strange animal shapes. The set was built on a huge revolve, and the wood was dominated by an animal-like tree structure, which was the primary home of Puck. He was played by Klaus Maria Brandauer, who sprained his ankle a week before the opening and had to be replaced by his understudy.

MR When you designed Mozart's *The Marriage of Figaro* for the English National Opera at the Coliseum in 1978, what prompted you to give it a French setting?

PR Jonathan had seen a château which he thought would be the ideal setting for *Figaro*. By chance I happened to have a couple of pictures of this château in a book so I tried to recreate the essence of its structure as best I could.

The set itself became deeper with each scene, and at the same time it widened. So we started off with a narrow space and ended up with the full width and depth of the Coliseum stage. For the final scene we removed the château walls so that the garden could be even larger – its layout was inspired by a picture of an ornamental garden which Jonathan had found in France. The centre area of the stage was filled with an arrangement of small, heart-shaped box-hedges, which we surrounded with outer walls containing lots of alcoves and entrances for the characters to hide in or disappear through.

MR Britten's *The Turn of the Screw* always poses the problem of representing a series of constantly shifting locations on stage – did Jonathan see slide projection as a solution to this when he staged it at the Coliseum in 1979?

PR Absolutely – he thought that it would give the piece great fluidity of movement and do away with the need for lengthy scene-changes. He said to me, 'It's a piece about ghosts, so you can use your projections to tremendous effect.' The side-screens were staggered so that the singers could make their entrances through them, and projected onto from several directions to create a sense of depth. The slide projections gave the production such a cinematic style that at times it really felt like you were watching a film – the only solid objects onstage at all were a few pieces of furniture on small trucks which rolled on from the sides.

All the images on the slides were in black and white, as Jonathan had suggested that we refer to the style of early Victorian photographers like Fox Talbot at Laycock Abbey. I used up several rolls of film taking prints of a place called Ashridge Park, which was an amazing Gothic structure by James Wyatt & Son out in Hertfordshire, and then had them specially developed to get the grainy effect of those Victorian photographs, which was later further enhanced by the metallic quality of the aluminium screens. Jonathan took great interest in this process, as he loves the art of photography.

MR What line did Jonathan take on the ghosts?

PR We all read the Henry James story during rehearsals, and that is very equivocal about it all – whether the ghosts are just a figment of the Governess's imagination, or in fact the children are actually possessed. I think that Jonathan took a similarly equivocal view, which is probably the right thing to do. The ghosts were certainly not intangible presences, though – they were plainly there on stage, dressed in the costumes they would have been wearing at the time the story took place.

MR When you went on to *Otello* with Jonathan at the Coliseum in 1981, you reversed the principle that you had used there for his *Figaro*.

PR That's right *Otello* – started off with a large stage space, and then became progressively smaller and smaller. The idea for the set stemmed from a picture I'd seen of a circular building in Cyprus, which Jonathan encouraged me to translate into a stylisation of the Elizabethan 'O' theatre shape, with sixteenth-century dress for the cast. So we constructed a wooden set on a raked stage, backed by triple arches which were open at the beginning but became gradually filled in with wooden Venetian blinds until everything was completely enclosed for the bedroom scene in the last act.

MR And then, of course, came Jonathan's famous 'Mafia' *Rigoletto* at the Coliseum in 1982.

PR A couple of things sparked that off. Jonathan was sitting in a bar in New York with his wife one day, when the juke-box suddenly began playing music from *Rigoletto*. Soon afterwards, while watching *Some Like It Hot* he was struck by the moment when one of the mobsters says that he was 'at Rigoletto's'. That, combined with hearing 'La donna è mobile' come out of a juke-box, gave him the idea of setting *Rigoletto* in the Mafia community of 1950s New York.

MR Did he have problems initially in trying to convince the Coliseum of the validity of his concept?

PR There were long arguements with them. At one point, Jonathan even thought of changing the setting to post-war Italy, but then became abso-lurely certain that the New York Mafia setting was the only way to do it.

There were long arguements with them. At one point, Jonathan even
The principals among the cast immediately embraced the idea, but some of the chorus thought it was nonsense to do it in modern dress and wanted to return to traditional tights and doublets instead. However, they quickly became totally converted and Jonathan showed them the *Godfather* movies to get the right mood of these plausible gangsters in their smart suits.

When the production eventually opened, it proved a colossal hit with audiences and drew a whole new audience to the Coliseum. It probably converted thousands of people to opera by presenting them with some-thing which was understandable to them rather than fancy dress, and it's since had a very far-reaching effect on opera production.

MR How did you research the set designs?

PR I started off by going through reference books on cast-iron architecture in New York and found pictures of these wonderful nineteenth-century buildings with little mock-Renaissance decorative touches, which provided a neat allusion to the opera's traditional setting.

Then Jonathan persuaded the Coliseum that if we were going to do *Rigeletto* like this we really had to get it absolutely right, so they sent me over to New York for a few days, which I spend wandering around the streets of Soho and Little Italy taking hundreds of photographs. These photographs, my book on New York architecture and the colours of Edward Hopper (especially his redbrick and greenish shades) all combined to form the basis of the settings.

The bar in the hotel set for the opening scene was based on the Odeon Café on Lower Broadway, which Jonathan knew from his *Beyond the Fringe* days in New York – it was an extremely successful restaurant run by a pair of ex-actors, decked out in this marvellous art deco style.

Rigoletto's house was based on the tenement blocks that I'd seen in Little Italy, with lots of fire escapes running down the sides. The set for the last scene was based on the bar in Hopper's *Nighthawks*, complete with a Wurlitzer juke-box which we were able to find in London. Jonathan even managed to track down a poster of a film which would have been showing at the time and put it up behind the bar.

MR You last worked with Jonathan in 1982, on *The School for Scandal* at the American Repertory Theatre at Harvard – was this intended to be one of his final productions?

PR That's right – he had promised Robert Brustein that he would do the play, but apart from that he was trying to cut the Gordian knot with the theatre in order to return to medicine.

He seemed rather disenchanted with the stage at that point, and I got the impression that he had a guilty conscience about concentrating on theatre instead of medicine. I remember his saying, 'I'm going back to neurology – I'm sure my father would approve. I'm not wasting my time with this frivolous activity anymore – I ought to be doing serious work.' He was quite definite about abandoning the theatre for good, though I never gave it much chance of lasting.

MR What do you remember of Jonathan's direction of *School for Scandal*?

PR He had a wonderful ability to communicate with his actors or singers. He was always able to keep the ball rolling in rehearsal and entertain the cast, so it became a very enjoyable experience for everyone involved. In

6 Margaret Marshall (Pamina) and Ben Luxon (Papageno), *The Magic Flute*, Scottish Opera 1983

that way he managed to get the best out of people, which he wouldn't have done had he been a dour and boring director. He was very instructive in his demonstrations and analogies in rehearsal, so the performers found him immensely stimulating to work with.

His work could vary depending on the material. In certain productions he knew exactly what his interpretation would be and what he wanted from the performers, and these would always be extremely successful. When he was given a production that was not his own choice – *The Freeway* at the National, for example – he would sometimes flounder a bit. These shows certainly worked, but they didn't have the conviction behind them that something of his own choice would have done.

PHILIP PROWSE

Philip Prowse designed *The Magic Flute* (Scottish Opera 1983 and English National Opera 1986) and *Don Giovanni* (English National Opera 1985).

Michael Romain   You designed Jonathan Miller's Scottish Opera production of *The Magic Flute* in 1983 – what was the starting-point for that staging?

Philip Prowse   Jonathan was quite clear right from the beginning that his *Magic Flute* was to be set against the background of the Enlightenment. How to represent this on stage, though, was more a matter of discussion.

In fact, we only had a few meetings and worked very fast. We talked a lot about the visionary architects of the Enlightenment, Etienne Boullée and Nicholas Ledoux. And then he showed me a rather odd, surrealist Hogarth engraving of a room full of unrelated objects. We started talking about a lumber-room, and then hit upon a library, which Jonathan had already mentioned in passing. What I eventually came up with was the classical galleries at the British Museum, but looking as if they had been relocated inside a monumental eighteenth-century library. It epitomised the mood of the late eighteenth century, that reassessment of the classical experience, set against rather Gothic Catholicism.

The Enlightenment setting enabled us to avoid the usual representation of ancient Egypt, but we were still able to retain its essence by having bas-reliefs, sphinxes and a pyramid on stage as ancient artefacts in the context of the reinterpretation of the ancient world by the late eighteenth century. When I began work on the designs I'd just come back from New

York, where, in the Metropolitan Museum, a whole small Egyptian temple, surrounded by water, is housed in a gigantic greenhouse. You look through the glass windows at the muggers and joggers in Central Park, then turn round to be confronted with this ancient temple. It was very much in my mind when I came to design *The Magic Flute*.

MR One of the remarkable features of Jonathan's *Magic Flute* was its multi-layered portrait of late eighteenth-century society – how did you build this up?

PP The point about that sort of staging is that if the initial idea is fundamentally right – which this was – then everything will fall into place within it.

The Queen of the Night, for instance, was based specifically on Maria Theresa. 'She *is* Maria Theresa', were Jonathan's words. There's an immensely pompous court painter's portrait of her, but I didn't work from any particular paintings – I just knew that she was dumpy and imperial, and worked from that.

The Three Ladies consequently became the sort of dowagers that Maria-Theresa would have had hanging around her, in strict order of precedence. When she made her first entrance, she was surrounded by a Catholic retinue of bishops and altar boys – it was based on El Greco, and was supposed to be every sort of black Catholic nightmare. Sarastro's retinue were right at the other extreme – they were eighteenth-century masons. Jonathan didn't labour this point, but simply used images such as a table with masonic insignia on it.

Monostatos was based on black revolutionaries like Toussaint, while his retinue were simply Robertson's gollies – I suppose it was the last racist joke ever allowed in the theatre.

For the final chorus tricolours were worn to symbolise the natural progression in the late eighteenth century from Enlightenment to the adoption of revolution – a liberal revolution, though, before the Terror. In this way, Jonathan reflected all the different concerns – social, political, religious etc. – of the Age of Reason.

MR What happened when the production joined the English National Opera repertory at the Coliseum in 1986?

PP The ENO were in the middle of heavy labour disputes at the time, and clearly brought the production in as a stop-gap. I don't know the backstage politics of it all – all I remember is that the place was in chaos and they really were not able to handle anything quite as elaborate as our *Magic Flute*. Having been immensely proud of it at Scottish Opera, I thought the Coliseum version was a travesty. But Jonathan, of course, has the most astonishing resilience, so he was able to make the best of it despite all the technical problems.

MR You went on to design another Mozart opera for Jonathan, *Don Giovanni* at the English National Opera in 1985 – what was the inspiration for that production?

PP The work of Goya, chiefly.

Very early on we talked about using the actual walls of the Coliseum as a background, but we were told that we couldn't do that because they were needed for storage space. Jonathan knows the theatre very well, and said that the sides were full of the most extraordinary niches, detours, alcoves and domes, so it might have formed a very effective background indeed to the pieces of architecture that I was using, and consequently enable us to suggest a whole city. But unfortunately it proved impractical.

Jonathan was very familiar with my work at the Glasgow Citizens', and had liked the *White Devil* that I staged at Greenwich. We discussed that production and he asked me to recreate the same effect of the walls shifting around the characters. So eventually I came up with three mobile towers for *Don Giovanni* which, manoeuvred by actors in eighteenth-century costume, would revolve to create warrens of streets. They were naturally ideal for all the escape scenes, and actually made them credible for once; and they also had a rather claustrophobic effect, as if hemming the characters in.

The central design was based on a building in Palermo – I asked my model-builder to make a whole façade of it, which we then just broke into three pieces. This resulted in the rather surrealist effect of the three towers, which, if they had ever joined up in a straight line, would in fact have formed a complete building.

The tomb of the Commendatore is usually rather short-changed, but a man like that would have had an immensely elaborate and important monument. Jonathan had seen a statue of the Maréchal de Saxe on top of a tomb by Pigalle. So we reproduced it exactly and just put a singer into the middle of it – this was entirely Jonathan's invention, and it worked superbly.

Another thing that Jonathan came up with that I thought was absolutely sensational was his idea of having a group of drowned women, the Don's

7   William Shimell (Don Giovanni) and Richard Van Allan (Leporello), *Don Giovanni*, designed by Philip Prowse, English National Opera 1985

suicidal lovers, coming on to claim him at the end, clutching their dead babies. It was a really brilliant piece of invention, and I can't imagine the descent into hell being done more evocatively than that. The Commendatore came back in the final scene in the image in which he had been killed, instead of as a statue, wearing the dirty old dressing-gown that he had on when he rushed into the street in the opening scene.

Actors

JOHN SHRAPNEL

John Shrapnel played Charles Surface in *The School for Scandal* (National Theatre at the Old Vic 1972), Andrey in *The Three Sisters* (Cambridge Theatre 1976) and Claudius in *Hamlet* (Donmar Warehouse and Piccadilly Theatre 1982), as well as appearing in the BBC TV Shakespeare productions of *Timon of Athens*, *Troilus and Cressida* and *King Lear* (1981/2).

Michael Romain   How did Jonathan fit in to the National Theatre when it was based at the Old Vic in the early 1970s?

John Shrapnel   I was quite surprised by the ease with which he fitted into Olivier's establishment at the National, and by the fact that he committed himself to the company as an Associate Director, as he has never liked working in big institutions. But he seemed completely at home there: we used to rehearse in pre-fab huts in Aquinas Street, an army-billet environment which was the heartbeat of the National during its Old Vic days, and you would often see Jonathan locked in discussion there with Olivier and Kenneth Tynan.

My first major role at the National was Charles Surface in Jonathan's 1972 production of *The School for Scandal*. He had already directed it at Nottingham, and we had heard all sorts of stories of actors standing on tables, urinating into pewter pots, etc. Apparently Olivier was rather worried about background colour of this kind and tried to persuade Jonathan to tone it down a bit. Tynan loved it, but I think Olivier sometimes regarded Jonathan as a bit of a naughty boy who, allowed to run away with himself, might bring the National crumbling around his head.

MR   In his production of *The School for Scandal*, Jonathan aimed to 'reproduce as carefully as possible the quality of life in Georgian London in the 1770s' – how successful was his attempt to strip away the traditional prettified 'chocolate-box view of the eighteenth century' and replace it with social and historical realism?

JS   I think, very successful indeed. Without the usual thigh-slapping and roistering, Sheridan's world became a very dangerous place. Charles Surface's lodgings became every parent's worst nightmare; a bachelor residence dedicated to drink and revelry (and perverse use of pewter pots).

The thing was heightened by this gritty approach to the play, and the fact that none of us were lovable – we were actually dishevelled and sweaty figures, and there were all sorts of things going on in dark corners. My room would be full of smoke, drunkards and pugilists, people sprawled under tables, and 'loose women' in déshabille draped over couches. It was a real Rake's Progress. Hogarth and Gillray were Jonathan's sources of reference for the staging.

He wanted to get us away from the Edith Evans diction, the poised exchange, the fluttering handkerchief and all that rather arch way of playing Restoration comedy. He had a fairly young and spirited cast, who were prepared to take risks, and I think his approach gave the play a real bite.

People don't realise sometimes what a vicious play this is – Sheridan presents a Jew, for instance, in the worst kind of patronising stereotype. Jonathan was quite fearless about bringing this out – it would have been a typical attitude of the 1770s – and by highlighting this anti-Semitism he generated a tension and consequently sympathy for the character. A more predictable production of the play might gloss over this and end up merely bland, without telling the audience anything about the society that produced such a work. What Jonathan achieved by stripping away a hundred years or so of theatrical embellishment was a sense of what it might have been like to see the play in its own time.

Jonathan's staging also heightened the moral structure of the play. In a traditional 'chocolate-box' production there is no sense of risk, so the audience does not really care very much what happens. But if you've seen a Jew being insulted and people damaged by vicious and compromising gossip, then through the comedy of the play a natural justice has to assert itself.

MR Jonathan has said that the best work within rehearsals for *Three Sisters* was done during coffee-breaks: are informal discussions between the cast and the director typical of his working methods?

JS Very much so. Jonathan has a habit of working through the day without the distraction of hour-and-a-half-long lunch-breaks, but will frequently pause for coffee to talk over ideas about the play with the actors. So you find that however larky and casual a day has apparently been, by and large it has always been tied down to solving the problems of the play. He has a very flexible way of working: there's none of the formal 'Welcome everybody, first I'm going to show you a model of the set, then you can have a look at your costumes before we start reading through the play.' That's not

Jonathan's style at all. Even when he was directing Shakespeare for the BBC, I don't think we ever sat down for a formal read-through.

He always generates a very happy working atmosphere, and (as with *Three Sisters*) is able to make great progress in a very short space of time. There was a fairly disparate group of people, and we spent several afternoons at his house prior to rehearsals looking through Chekhov's short stories and discussing which version of the play to use, which broke the ice well before we actually started work. So once we got into the rehearsal room – which somewhat bizarrely turned out to be a disused ballroom in a hotel off Tottenham Court Road – we worked very fast indeed. The decisions we arrived at about the play all seemed to be mutual, and there were no agonising divisions of opinion. We had the chance of opening the production at the Yvonne Arnaud Theatre, Guildford, earlier than was originally planned, after only three weeks of rehearsals, and, as everything was going so well, we decided to take it. So we opened prematurely, probably rather tentatively, and it went very smoothly – the whole thing was an amazingly painless operation. We all got on very well, and the production came together even more when we took it on tour before transferring to the West End, where we opened at the Cambridge Theatre in the summer of 1976.

At the Cambridge, the production was praised by the critics and became a big success, but we had arrived at it so naturally that it seemed simply a rather easy and immensely enjoyable experience.

MR Did Jonathan try to get away from the tearful English tradition of acting Chekhov and concentrate instead on the routine, ordinary aspects of the characters' lives?

JS Yes, he approached the play with respect, but not with the slavish reverence sometimes given to Chekhov as a Bleak, Yet Universally Truthful playwright. The humour, the human points of contact and the little incidental details appealed to Jonathan very strongly, as well as the fact that he was dealing with a doctor/writer. Chekhov was portraying the boredom of everyday lives, not three tragic heroines demonstrating some Universal Truth to the rest of the world through their own suffering.

As Jonathan saw it, what happens to the characters in the play – a woman falling in love with a visiting soldier, and so on – is actually very uncomplicated. The sisters are going through mundane periods in their lives, and facing this with a mixture of fortitude and frailty, and Jonathan pinpointed their emotions and nuances in a way that audiences could sympathise with, and be moved by. It was one of his more emotionally engaged productions, and generated a very strong ensemble feeling that really brought us together as a family – a lot of that company are still close friends to this day.

MR   Irving Wardle commented in *The Times* that 'the sympathetic characters are viewed more dryly, the unsympathetic with greater kindness' – how was this reflected on stage?

JS   Well, for instance, take Jonathan's treatment of Natasha, and her relationship with the sisters. Natasha is often portrayed as a vulgar intruder into the family who tries to establish herself (through Andrey) among the sisters, so that their efforts to exclude her appear perfectly understandable. Jonathan used her more as a means to focus the sisters' frustrations; they take it out on her. Where, for example, Olga criticises Natasha's belt just before they go in to dinner, 'Oh, my dear, a green belt ... it's quite wrong ...' if the error is obvious, you side with Olga and there's merely a consensus with the audience about taste. (Usually the way this is carried off.) Jonathan's idea was to present her as only slightly mis-dressed – one shade of green out, as it were – so that Olga would appear rather cruel in trying to ostracise her by seizing on a minute sartorial irregularity.

In criticising the sisters in this way, I thought that Jonathan was being truthful and accurate. He was emphatic that the sisters should be allowed to snap at each other, lose their tempers and do the things that people in families normally do. Although there is evidently great love between Andrey and his sisters, Jonathan pointed out that there is also considerable tension – living with close relatives is not necessarily easy.

MR   How did Jonathan come to direct *Hamlet* at the Donmar Warehouse in 1982?

JS   He had been working on the BBC TV Shakespeare series for some time, and I think he was eager to get back into a theatre and make contact with a live audience again. He had already directed *Hamlet* twice before, and he wanted to stage it in a small space without any fuss – I think he's happiest in small theatres. The Donmar offered him the intimacy he was looking for, and proved very effective – the Ghost scene, for example, played on the bare stage in hard daylight, with Philip Locke and Anton Lesser simply sitting on a bench and talking as genuine father and son might, no dry-ice and weird effects.

MR   John Elsom described the production as 'the first *Hamlet* I've seen which asks why Claudius cannot bring himself to kill Hamlet, instead of the other way round' – how did Jonathan develop this interpretation?

JS We came up with something of a reappraisal of Claudius, which made it very exciting to play. It was as though Hamlet and Claudius spend the play stalking each other intuitively and intellectually.

Jonathan reckoned that the murdered King Hamlet was not necessarily the greatest ruler of all time; that Denmark might actually be better off under the usurping Claudius. To some extent the play asks this question, which you can begin to answer by the way you play it. In the Olivier film of *Hamlet*, Basil Sydney plays Claudius as a glamorous villain, kebabed by a horizontally flying Olivier at the end, but much as I admire that film, I think that we've got beyond that sort of romantic presentation. We can look more seriously at other possibilities.

Jonathan's view was that it all boils down to how far you believe what one character says about another in the play: we don't know, after all, how reliable Hamlet's descriptions of Claudius really are. We tried to portray Claudius as truthfully as possible, so that I should try to win some sympathy for the character. We looked hard at Claudius's line about Gertrude: 'She's so conjunctive to my life and soul, / That, as the star moves not but in his sphere, / I could not but by her.' I found this insight very moving, as well as revealing. Claudius and Gertrude were obviously deeply in love with each other, so that the murder of King Hamlet – whether or not Gertrude connived in it – became the only way to resolve the situation. Claudius is doubly vulnerable – because of his love for Gertrude, and because he's committed murder. This guilt and the impossibility of tranquillity finally cracks the shell; we see him unable to pray. Jonathan called the Prayer Scene 'The Dark Night of the Soul'. I think he felt that if you can get at that, you can get at the man.

We talked about Bolingbroke in *Richard II*, who – before he has actually committed regicide – is shown as a very efficient politician and administrator. The same is true of Claudius. From the first court scene he is solving problems, sending Laertes off to France, dealing with Fortinbras's invasion, and so on. We're dealing with a high level of subtle pragmatism here, and you're tempting fate if you underestimate him.

Also, by presenting him as an effective and ingenious ruler, you make Hamlet's position much more difficult – he's not just up against some drunken oaf he'll be able to stab after three and a half hours. It's much more interesting and dramatic if you show parallel intellects at work, locked in rivalry.

The production is a very good example of Jonathan's ensemble work. Attention would be paid to every corner of the play. Among many intriguing interpretations, Kathryn Pogson's Ophelia, in her mad scene, was quite difficult for us to watch, and I'm sure extremely difficult to do. It was very graphic, and (naturally) accurate in medical detail and Kathryn was very nervous about performing it in rehearsal – rather like doing a nude scene on a film-set. It aroused strange, nervy reactions in our audiences – school parties at matinees seemed to be particularly startled by it.

JANET SUZMAN

Janet Suzman played Masha in *The Three Sisters* (Cambridge Theatre 1976) and the title role of *Andromache* (Old Vic 1988).

Michael Romain   What were the rehearsals like for *Three Sisters?*

Janet Suzman   It was a strange maverick fate. It doesn't often happen – sometimes you can have very unhappy rehearsal periods and have a very fruitful product at the end of it. The happiness of rehearsals does not always affect the work. But in this particular case – and it's the only time I've known it in my life – rehearsals were a total joy and the end result was very good indeed. It was literally a once-in-a-lifetime experience.

Jonathan would take from the actors what they gave him and then transform the ideas – he is able to stimulate the actor's ability to invent. What's vital about him is what a good audience he is – it's very important for actors in rehearsals to see his responsive face taking everything in and delighting in it. He uses his own emotions as a sounding-board, and if something moves him or if he likes it he will always encourage the performer. Sometimes you can feel a real fool in rehearsals, but he will always be warm and supportive. So the inventiveness in the rehearsal room was at pitch from the word go, and we covered a lot of ground very quickly.

In the end, that *Three Sisters* almost ran out of control because it was so overwhelmingly ordinary and human, which is a very un-Milleresque trademark. In a sense, it was a departure from his usual style. Many of his productions remind me of those comic strips where you see a light bulb light up over someone's head when they have an idea.

MR   What characterised that *Three Sisters?*

JS   I think that the tone of that whole production was caught in the scene in Act 3 where Masha confesses her love for Vershinin. When we came to rehearse that, I got the most terrible giggles about something stupid, as I'm a dreadful giggler. I really couldn't stop, so what Jonathan did was to keep it in the scene. Then, of course, it all began to sink down much deeper and made absolute sense about how a very great emotion can sometimes send you tumbling in the opposite emotional direction. It was quite unexpected, as it was the reverse of the way the scene is normally played – instead of being a great tragic confession, it simply became panic-stricken.

There were a lot of those sorts of touches, which simply began to sow themselves throughout the production. Maybe because there was a terrific sense of freedom amongst all of us – Jonathan created the sort of atmosphere in the rehearsal room where people could stand on their heads and nobody would care. We all became pretty shameless, and therefore rather creative. The rapport between the three sisters became particularly sisterly – we girls actually romped together very well. Natasha, for instance, is always going to be a total pain in the ass, but here she also became very funny indeed – her vulgarity was stunningly comic.

MR Much of *Three Sisters* revolves around family conversation – how did Jonathan approach that?

JS He used his technique of overlapping dialogue, that cross-cutting of conversation which he developed much more when he did *Long Day's Journey into Night*.

He is also very strong on words and language. He loves philosophising, as do all the characters in the play, particularly the Baron and Vershinin. Jonathan treated their exchanges not as something to pass the time, to kill a few dead minutes in the sitting-room of the Prozorovs' house, but as quite the reverse – as a relish of the idea of voicing thoughts on whatever subject might arise, which Jonathan, of course, enjoys doing himself.

MR You next worked with Jonathan in 1988, when you played the title role in his production of *Andromache* at the start of his first Old Vic season.

JS Jonathan phoned me a year before that, which was a very long time in advance, and I said yes to the role immediately because *Three Sisters* had been so good. *Andromache* was much more difficult, because of the problems we had – inevitably, with a Racine play – with the translation.

When we did *Three Sisters*, he borrowed the suitable phrases from quite a lot of versions of the text until they began to sit easily on everybody's tongues. He simply used an amalgam of the best translations rather than one with the author's personal stamp on it.

That was not the case with *Andromache*, where he first of all determined to do something new with the terrible problem of French into English and gave it to Craig Raine, which didn't work out at all. Then he turned to Eric Korn, an old friend and colleague of his, and out came this very fresh, very anglicised, Anglo-Saxon even, version of the play. On the whole it was very successful, but there were one or two colloquial phrases here and there which had the effect of deflating the tragedy somewhat. The translation was so good that it should have been better – had those small points been altered, it would have been magnificent.

MR   How did rehearsals compare to those for *Three Sisters*?

JS   Jonathan was not so happy this time. I think that he responds more to the human situations of Chekhov than to the idealised and remote world of Racine – he's more at home amongst the samovars.

He didn't work as fast on *Andromache* – the pace of rehearsals was even, and at times slightly plodding. Rehearsals were very difficult, mainly because of the problems we faced in finding our way through the language to the heart of the matter.

What we did find thrilling was the discovery of how passionate and immediate a playwright Racine really is, whereas I had always previously regarded him as rather remote and intellectual.

I liked the sparseness of the world which Jonathan and Richard Hudson, the designer, created for us to inhabit. Though in an attempt to make it stratospheric and hieratic, Jonathan spent a lot of time showing us those strange, pleading gestures in baroque paintings – that pictorial image seared itself onto his mind, but we found it very hard to recreate those painterly attitudes.

MR   How did the production turn out in the end?

JS   Racine is very badly served in Britain, and I have to say that I think we did a damn sight better than previous attempts. Most of those were distant and Tragic with a capital T, whereas ours was much more warm and accessible – it was surprisingly human. Jonathan left space between the actors, so that there was an emptiness and a sense of reaching out across a distance that gave it a strange nobility. And there was certainly great excitement that we were opening Jonathan's reign at the Old Vic with such a rarely seen classic.

MR   What makes Jonathan stand out above other directors?

JS   He's a maverick figure – his productions are always very daring, and he's put on plays at the Old Vic that nobody else would do. He doesn't really like to belong to Establishment organisations, because he won't toe the line. He has done a lot of work for the subsidised companies, of course.

But they're too big for him – he's not comfortable there, because he feels a bit of an outsider. He is from medicine, after all, which has actually served him very well in his productions.

Jonathan's particularity as a director – more than any other director I know – is the fecundity of his mind. Some actors are wary of Jonathan's so-called intellectualism, but that's just the English disease – they are terrified of people whom they call 'intellectuals'. I don't have that, because I'm not English. Jonathan's extraordinary intellect is probably the thing that annoys people the most about him, but for people who are on his side – as I am – it delights them the most.

He's also quite a lateral thinker – he thinks sideways rather than thinking obviously. That's got to be his strongest point as a director – he will never settle for the obvious.

JOHN CLEESE

John Cleese played Petruchio in *The Taming of the Shrew* (BBC TV Shakespeare 1980).

Michael Romain How did you come to play Petruchio for Jonathan?

John Cleese I phoned Jonathan up one day about something completely different, an idea that I had for a TV show or something. He was doing a television series in the same area, so I wanted to see whether we might overlap. Then he called me back the next day and asked me if I would play Petruchio for him in *The Taming of the Shrew*.

I told him that I thought it was rather a silly play, with a lot of male thigh-slapping behaviour. But Jonathan asked me to read it again, and I did so because I had enormous respect for his opinion. A couple of days later he came round to my house, and I put to him a whole load of questions about the play which were worrying me. He immediately gave me answers that made perfect sense, and that also revealed the play in an intelligent light. Then I asked him the big question for me – does Petruchio need facial hair? Jonathan thought that it would be a good idea, so I started to grow a beard.

MR Petruchio's extreme behaviour poses a problem for actors and directors today – how did you tackle it?

JC Jonathan had obviously seen in my sketch acting the ability to play Petruchio in the way that he envisaged the part. We tried to do it in as

8 John Cleese (Petruchio), *The Taming of the Shrew*, BBC TV 1980

subtle and intelligent a way as possible – if you do it the other way you give off a totally different message, which is that here is a man who likes hitting women.

Jonathan was very keen on the idea that Petruchio is an early Protestant

135

who is thrilled by the idea of direct communication with God. His conscience is a matter between him and God, so he is not at all worried if other people find his behaviour scandalous. He's not at all concerned about the effect that his outrageous behaviour in the church has on the congregation, because he and God both know that it was done for the right reasons.

Jonathan pointed out that Petruchio doesn't believe in his own antics, but in the craftiest and most sophisticated psychological way he needs to show Kate certain things about her behaviour. He takes one look at her and realises that here is the woman for him, but he has to go through the process of 'reconditioning' her before anything else. So he behaves just as outrageously as she does in order to make her aware of the effect that her behaviour has on other people.

The play starts off with a patriarchal, almost chauvinist, attitude, yet I felt that in Jonathan's production Petruchio and Kate finished up very much as equals, which made the ending rather touching. Petruchio, a very experienced man of the world, saw this extremely attractive girl with tremendous qualities who simply didn't know how to behave because her parents had never been able to contain her anger and anxieties. He realised, therefore, that he was going to have to teach her a few things, and when she had learned those lessons she would be the perfect partner.

When a psychiatrist friend of mine read the first scene between Petruchio and Kate he said that it reminded him basically of what he did with shrews in therapy, which was to tease them. Not in an aggressive way, which is just destructive – he would only ever tease shrews if he knew that they sensed his affection and support. This is the constructive way of teasing people, which is a gentle, humorous way of making them start to think about their own behaviour. That's what Petruchio is up to, and to some extent what a therapist gets up to. Kate needs to be made happy – she is quite clearly unhappy at the beginning of the play, and then extremely happy at the end because of what she has achieved with Petruchio's help.

I loved working on that very tired speech of Petruchio's with Jonathan, where he says something like 'Now is my hawk tamed.' Jonathan brought out wonderfully the fact that poor old Petruchio is thoroughly exhausted by the whole exercise, and is looking forward longingly to the moment when it would be over, when Kate had learned what she needed to learn and could take her place alongside him.

MR   How did you find Jonathan's direction?

JC   I remember seeing a swashbuckling movie called *Scaramouche* when I was at Clifton College in 1953, in which a fencing-master said you should hold a sword as though it was a bird – too tightly and you will crush it, too lightly and it will fly away. Jonathan's direction is exactly like that – he knows *precisely* the amount of support to give his actors. He would encourage us to play, and made us feel that every contribution we made was of value.

I was very impressed with the way that he cast the play, so that even the minor roles were fully fleshed out. He works very well with actors because he makes them feel creative. He's a very generous director, and gives actors great freedom to find things out for themselves – he holds them lightly enough for them to feel supported yet also free, and they always sense that he's basically got it together. I think that a director has got to be a parental creature. Actors are naturally frightened – they are the ones up on the stage with the potential for really making fools of themselves.

I also found that Jonathan's knowledge and experience of psychology was very useful in exploring the problems of the characters. He offers ideas in a very nice way, so that you can try them and then move on to something else if they don't seem to work.

There is a school of acting which you get a bit in America where it is considered enormously insulting to the actor to show him what to do, or even to suggest an inflection – the actor, they maintain, must discover it for himself. That's a way of thinking that I'm pretty contemptuous of. I understand the reasons behind it, but on the whole I think it's just egotism. If you can work with a director like Jonathan who will sometimes show you a posture, a gesture, an inflection or an expression, then rehearsals go much quicker than having a long theoretical discussion in order to get to exactly the same point. Sometimes it's much easier to mimic someone than to go on a whole roundabout route to arrive at the same conclusion.

I remember marvelling at the way that Jonathan brought us all to a state of readiness. Four days before we began filming in the studio, he suddenly added little touches to the production – a silly hat for me, for example, with huge quills sticking out of it. Having brought us to an advanced stage of preparation, he then gave us extra stimulus by giving us something new to play with.

MR Did you find that humour was an essential part of his rehearsals?

JC Yes I did – humour is a very important part of the way that Jonathan works. He's looking for humour when he directs.

Jonathan's sense of humour is why his productions are so successful. Unless you have an atmosphere in which there is the possibility of humour, you're not going to get the actors at their most playful and inventive. If you work in an atmosphere where everything is enormously serious, it is inhibiting in terms of creativity.

MR Where do you think Jonathan's comic forte lies?

JC Jonathan often refers to Erving Goffman, particularly his *Presentation of Self in Everyday Life*, and I think that he is fascinated by bits of behaviour. He did a sketch in *Beyond the Fringe* about what people do when they're alone in a railway carriage. That's very much what intrigues him – he loves to watch what people do in those little private moments. What happens, for instance, if they trip over a paving-stone while they're walking along the street, and how they cover up this appalling damage that they've just done to their egos by then becoming angry with the paving-stone.

So I think that Jonathan's particular forte is his very, very accurate observation, rather like Alan Bennett. Alan's observation is more verbal – he keeps little notebooks in which he writes down things that he's over-heard people saying on buses; whereas Jonathan is probably slightly more interested in the physical aspects – the postures, gestures, quirks and so on.

MR Have you ever performed comedy with Jonathan?

JC He directed the first show that we did for Amnesty International, then in the next one I performed the Philosopher's sketch from *Beyond the Fringe* with him, which was a great joy. He's a wonderful actor but, rather like me, I don't think that he wants to have to get up and do it every night. As a director, he's able to enjoy his acting ability in a very constructive way without having to get up and do it onstage six nights a week.

MR Was *Beyond the Fringe* an influence on you?

JC Oh yes, I don't think there is any question about that, because it was quite simply the funniest show that I'd ever seen in my life, and I think it remains so today. I can still recall just being amazed at how good it was. I saw it in Cambridge the week before it went to London, and the great delight of it was that there were four people onstage who were all somewhere near the genius level. When a sketch with Peter Cook finished, you would have a momentary flicker of disappointment that it was over and then five seconds later the lights would go up and there would be Jonathan Miller carrying a torch. And then so on with Alan Bennett and Dudley Moore.

When I was working out the plot of *A Fish Called Wanda* I was really operating on exactly the same idea – having four characters who were funny in different ways, having them coming on one after another, and then mixing up the combinations of them all. The richness of having four separate comic identities and then being able to combine them in various permutations means that the audience doesn't have much chance of getting bored. The terrible thing about comedy is that once the audience gets the point of a joke, you've got to move on immediately. If comedy is going to succeed, you actually have to have a lot of development and several different comic ideas, and that comes relatively easily if you've got a number of funny characters who you can then combine in different ways. That's why *Beyond the Fringe* worked so well.

The interesting thing about *Beyond the Fringe* is that when I and my contemporaries saw it at Cambridge, we simply accepted that we had seen something funnier than anything we had ever seen before and probably funnier than anything we would ever see. It never occurred to us, though, that it was satirical. Nobody used the word in Cambridge, and it was only when it reached London that it was labelled 'satire'. To us it just seemed the natural content of comedy, the sort of things that you would make jokes about. It was the skill with which the material was played that we found so remarkable.

ALEC McCOWEN

Alec McCowen played David Hume in *Dialogue in the Dark* (BBC TV 1988).

Michael Romain   When did you first encounter Jonathan Miller?

Alec McCowen   In 1961, when he was appearing in *Beyond the Fringe* in the West End. At that time, I was appearing in a very old-fashioned revue called *Not To Worry* – we should have done. The day after we opened one newspaper headline called us 'The Worst Revue Ever!', and I was rather hurt by that until I went to see *Beyond the Fringe* a few weeks later and then thoroughly agreed with it. At *Beyond the Fringe* you were just knocked out by a combination of humour and intelligence in those four young men who had never been seen on stage before; the revue that I was in, on the other hand, was about fifty years out of date.

MR   You played David Hume in Michael Ignatieff's philosophical conversation-piece *Dialogue in the Dark*, which Jonathan directed for television in 1988: how did he tackle such complex material?

AM He didn't spend ages exploring the philosophical concerns expressed in the text – his analysis was so clear that he was able to convey the meaning of the lines very quickly indeed, without getting weighed down in it. I wouldn't like to do that piece with any other director.

In order to make the piece work as a conversation, it had to be played at some speed. Jonathan was extremely enthusiastic about his technique of overlapping dialogue, which he used to remarkable effect in *Long Day's Journey into Night* and other productions. I didn't think that it would work with this material, though, because it was so deep that I found some of it difficult to follow even when we were saying it slowly. But he encouraged us to overlap the lines, and I was delighted when I eventually saw the piece as it worked superbly and made the dialogue very sparky.

In fact, he gave us a lot of freedom in rehearsals, though, not having worked with him before, I was a little worried that he might come up with too many suggestions and confuse me. But he hardly gave me any notes at all for the first ten days, because he knew that I was still learning the lines. He would discuss the meaning of the piece, but didn't put a lot of ideas to me until well into the rehearsal period, by which time I felt at home with the lines and knew roughly what I was doing. And then he would start putting ideas to me, which was very exciting.

You see, Jonathan has an instinctive understanding of actors – their moods, their problems, their worries. At the end of the play, for instance, I was supposed to strip off completely, which was not worrying me desperately but was certainly lurking at the back of my mind – you tend to think about these things if you have to strip in a crowded TV studio. And I think Jonathan must have sensed this, because well before we started filming he said 'I don't think it's necessary at all for you to strip – you don't have to bother with that.'

MR Did Jonathan try to recreate a sense of the eighteenth century in his production?

AM He certainly did from a visual angle: the costumes, make-up and designs were all accurate, and he took enormous care over the lighting so that the piece was lit like a painting from the period. We spent three days in the studio, which is a long time for a play that lasted barely forty-five minutes. This enabled Jonathan to do extremely long takes, which is quite rare nowadays and a great help to actors doing dialogue scenes like that. He would shoot twelve-minute takes, and perhaps do them as much as three times to get them exactly right.

He was also very precise about the illness and death that feature in the play, particularly about the form that David Hume's physical decay would take. He went into great detail showing me how fast Hume would walk, or how he would eat – that he would look forward to meals but find himself unable to eat the food when it was served up, then all of a sudden make a huge attack on it and eat very greedily for a short time. Jonathan also developed the relationship between Hume and Boswell in emotional terms, such as the older man's envy of the younger's sexuality and appetites.

MR Jonathan is a director who works primarily in the classics, without the playwright or composer present – how closely involved was Michael Ignatieff?

AM Michael was actually very closely involved in the production. In fact, Michael became really caught up in it, and would sit nodding in agreement with Jonathan on the set or in the rehearsal room.

MR Which feature of Jonathan's personality struck you most when you worked with him?

AM His energy, without any doubt. It is phenomenal. I wondered before-hand whether his attention would be divided on *Dialogue in the Dark*, because he was running the Old Vic at the same time, as well as writing and lecturing. But, for the two and a half weeks that we were doing it, you would not have known that he was doing anything else in the world except that little television play. He never left the rehearsal room for a moment, and concentrated entirely on the play despite the fact that he had so many other things on at the same time.

MR Have you worked with any other director like Jonathan?

AM Only Tyrone Guthrie. He was similarly open-minded, with a terrific sense of fun. The ideas just bubbled up from him in rehearsals. Like Jonathan, he would follow clues in the text to explain a character's behaviour, or take off on sudden flights of fancy. There's a great similarity between them – Guthrie would also hold back until the later stages of rehearsals, when he would give his ideas free rein.

I remember doing a run-through of *The Matchmaker* in the fourth week of rehearsal, and Guthrie saying at the end of it 'Well that's very neat, very clear, you all know what you're doing. Now we're going to mess it up a little.' And that was when it started to come alive. Jonathan could well say something like that, and turn something that was rather formal and careful into something dangerous and exciting.

GEMMA JONES

Gemma Jones played the Countess in *The Marriage of Figaro* (National Theatre at
the Old Vic 1974) and Goneril in *King Lear* (Old Vic 1989).

Michael Romain   You played the Countess in Jonathan's production of the
Beaumarchais *Marriage of Figaro* for the National Theatre in 1974 – how
much emphasis was put on the politics of the play?

Gemma Jones   Jonathan didn't stress its revolutionary aspects, but made it
more of a domestic romp. It veered towards being stylised farce, without
being held back by any reverence for its status as a classic. Even my
performance as the Countess bordered on the farcical. I was actually
pregnant at the time, and as I grew bigger and bigger my corsets were let
out more and more.

  We had a very productive rehearsal period and laughed a lot, as one
always does with Jonathan. He encouraged us towards a rough-edged,
anarchic and joyous reading of the play, and we enjoyed ourselves so much
that we presumed the audiences would too, as indeed they did once the run
was under way.

MR   When you worked with Jonathan fifteen years later playing Goneril in
his *King Lear* at the Old Vic, he had already directed the play three times –
did this mean that he came to the production with a set interpretation?

GJ   Not really – he was obviously very familiar with the text, but he came to
it totally fresh, thinking on his feet and ready to react to the different
chemistry of a new cast.

MR   Did he outline an initial approach to the play at the read-through?

GJ   He said that he didn't want to set *King Lear* in the First World War or
anything like that – he wanted the production to have a strong allegiance to
the concerns of the play rather than anything else. And that's what he came
up with – he used a bare and abstract set, against which the input of the
actors and the text was paramount. He gave it a timeless style rather than
the traditional 'Stonehenge look'.

MR   How does he deal with characterisation?

GJ   He leaves a lot of room for the actors to experiment, as long as they are
capable of making some creative input. He's very open to discussion of a
role, and doesn't overwhelm you with suggestions unless you get stuck.

Frances de la Tour and I worked very well together as Regan and Goneril, evolving our performances in the the process – it wasn't so much a case of Jonathan telling us what to do every second as the fact that he had obviously given us the roles in the first place because our personalities fitted in with his ideas about the characters. He gently encouraged us, and then polished the edges – he would improvise moments himself for us, as he is very good at playing women.

He was keen to show – as I was too – that Goneril was a human being rather than the usual vampire woman, and that some psychological trauma made her behave the way she did. Being a psychologist himself, he would naturally analyse the characters for us, but in a domestic way rather than just quoting Jung and Freud at us. He's quite right – it's no good relying purely on theory, because you can't put a theory onstage when you need visible characterisation.

I remember him saying to me during one scene, 'I think that Goneril has got a migraine.' Her travail was making her ill, and her actions immediately became clear. That's much more effective than saying, 'Well, if her father hadn't done this, and of course she hasn't got a mother, etc. etc.' That's the thing about Jonathan – he's very practical. He had Albany portrayed as an intellectual with his head permanently buried in his books, which must have driven Goneril crazy too. So he made the characters into people who could sit round a kitchen table and eat Weetabix as well as commit murder and behave in the most extraordinary manner.

MR What was his feeling about the verse?

GJ He is quite resistant to what he calls 'RSC and National Theatre verse-speaking'. He doesn't like actors to get weighed down in dogmas about the verse; instead, he is very open to the diverse styles of his group of actors, which is always very eclectic. He is not at all dictatorial about it – his sole concern is that we should get the meaning of the words across to the audience. He likes us to use subtlety and irony in the lines, though, slipping them in through the back door rather than throwing them in someone's face.

MR How do actors respond to the fact that he is a doctor as well as a director?

GJ When you work with him in the theatre he will wear his director's hat. That said, there was actually quite a lot of medical chat during *King Lear* rehearsals – Jonathan is very interested in the nature of madness and senility, so there was a lot of talk about Alzheimer's Disease in relation to

Lear himself. There was not a great deal of spiritual talk, though – Jonathan is much more interested in blood, brains and guts than stars and spirits. But then he is like that as a person – he is absolutely practical. He thinks that when we die we get buried in the ground and that is it, so it's quite hard to get him talking about the afterlife or the influence of the elements. Any excuse to talk about blood and guts.

MR   In many ways Jonathan is similar to Peter Brook, both being boldly innovative directors equally fond of visual imagery and textual exploration – having worked with Brook on his famous *Midsummer Night's Dream*, how would you compare the two?

GJ   They are indeed similar, and at the same time quite, quite different. Brook works in a narrow channel and if you're lucky you can join him on his tightrope, which is very concentrated and thrilling. Jonathan sort of swings a safety net around his cast, so that they can all make it – his style is ultimately freer.

There is a kind of security in knowing the confines of working with Brook, but there is also security in working with Jonathan because he gives you a sense of responsibility. Brook is more spiritual and Jonathan more practical – I suppose that Brook's approach is finally more rigid. Once he has pulled all his elements in, you know exactly where your track is; whereas working with Jonathan sometimes makes you feel as if you are in danger of maybe falling off the stage.

Their characters are very different. Jonathan is very open, whereas Brook is very shy. He is more like a teacher, while Jonathan is more like a friend. In a way, Brook's way of working is more cerebral; whereas Jonathan, although an intellectual in every sense of the word, doesn't let that overwhelm his direction – he works out of a spontaneity and generosity that isn't necessarily book-bound. I've been jolly lucky to have worked with both of them.

JACK LEMMON

Jack Lemmon played James Tyrone in *Long Day's Journey into Night* (Broadhurst Theater, New York, and Haymarket Theatre, London 1986).

Jack Lemmon   I happened to be in England in 1962 for a picture with Sam Spiegel, and everybody told me that I had to go and see *Beyond the Fringe* in the West End. I loved it, and that was my first encounter with Jonathan. I met him briefly a couple of times after that, and when *Long Day's Journey into Night* came up in 1986 I accepted immediately when they said that he would be directing it. I'd never seen a production of the play, I'd only read it once, and I didn't even know if I could play the damn thing. But if Jonathan thought that I could, then that was all I needed. I didn't even know who was on the phone – I just said 'I'll do it!' Subsequently, Jonathan and I became as close as you get in that rather incestuous world of the theatre.

Michael Romain Your portrayal of James Tyrone was a departure from tradition in many respects – he was not the usual Great Actor but a much more human and domestic figure, vulnerable and irritable, yet surprisingly sympathetic in his genuine concern for his wife.

JL He would never have put up with his wife's morphine addiction if he had not been deeply in love with her. He simply would have had her committed – it wouldn't have cost him more than ten cents. But he didn't because, underneath it all, he adored her, without any question. Otherwise it just doesn't make any sense.

That, like almost all of the characterisation, stemmed from Jonathan's perception of our roles, and we all went along with that. His whole approach to the play was entirely natural. Sacriligious to a few, of course, because we overlapped many of the lines, but who the hell isn't going to overlap when they're screaming and shouting at each other in their own house? When you have people drunk and doped up, on top of the incredible tensions that already exist in the family, then they are going to interrupt and yell at each other. As Jonathan showed us in rehearsals, they don't listen to each other because they've heard the same old lines again and again over the last twenty years. They're even repeated again and again during the course of the play itself.

The timing of the play originally, according to the notes that O'Neill left, was considerably shorter than the standard playing time, so the dialogue must have been overlapped. There's no other way of doing it.

We knew precisely where we were supposed to be overlapping – we didn't just do it whenever we felt like it. We worked out all the interjections in fine detail and orchestrated them at specific moments. In fact, Jonathan almost directed it like an opera, which he's damn good at.

At one rehearsal, Jonathan brought in a tape of Beethoven's 'Grosse Fugue' and played it to us. Immediately, we knew what he was aiming for. It was a way of making us understand the play. Suddenly I could see and feel all of its levels – where we were going and what was happening to us.

Somehow, that music evoked the shadows over the light that you find in every relationship in the play. It's akin to what I look for, at a much more simplistic level, in any play or movie – not a comedy and not a drama, but both together. Some of both, because that is what happens in life. But finding the real comedy is not easy.

Lasting comedy, very often, is not funny for the people involved. It's only funny if you're looking at it and it's not affecting you. This goes right back to an audience roaring with laughter when somebody slips on a banana skin. What the hell is so funny about that, except the fact that you can break your back or split your head open or kill yourself? But, oh God, it's funny as long as it's not happening to you. Jonathan would be the first person to point this out, and his awareness of these ironies enables him to pinpoint the best means of expressing humour.

When you're doing an apparently serious drama, you can find comic moments which even the author did not necessarily anticipate. But O'Neill definitely knew that there was a lot of humour in *Long Day's Journey into Night*, and we evoked laughs with Jonathan's help that were absolutely legitimate but had simply never been tried before.

MR   The use of overlapping dialogue in the production built up an almost Chekhovian sense of family – did this generate an ensemble feeling amongst the cast?

JL   Oh yes, very much so. Jonathan's approach to the play demanded a sense of timing and a real company spirit from his actors, and he cast people who would quite naturally blend together into a family. Bethel Leslie, who played Mary Tyrone, was already a close friend; and the two boys, Peter Gallagher and Kevin Spacey, have since remained very close. So it was a very close, intimate company, partly due to the way Jonathan worked at crafting the production itself.

MR   Jonathan's production – with its use of overlapping dialogue to build up normal layers of conversation, and its reappraisal of previously stereotyped characterisation – was radically innovative compared to most revivals: how was it received when you opened on Broadway?

JL   Most people welcomed it, but some were a little ambivalent. They wanted to like it more, but the O'Neill tradition in them prevented them from wholeheartedly embracing such a novel concept, and they were rather hedgy. They completely forgot, of course, that for decades now it's been perfectly acceptable to overlap Shakespeare or update it or do whatever the hell you want with it. That's OK with Shakespeare. But not with O'Neill!

Maybe it was because they were American critics, with only a handful of native playwrights that they could put up on that kind of level. But it's asinine to treat O'Neill that way and insist that you have to be able to hear every word in his script loud and clear.

That's the biggest problem that you face when you do an O'Neill play – reverence. The awe! 'Oh, it's O'Neill! I – must – say – ev-ery – word – in syll-ables!' Rubbish! In the play, you have a bunch of screaming people, an Irish-American family that are going for each others' throats. There's got to be a certain bar-room level of behaviour there, and that's exactly what Jonathan achieved. And he was dead-on in his aim: not one dramatic note was missed. It was incredibly exciting for audiences – sometimes they would be just stunned, as they'd never seen O'Neill played like that before.

There was the occasional criticism that Jonathan's direction was too innovative. They seemed to be implying that he was being innovative simply for the sake of it. That's utterly wrong – he's never worked that way. He will only direct a particular play or opera for a reason, because he'll see something in it that will excite him and spark off an idea. He won't do something just to be different. And if it is different, then it's for a good reason.

RONALD PICKUP

Ronald Pickup played Saint-Just in *Danton's Death* (National Theatre at the Old Vic 1971), Joseph Surface in *The School for Scandal* (National Theatre at the Old Vic 1972) and Edgar in *King Lear* (BBC TV 1975).

Michael Romain What were your first impressions of Jonathan when you played Saint-Just in his production of *Danton's Death* for the National Theatre in 1971?

Ronald Pickup Very much those that I'd gleaned from seeing him in *Beyond the Fringe* – he was no less funny offstage. I'd energetically proffered myself to Olivier for the role of Saint-Just, so I don't know if I was Jonathan's first choice for it, but I found him highly engaging right from the start.

MR Was there much discussion in rehearsals?

RP The rehearsals were a mixture of Büchner's play and seminars with Jonathan on any subject that you chose to come up with. Sometimes these would be so fascinating that the play almost got in the way. There always comes a moment when you sometimes wonder whether you've talked too much one day and not done enough work on the play, but you realise later that it has had a percolating effect on the production, like filtering coffee. It was an immensely enjoyable rehearsal period.

MR   How did Jonathan work with you on the role of Saint-Just?

RP   For Saint-Just's big speech, Jonathan helped me to find certain stylised rhetorical gestures of a kind that anyone who's ever watched Hitler or Mussolini could use. Then we worked out the way that I should deliver the speech – it rose to a mounting crescendo, almost note by note, a semi-tone each time. It was as technical as that – I would practise it over and over again like a musician, and he would be there all the time to tell me whether it was working or not.

When Jonathan gave notes he would draw all sorts of analogies, and his most effective notes were always metaphorical. When we were having our first conversation about the role, he said, 'Saint-Just is one of those people you imagine tearing off reams and reams of lavatory paper.' That captures precisely this cut-glass, ferociously clean, obsessive character. Those are the kind of notes which are most useful to the actor, and they have the added benefit of being extremely funny as well – a sense of humour like Jonathan's is absolutely vital in rehearsals.

MR   What exactly was the style of Jonathan's production?

RP   Very still, sparse and simple, which is exactly right for that play. The scenes between Saint-Just, Danton and Robespierre were very concentrated – they were staged as an intense argument between the three of them, without the attendant noise of crowds punctuating the conversation.

Because we were a small company at that time, there were no huge crowds in *Danton* – rather than having a small, unconvincing crowd, Jonathan cut them altogether. So when we came to our revolutionary speeches, we played them out to the front. It must have looked rather weird, and therefore very compelling – I imagine it would have had the effect of people speaking from a distance, and thus in a curious way seeming rather insignificant. This momentous event suddenly seemed like a little blip. Certainly the slightly crooked and off-centre set, a raked series of boxes, contributed to this sense.

The make-up, too, was very stylised – it was greenish in shade, and looked very Germanic, like something out of those early Expressionist films. It was also very romantic – the long hair, greenish make-up and French Revolution costume combined to give us a kind of spooky glamour.

The make-up added to the 'museum cabinet' effect that Jonathan was after, matched by all the dolls in glass cases positioned around the stage. We all became objects of scrutiny.

This stylised staging, and the way that we did some of the speeches in an almost robotic manner, worked very well onstage. It had a frightening intensity about it.

MR   You next worked with Jonathan on *The School for Scandal* at the National the following year.

RP   After continuously playing *Richard II* and *Long Day's Journey into Night* I was very tired during rehearsals, and I didn't seem to be able to make Joseph Surface work. Jonathan gave me an awful lot of uplift and support by convincing me that whatever it was that we had both worked out was funny. I was greatly helped by the fact that he came up with all sorts of business which suited my rather lean, manic figure – leaping around chairs and things, which is not the way that Joseph Surface is normally played. But it suited me – he adapted the role to my personal characteristics as much as we adapted to his direction. Jonathan is hugely inventive and loves comic business – sometimes there was so much of it going on across the stage that you weren't quite sure where to look.

Rather than just playing Surface as the ultimate smoothie in a very well-oiled Haymarket style, Jonathan encouraged me to play him as an edgy, neurotic figure, as a man who lives on that kind of hypocritical level would have to be. This fitted in with the style of his production – there was a strong feeling early on of these smelly rooms, of the body odour of the characters and the murky lighting. There was nothing prettified about it at all, which was very arresting for our audiences. It made the play much fresher, and brought a lot of younger audiences into the theatre.

MR   How did Jonathan fit in to Olivier's National Theatre company?

RP   He was very fond indeed of the National when it was based at the Old Vic under Olivier, as we all were. The irreplaceable personal touch of Olivier's management combined with that small, overcrowded atmospheric building to generate a kind of energy which, although it was often chaotic, formed the essence of what theatre is all about. It tapped deep into hundreds of years of that kind of work – however much styles may have changed, the slightly dusty, musty things-might-fall-apart atmosphere of the Old Vic was absolutely right for someone like Jonathan, as it was for most of us.

Olivier had built up a genuinely close-knit company. It was like a family, with the natural rows and tensions of any family, but underneath it all there was great mutual affection and respect. It was chemically vibrant – people sparked off each other in a huge variety of plays and productions. Jonathan loved all this, and he was there on a regular basis from his debut production onwards.

In fact, I'm sure that he would have liked to be there on a permanent basis, rather than just coming in to direct his shows. He used to pop into the Old Vic as often as he could, particularly when one of his own productions was on. He would come and see it again, or sit around dressing-rooms listening to it over the tannoy. He adored the company of actors. He wasn't a director who necessarily wanted to sit out front every night and take a lot of notes – he just loved being around his creation, which was very endearing.

MR You played Edgar in Jonathan's 1975 TV version of *King Lear* – how did this become such a pared-down production?

RP We filmed that *Lear* at the time of the three-day week and the power cuts, and halfway through rehearsals Jonathan came in white-faced after being told that he suddenly had to cut about an hour and a half from the play. Once he had been forced to cut it, though, the actual cutting was marvellously done and may even – dare one say it – have benefited the play. It seemed to flow with the most remarkable simplicity. The whole production was very simple – we were essentially figures on a neutral background, based on the paintings of Georges de la Tour, and Jonathan left us free to get on with it in a totally uncluttered space.

MR How did Jonathan apply his neurological knowledge to the madness in the play?

RP Jonathan would tell us long stories of his trips to mental institutions, and demonstrate the behaviour of the patients in great detail. I remember him showing me how one of them would sit in one position, where he appeared to be leaning on something but in fact was not, and would out of the blue stab at his forehead with his forefinger every now and then. I was able to use that for the scene where Edgar is feigning madness. In fact, Jonathan gave me a crown of thorns to wear when Edgar disguises himself as Poor Tom, to suggest that he was one of those wandering madmen who dressed themselves up as Christ.

MR What is Jonathan's great strength as a director?

RP He is able to approach a play with some brilliant ideas but without ever getting weighed down in a rigid staging. He'll surround himself with the best actors he can get – knowing that he is often going out on a limb in his productions, he always pays his actors the respect of understanding that he needs just as much skill from them as they do from him.

He did this in *The Merchant of Venice*, when he got Olivier to play Shylock in a highly original way, against the seedy, nasty Victorian atmosphere of hypocrisy which formed the basis of that production. That's exactly what the play is about – they're all foul people, the nastiest bunch in Shakespeare. I can't imagine why it always used to be seen in such a popular, sentimental light, but Jonathan's production certainly knocked all that for six.

SIR MICHAEL HORDERN

Sir Michael Hordern played the Professor in *Oh Whistle and I'll Come to You* (BBC TV 1968) and King Lear (Nottingham Playhouse 1969, BBC TV 1975 and BBC TV 1982).

Michael Romain When you played the Professor in Jonathan Miller's TV film of M. R. James' ghost story *Oh Whistle and I'll Come to You* in 1968, did you expect that it would have such an alarming effect on the viewing audience?

Sir Michael Hordern The story is fairly shocking on the printed page, but I don't think we quite realised how terrifying Jonathan's film would turn out to be. It really frightened the life out of the viewers, and made a huge impact – people still talk about it today.

What made the piece so effective was its simplicity. Jonathan actually shot it very simply, and I had never worked like that before. We went down to film it in Norfolk without any fixed script, and Jonathan would say 'I think we'll do that bit where you come in late for breakfast and have this chat with one of the guests. We'll have you sitting over there in the corner, eating a proper breakfast.' It was almost entirely spontaneous.

The only part that was written down at all came when Jonathan said to me, 'After breakfast, you'll be left alone in the dining room with the old colonel and you'll begin a conversation with him about extra-sensory perception.' I said, 'Well, I couldn't possibly talk about anything like that!' 'Oh,' he said, 'I'll write something for you.' That was quite late at night, but by the next morning he'd already written a long speech on the subject for me. But the rest of it was simply improvised. 'I think we'll go out today and do the picnic lunch on the beach', he'd say. 'You'll take it out of your bag, have a sandwich and talk to yourself.' 'All right then', I'd reply. It was all done like that.

A few months later, quite out of the blue, Jonathan invited me to have lunch with him in Soho, where he propositioned me to play King Lear for him at the Nottingham Playhouse in 1969. I accepted immediately – you don't get offered Lear every day of the week – and I don't think that we discussed the play at all over the rest of the meal.

MR The Nottingham *King Lear* came quite early on in Jonathan's career, and was his first professional Shakespeare production – how much confidence did you have in his direction?

MH Complete confidence – I put myself totally in his hands. He had the most amazing grasp of the play. Again, we didn't have any in-depth discussions about it beforehand – he came down to my cottage in Berkshire for an evening, but we never went into *Lear* in great detail.

The staging at Nottingham was very bare, almost Brechtian. And when Jonathan directed it again for television it was equally bleak. He just concentrated on the relationships, as he saw the play as essentially a family drama and consequently did a lot of work on the interplay between the characters.

I played Lear three times for Jonathan – on stage, then twice on television. The last two *Lear*s really built on the foundations of the Nottingham production, because that initial interpretation of the play was so strong. But we got better at it each time, and the final *Lear* for the BBC in 1982 was undoubtedly the fullest.

I think that I learned from one production to the next, and certainly as I grew older myself so my understanding of Lear deepened. Jonathan displayed an incisive understanding of an old man's state of mind, and was invaluable for the mad scenes. He saw Lear in a very human and sympathetic light, and brought out a lot of the humour which surrounds him – unkind, ironic humour, but comic nevertheless, particularly in his scenes with the Fool.

I was very lucky to have Frank Middlemass playing the Fool in all three *Lear*s with me – it was Jonathan's idea, in fact, to have the Fool as a contemporary of Lear. He saw them as mirror-images – despite the fact that one had been brought up in the palace and the other in the stables, they had obviously developed an extremely close relationship over the years. But casting Frank, who is roughly the same age as me, as the Fool, was a very innovative stroke – he's often referred to as 'boy' in the text, and had always been played as precisely that, usually waving a balloon about on a stick. But 'boy', of course, used to be applied to servants whatever their age, and Lear and his Fool must go back a long way together.

MR What do you remember most about Jonathan's direction?

MH His spontaneity. His way of working is quite improvised, though he always has a clear end in sight. He's immensely open-minded and never dictates – he'll take what you can give him and use it if it's good. Tyrone Guthrie was like that – very spontaneous and fresh. But I think that Jonathan is really quite unique as a director because he moves about so much in both science and the arts.

JANE LAPOTAIRE

Jane Lapotaire played Jessica in *The Merchant of Venice* (National Theatre at the Old Vic 1970) and Cleopatra in *Antony and Cleopatra* (BBC TV Shakespeare 1980).

Michael Romain When you played Jessica in Jonathan's production of *The Merchant of Venice* at the National Theatre in 1970, how did he tackle the Jewish aspect of the play?

Jane Lapotaire Jonathan gave the play a late nineteenth-century setting, so that there was a great difference in appearance between the Jews and the gentiles, with a very beautiful and realistic set by Julia Trevelyan Oman which looked like St Mark's Square in Venice. Jonathan made Jessica much more of a central focus in the play than she normally is – she was portrayed as the Jew who tried to crack gentile society but was always doomed to be an outsider. He ended the play with me standing alone in the middle of the stage while the others went inside, completely abandoned by them. Jonathan spent a lot of time with me and Olivier building up a very real Jessica–Shylock relationship – he spent much time discussing the implications of Shakespeare's use of the words 'kin' and 'kind'.

MR What was your reaction when Jonathan asked you to star in his TV production of *Antony and Cleopatra*?

JL I was both flattered and terrified; it's a wonderful, challenging part but I thought that nobody in their right mind would offer me the role of Cleopatra. But once he explained his concept, it was easier to accept it.

He saw Antony and Cleopatra as middle-aged people grabbing at the image that the world had of them when they were younger – him as the glorious soldier, the hero of Rome, and her as this extraordinarily charismatic woman for whom Caesar and countless kings had gone down on their knees. But now, Jonathan thought, they were both over the hill. What splits their relationship is not so much Antony's decision to go off and marry Octavia in order to placate the rest of the triumvirate, but rather the fact that there is suddenly a big chink in her idea of the image of him as this world-conquering soldier when he fails in battle, and an equally big chink in his image of her as this powerful ruler and amazing woman when she turns tail and flees. Once they stop being in love with the romantic images that they have of each other, then they can actually see themselves for what they really are – Jonathan saw this as the turning-point in their relationship.

It's an oddly structured play because Cleopatra really only comes into her own in Act 5 after the death of Antony. Jonathan helped me to discover that although she loses her kingdom and her queen-like aura, she in fact becomes a greater human being – that's the tragedy of the play. She becomes a tragic heroine after Antony has died because she rises to and carries out her own death in such a heroic way.

MR   What do you remember of the rehearsals?

JL   Great fun. He shares his incredible knowledge in a very un-pompous way. He worked very quickly on *Antony*, as we had only four weeks to do it in. He was thinking on his feet a lot, as it was one of his first productions in the BBC TV Shakespeare cycle. I was filming Cleopatra by day and playing Piaf by night, so it all passed in a terrible blur of exhaustion and nervous energy. I still had my Piaf arthritis in my hands when I played Cleopatra – I couldn't shake it off, as I was doing it every night.

In fact, Jonathan thought that there was a strong similarity between Cleopatra's voracious appetite for life – drink, fun, sex and Antony – and Piaf's. I'm not exactly everybody's idea of Cleopatra, but he put my worries to rest by saying 'There is only one extant portrait of Cleopatra – on a coin – and she is not by anybody's terms a beautiful woman. She may have been charismatic, attractive and striking, but not beautiful.'

He told me all sorts of information about her – that she was the last of the Ptolemys, and could speak and write thirteen Greek and Egyptian dialects, and so on. I remember him saying to me at one point – 'You know why she's in love with Antony – he's her bit of rough trade!' He's wonderful at finding very real analogies to de-mystify all the awe about Shakespeare, and then of course you can immediately grasp the human being behind the writing.

MR   What was it that Jonathan admired so much about Colin Blakely, who played Antony?

JL   He admired Colin's workman-like attitude to his job – Colin would come in, hang his coat up, do his day's work and then go home. He was the least theatrical of actors, a very hard worker, and above all a wholly honest performer. That was why he was such a great actor. Antony demands a difficult combination from an actor: the ability to play a 'real' soldier yet rise to the great poetic heights of some of the verse.

MR   What was Jonathan like behind the camera?

JL   He always used a lot of long shots, so that he could arrange a kind of Caravaggio or Veronese grouping. He gave *Antony and Cleopatra* a visual style based on Italian Renaissance paintings – he said that would have been the way that Elizabethan audiences would have perceived the decadence of Egypt, their knowledge of decadence being sixteenth-century Venice.

Jonathan used real snakes at the end of the play. I have a phobia about snakes, and the girl who was playing Charmian had an even bigger phobia – and she was pregnant at the time. One day, three tupperware boxes turned up in the rehearsal room – a daddy box, a mummy box and a baby box. And out of these boxes came the snakes. We said, 'Oh, are those asps?' And as a complete *en passant* remark Jonathan said 'There's no such thing as an asp – asp was just a general name for snake. These are boa constrictors.' We said, 'What? Boa constrictors? You must be crazy – they squeeze people to death!' 'Oh yes,' he replied, 'but these ones are only eighteen months old, so they are not strong enough yet for that. They'll just give you a gentle little squeeze, but they won't actually do anything.' He knew that we were all absolutely terrified of these snakes, so he handled us very cleverly by simply undermining all the horror stories about snakes, and making it fun.

He makes the actors feel comfortable. He makes you feel that because he's cast you in a role, there is absolutely no doubt in his mind that you can't play it superlatively well. Although that may sound like a cliché, it is the most wonderful comfort – if you've got any qualms yourself – to have a director who has complete confidence in you. He simply takes it as read that his performers can use the basic actor's craft on the text, and he will concentrate on focussing and choreographing them in the direction that he wants.

A profile of Jonathan Miller

ERIC IDLE

Eric Idle played a Top Hat in *Alice in Wonderland* (BBC TV 1966) and Ko-Ko in *The Mikado* (English National Opera 1986 and Houston Grand Opera 1989).

Michael Romain   When did you first encounter Jonathan?

Eric Idle   I first saw him doing *Beyond the Fringe* at the Fortune Theatre in 1961, when I was still at school. I went to see it with a friend, but we found that we couldn't get seats because it was completely sold out. So we got standing-room tickets, and rolled about against the wall at the back of the stalls for two hours. It was so funny that we could hardly stand up. Like everybody else of my generation, I immediately bought the album and learned it all by heart – it really determined my career in comedy.

MR   Was it a direct influence on *Monty Python?*

EI   I think so, yes, though nobody ever says that except me. It started that Oxbridge/Edinburgh Fringe late night revue format. That has since become an ongoing strain of British humour, which still exists today – that sort of cabaret with four very bright guys being silly. We certainly did that at Cambridge and Edinburgh when I was in the Footlights. It's definitely a branch that goes straight into *Python*, though we tended to be a bit more silly – we tried to break it up a bit and not be quite so smart, bright and sophisticated Oxbridge. But *Beyond the Fringe* is definitely underneath – you can't hide that.

MR   What do you remember of Jonathan's film of *Alice in Wonderland?*

EI   I only played a small part in that – I was a Top Hat, and appeared in the Pool of Tears and various other scenes. It was 1966, the year of the Beatles, and we all went on this huge Magical Mystery Tour of country houses to film it on location. It was one of the best times I've ever had, because I had no responsibility and almost no lines. It was just like dressing up with a lot of funny, clever people – Peter Cook, Alan Bennett and Peter Sellers.

MR   What was your reaction when, twenty years later, he asked you to play Ko-Ko in his production of *The Mikado* for English National Opera?

EI   I was very intrigued. My first instinct was, 'Gilbert and Sullivan, my God! I've managed to avoid Gilbert and Sullivan all these years!' I said to Jonathan, 'What are you going to do with *The Mikado?*' He replied, 'Well,

I'm going to get rid of all that Japanese nonsense for a start.' That just hooked me – if he was going to take the Japanese stuff out of *The Mikado*, I wanted to know how on earth he was going to do it!

MR   How did you arrive at your characterisation of Ko-Ko?

EI   Once Jonathan had liberated the piece from its Japaneserie, it was suddenly free of years and years of accretions and jokes that had been built into it by each generation. Consequently we were able to approach it as if it was a totally new text, without worrying about everything that had gone before, and this gave us tremendous scope with Ko-Ko.

Jonathan picked up on the fact that Ko-Ko is identified as a 'cheap tailor'. So we gave him that slightly camp quality of 'I think we could take in the inside leg a little bit more, Sir.' He certainly wasn't gay (he clearly spends most of his time flirting with women), but there was a hint of the pretentious tailor about him, that air which you see very much in dressers backstage.

Then I added a bit of that style we developed in *Python* – particularly John Cleese – where you're trying to hide the fact that you did not go to public school by attempting to speak quite nicely and taking elocution lessons. That sounded very 1930s, so it was ideal for this production. And my wig also looked very thirties. It enabled me to go through the show permanently flicking back my hair – when we did it in Houston, somebody dubbed it 'Ko-Ko Chanel'.

MR   Jonathan showed the cast videotapes of the Marx Brothers and Jack Buchanan during rehearsals to get the right style of thirties comedy for the production – did you find those useful references?

EI   Jack Buchanan was much more of a key for me and for Ko-Ko – he came from the Cambridge Footlights too, and I was very fond of his work. I have a blank spot with the Marx Brothers, though – I don't find them very funny! I only like Chico, which is very eccentric.

My own feelings about the Marx Brothers aside, though, they were certainly one of Jonathan's principal motifs for the production. He unashamedly pinched the whole of Groucho's Freedonia entrance from *Duck Soup* to build me up a terrific effect. Somebody does a false 'Here he comes!' and of course I don't show up, so they have to do this great big fanfare and chorus all over again for me when I do come on a minute later – it was the double entrance of all time.

MR   Did Jonathan ever talk about his method of direction?

9 Richard Van Allan (Pooh-Bah), Eric Idle (Ko-Ko), and Mark Richardson (Pish-Tush), *The Mikado*, designed by Stefanos Lazaridis, English National Opera 1986

EI He said to me recently that what he likes to do is just throw out
stream-of-consciousness ideas from which the actor can grab what's
useful and bring it into his performance. I think that opera singers
sometimes assume that they're supposed to do exactly what he says, which
is the last thing that he intends. In a sense, what he does is come in and do
a cabaret during the rehearsal, from which the cast will grab bits and
pieces.

MR Humour has always been a keynote of his direction – what makes him
so funny?

EI There is something irresistible about such intellectual brilliance coupled
with such comic flair. Humour is basically an ability to see the absurdity of
everything, and it's at its most effective when it is backed by intelligence. I
wish that he would direct more comedy. He sometimes feels that comedy is
not a serious business, that it's a rather childish thing to be doing.

I keep telling Jonathan that in fact it's an absolutely magnificent thing to
make people laugh and feel good – it's one of the most beneficial things he
can do in their lives. *The Mikado* is actually one of the few things Jonathan
has ever directed which is an out-and-out comedy. He said to me recently,
'Do come and work with me at the Old Vic – would you like to do some
straight acting? We could do something serious.' I thought, sure, but why,
having spent twenty-five years trying to learn how to make people laugh,
do you then try to compete with the Antony Shers of this world, who have
spent twenty-five years in another tradition altogether? I suspect that
Jonathan feels that you shouldn't quite respect comedy. But then he's so
good at it.

One of the best things about having him direct you is that if you make
him laugh, then you know that what you're doing is genuinely funny. It was
the same with *Python* – I knew that if I made Graham Chapman or Terry
Jones laugh, then I would also make the audience laugh. When we first
started rehearsing *The Mikado*, we were filmed with 'fly-on-the-wall'
cameras for a TV documentary, which meant that they put up huge bright
lights and everybody became inhibited. One day I began to rehearse my
grovel at the feet of the Mikado while the cameras were rolling, and
Jonathan nearly died laughing – he just rolled around on the floor because
I was making him literally helpless with laughter. When I play back the
videotape, I can say, 'This is the bit where I totally crack up the director.' I
think his sense of humour is his greatest asset as a director – after that, we
all knew that the grovel was a very funny moment. The audiences subsequently laughed at every performance, but Jonathan was the first to show

us that we were on solid ground. 'Keep going in this direction!' was our instinct from then on.

ROBERT STEPHENS

Robert Stephens played Trigorin in *The Seagull* (Chichester Festival Theatre 1973 and Greenwich Theatre 1974), Claudius in *Hamlet* and Pastor Manders in *Ghosts* (Greenwich Theatre 1974).

Michael Romain   When you played Trigorin in Jonathan's production of *The Seagull* at Chichester, did you find that he displayed a personal empathy with Chekhov?

Robert Stephens   Very much so – he is a doctor/director in the same way that Chekhov was a doctor/writer. There was none of the usual melodramatic fat on the production – it was so clean that it was like a skeleton. Jonathan can get to the heart of things in a very clinical way. There were no indulgences, no Chekhovian melancholy, or any of that kind of traditional nonsense. The emphasis was not solely on Nina, but on the whole ensemble. The open stage at Chichester meant that it had to be simple – there were no great heavy sets, no elaborate sound effects, nothing. Jonathan's skill was to treat it lightly as Chekhov wanted – Chekhov insisted it was a comedy.

MR   When *The Seagull* was revived at Greenwich as part of Jonathan's 'Family Romances' season, it was joined by *Hamlet* and *Ghosts* – was he able to get rid of Ibsen's reputation for doom and gloom?

RS   Yes he was, and he achieved this by lightening *Ghosts* with humour – he realised that there was a lot of implicit comedy in the text and brought it out very cleverly. Irene Worth and I actually got quite a few laughs in our scenes as Mrs Alving and Pastor Manders. I myself helped this by drastically cutting most of the boring and 'plot-laying' text of Pastor Manders.

Another way in which Jonathan achieved this very fresh style of playing Ibsen was by playing down the 'Pastor' image with Manders, so that he became an ordinary sort of man. On the page, Manders looks like the most boring character in dramatic literature. But Jonathan encouraged me to make him much more human and amusing, and in the end he became quite a touching figure. Consequently I got very good reviews – when you're playing Manders, you don't expect to steal all the notices.

MR   Did Jonathan display the same reappraisal of the text in *Hamlet*?

RS   Yes, he did, and he gave me the most wonderful effect in the play-within-the-play scene by bringing out the play on words. Obviously the relationship between Hamlet and Claudius is very uneasy by this point. I simply went to Hamlet and demanded from him 'Give me some light!', as though Claudius, in public, is 'calling Hamlet out', in the sense of 'Be honest with me!' That nearly blew Hamlet off the stage, and gave a real sense of the power in Claudius when someone pushes him too far.

MR   How did you feel about Jonathan's idea of juxtaposing *Hamlet*, *Ghosts* and *The Seagull* under the umbrella title for the season, 'Family Romances'?

RS   The whole concept of doing three plays with very similar themes worked very well, because the audiences could measure one against the other, particularly with the same actors playing corresponding roles. It also helped to build the company into a real ensemble.

FRANK LANGELLA

Frank Langella played Don Benito Cereno in *The Old Glory* (American Place Theatre 1964).

Michael Romain   How did you come to be involved in Jonathan's production of Robert Lowell's *The Old Glory*, which he directed at the American Place Theatre in 1964?

Frank Langella   Simply by turning up to audition. I came in one day and met with Jonathan and Robert Lowell, and Wynn Handman the artistic director, and read from a script placed on a pedestal in front of me. When I stopped, Jonathan immediately offered me the role of Benito Cereno and I said no, which was always my act at the time – I was only aged 24 then, and very independent. I wanted to do another play, or travel or something. Then Wynn said to me, 'Look, we're offering you a leading role in a Robert Lowell play directed by Jonathan Miller as the opening production of the American Place Theatre – how can you possibly refuse?' So what else could I do but agree?

  In New York in those days things were very casual, as there was an extraordinary amount of work available for actors. And of course you can never tell at the time whether a production is going to go down in theatre history, as *The Old Glory* did. It proved to be a major turning-point because it established the American Place Theatre, which has since become an enormously important outlet for new writing.

MR   *The Old Glory* is a highly demanding play to stage, with a huge cast; and on top of this, the production had a lot riding on it for the future of the American Place Theatre. It was, though, the first full-scale production that Jonathan ever directed.

FL   I don't think that any of us realised this at the time – you would never have guessed it from the confidence with which he worked. He knew exactly what he wanted from us, and how to get it. He loved to do run-throughs, for instance – we did a run-through on our feet on the second day of rehearsals, and did at least one every day from then on. That gave us tremendous confidence at a very early stage – it gave us a sense of the whole span of the play, and made our work much more cohesive.

    I had not worked with a British director before, and Jonathan was very, very different indeed from the American school of Method direction. He was direct about the characters, and there was no talk about their 'inner-life' or anything like that.

MR   How did he approach characterisation?

FL   Jonathan was immensely liberal in his relationship to the development of a role – he felt that the actor owned the part, the actor should create it, and the actor should live it, while his job as the director was simply to guide you as if you were in a funhouse. He'd push you out of the way of that kerb or that slant, and offer mild and gentle suggestions along the way – for example, I played Benito Cereno as a neurotic figure, and Jonathan encouraged me to tremble constantly and keep my eyes fixed firmly on the ground.

    American directors have a tendency to get inside and really muscle around with you about a role, whereas Jonathan doesn't. He's more interested in letting you get on with it, and pointing you in the right direction while you do it. Then he's happy when you start to do it well.

    I trusted him completely, because I knew that he wouldn't let me give a bad performance or go off on the wrong track because his overview was so strong. He realises that actors are cogs in a wheel, and that you must make each cog as strong as possible. When we saw that he had this gift, we could relax and feel confident – we didn't have to fight for our space, because we knew that our director had the right idea. Consequently we did better work, because we didn't have to keep one eye watching out for what we thought a director might be missing.

MR   What part did Robert Lowell play in the production?

FL   Lowell was closely involved in rehearsals, and had a very good working relationship with Jonathan. He was sweet, shy and not very verbal – in fact, he was unwell at the time and would frequently leave us to go off for treatment – but he was always anxious for us to succeed.

MR   How did Jonathan approach the two-play structure of *The Old Glory*?

FL   He rehearsed them as if he was staging two entirely separate evenings in the theatre. Another director of lesser imagination might have somehow tied them all together in some form, but Jonathan treated them both individually. I remember asking Lowell at one point if he had intended to link the plays together, and he simply said that they both displayed a common theme – idealism hardening into violence.

   The first play, *My Kinsman, Major Molineux*, was staged in a very stylised way, with all the make-up and costumes purely in black and white.

   Jonathan's approach to the second play, *Benito Cereno*, was much more straightforward – he just knew that it had to be on a slow burner, and he was sure that it would explode when the time came. The staging of *Benito Cereno* was very stark and simple, and extremely brave from a directorial point of view. The audience would sit there for nearly two hours, and this slow, creaking tension of the production would gradually build on them.

   At the time, it didn't occur to me – I was very young, after all – that there was anything difficult about the staging. That was probably Jonathan's gift – listening to him, I just saw it as 'Oh, this is how it's done – I go there, he goes there, a skeleton comes in, I fall down, and so on.' It all made perfect sense. I will never forget having to kiss that skeleton, though, and there was another wonderful moment where I was shaved by my slave with a Spanish flag draped around my neck for an apron – the imagery was tremendously powerful in this way throughout the production.

MR   What happened when the production opened?

FL   It was immensely successful. It wasn't until I experienced routine and unadventurous productions later on in my career that I realised how extraordinary *The Old Glory* was.

   The production became a big hit, much bigger than I ever expected. At the time, it was just another play for which I was being paid the rousing sum of fifty dollars a week without a long contract or anything. However, a measure of its power over me is that when it closed at the American Place I went home after the party to lie down and slept for three days. I then declined to play it in a larger theatre. We taped it for PBS TV and recorded it for Columbia Records. I saw the black-and-white tape about ten years ago. It is slow and pedantic but relentlessly powerful still.

After the run at the American Place Theatre was over, the play transferred to a much larger theatre, where it stayed for a very long time. It was completely different from anything that had gone before in American theatre – very original, very innovative, and really way ahead of its time.

SARA KESTELMAN

Sara Kestelman played Tamyra in *Bussy D'Ambois* (Old Vic 1988).

Michael Romain   You've worked with a wide variety of directors, ranging from Peter Brook and William Gaskill to Adrian Noble and Elijah Moshinsky: how does Jonathan Miller compare to them?

Sara Kestelman   I don't know any other director with such a strong visual sense as Jonathan. You can hardly see the walls of his house for all the books, and he has hundreds of scrap-books full of beautiful or interesting things. He has a wonderful eye for detail – the fold of a piece of fabric, for instance, will catch his attention in an advert, and he'll cut it out of the magazine and put it into one of his scrap-books, which he'll keep dipping into for inspiration.

He's always been torn between medicine and the arts. There was a time when he had serious doubts about staying on at the Old Vic to do a second season, as he had directed nearly all of the productions in the first season in a very short space of time and was very depressed by the negative criticism they had received. He said that he was thinking of going off to work in a hospital for a year, which he's talked about – and indeed done – before. But he admits that although he finds it immensely absorbing and rewarding working in medicine, it is not enough by itself – it has to be counterbalanced by his work in the arts.

MR   What was your reaction when Jonathan asked you to play Tamyra in his production of *Bussy D'Ambois* at the Old Vic in 1988?

SK   I found Chapman's long and convoluted sentences quite daunting at first and actually had to read the play several times, eventually out loud, before I fully understood it. But I was fascinated: Chapman has created in

Tamyra an astonishingly detailed psychological study of an intelligent, witty, articulate, and socially well-placed woman at the mercy of a completely unexpected physical attraction for a man she barely knows and with whom she has nothing in common; a woman who knows precisely the moral danger she's in; who recognises that by betraying her marriage she faces complete ruin and yet, turned mad by a fever of passionate longing, makes a choice from which there is no turning back, hopeless, helpless into the depths of hell, bloody discovery, torture and death. It is a very, very dense text which we had only four weeks to rehearse, an extremely short period for such a difficult play and especially one which had not been performed for over 300 years. Peter Eyre had done excellent work editing wherever possible and I worked extensively on the latter part of the play before we went into rehearsal, juxtaposing, editing and sometimes knitting together sections so that the heartbreaking emotional climaxes and the terrible twists and turns of the tragedy built to a crescendo with maximum dynamic.

Before I agreed to play Tamyra, I asked Jonathan why he wanted to revive the play. He said that he'd been very intrigued by it when he read it about ten years ago, and had decided that one day he would direct it. He saw it as a rich and extraordinary phantasmagoria, a study in the corrupt artificiality of office and power, as well as a very modern portrait of adultery and the psychology of jealousy.

Jonathan spent a lot of time building up the atmosphere of intrigue at court, and filled the doorways and passages of the set with silent, watching figures. All through rehearsals he kept coming up with new ideas – just before the first night, for instance, he decided to use the sound of amplified whispering voices as a background to the action.

When we came to the scene between Bussy and Tamyra after their night of passion, Jonathan said, 'This moment is the cadenza, when the conductor puts down the baton and holds back, very gently keeping the beat. He lets the soloist take off and then, as Adrian Boult used to, he shoots his cuffs and brings in the rest of the orchestra. So this scene is yours – do whatever you want.' Of course, it's wonderful when a director places that kind of trust in you, and David Threlfall and I really seized the opportunity – sometimes we did it well, sometimes we did it electrifyingly well, and sometimes it was terribly dirty.

For the torture scene, I remember Jonathan saying, 'You're going to have to scream all the way through this.' Chapman specifies that Tamyra is tortured on a rack, but Jonathan had her tied to a chair instead, and the action had to be very precisely choreographed so that I would not get hurt when the men began pulling me around. Jonathan's medical expertise came in useful for the gruesome cuts they had to make in my arm and neck. The knife that Lorcan Cranitch used pumped blood through tiny holes on its edge, leaving ghastly red gashes trickling over my white clothes onto the ground, the same blood which Tamyra uses to write to her lover. This very poignant and romantic gesture would nightly reduce the audience to tears. Especially the men.

He and Richard Hudson, the designer, had devised an entirely abstract set: it was so enormous that it dwarfed the cast, in itself an interesting and dramatic effect, though some of its configurations pushed the acting area dangerously close to the audience.

We opened to mixed and rather indifferent reviews, but our audiences built through word of mouth and after each performance Jonathan would phone from wherever he was (once it was Toronto airport) to find out how we all were and how the performance had gone.

Jonathan creates a wonderfully relaxed working atmosphere and the door of the huge company office on the top floor was always open, everyone working in their various corners of the room, design department, casting department, actors wandering in and out, coffee always on the go and Jonathan sitting in an armchair surrounded by his books.

PENELOPE WILTON

Penelope Wilton played Cordelia (Nottingham Playhouse 1969) and Regan (BBC TV 1975 and BBC TV 1982) in *King Lear*, Masha in *The Seagull* (Chichester Festival Theatre 1973), Isabella in *Measure for Measure* and Helena in *All's Well that Ends Well* (Greenwich Theatre 1975), Desdemona in *Othello* (BBC TV 1981) and Hermione in *Andromache* (Old Vic 1988).

Michael Romain You appeared in Jonathan's first three productions of *King Lear* – as Cordelia in his Nottingham revival, then as Regan in his two subsequent television versions of the play. What remained consistent about his interpretation?

Penelope Wilton His basic approach was always the same – it was done very sparsely, with everything focussed on the characters. Jonathan drew a lot on his knowledge of geriatric behaviour and madness for the characterisation of Lear, and also for Edgar's scenes as Poor Tom.

One of the best things about all his *Lear*s was his ability to make the play very much a story about a family – he knows how to reduce Shakespeare from the epic to the intimate. Trevor Nunn has since done that with his *Macbeth* and *Othello*, but Jonathan really started that style of production off – he also did it with a small-scale *Tempest* at the Mermaid.

He always made the smaller roles in *Lear* – Oswald, for instance – come to life by casting very interesting actors and giving them a lot of attention. He brought out all the relationships with great clarity – we all looked very etched and clear, these incredibly striking figures against an uncluttered background. When Gemma Jones played Goneril for him at the Old Vic, she really stood out on stage in this robe of brilliant red.

Jonathan has a strong visual sense – he'll arrange the characters into a moving painting onstage. For the *Lear*s he drew on the paintings of Georges de la Tour, where you had this reflected light thrown onto people's faces without actually being able to see the source of the light itself. The production consequently looked marvellous in a very under-stated way, rather like that beautiful *Marriage of Figaro* he did at the Coliseum.

MR When you played Masha in his production of *The Seagull* at Chichester in 1973, did you find that he brought out the humour of the play as Chekhov wanted?

PW Yes he did – he likes Chekhov's plays because they amuse him. He brought out the silliness and idiocy of the characters very strongly, especially the vanity of Arkadina and Trigorin.

Chekhov characters were traditionally played in a rather listless way because they keep saying that they are so bored and depressed. Jonathan pointed out that prolonged boredom and depression would actually make them quite emotional because of the sheer frustration, rather than melancholy. Because Masha always wears black, Jonathan suggested that she was quite an angry character, furious with what has happened to her life. I shouted a lot of her lines, particularly when the schoolmaster is following her around like a lap-dog and driving her up the wall. All the characters were played in a human light – Arkadina was especially mean and beastly with her money.

The characterisation was so strong and natural in this respect that the production came together very quickly. At first I thought it would be difficult to do Chekhov on that big open stage at Chichester, but Jonathan made it work surprisingly well – he actually used the vastness of the space to great effect in Konstantin's play at the beginning.

MR You next worked with Jonathan in 1975, playing Isabella in his *Measure for Measure* at Greenwich – how did he tackle such an ambiguous play, with its strong psychological subtext?

PW *Measure for Measure* is about sexual frustration and repression, so Jonathan set it in Freud's Vienna, which reflected all of the play's themes – particularly that puritan streak in Angelo, which was very evident in Freud's time. Again, it was very clearly portrayed – Jonathan's approach has never changed in that sense.

Jonathan is able to bring the enormous moments in Shakespeare down to a minimum of action, which makes them much more effective. He's very specific and accurate about gestures and emotions in these key scenes. When Angelo seduced Isabella, for instance, Jonathan suggested he do only one thing – he simply pleated my skirt with one hand, very neatly making little folds in the material as if he was fiddling with a piece of paper, while I was unable to look down because his hand was touching me. That was the only physical contact at all between us. It was very sharply focussed and frightening, rather like interrogation scenes where you don't know what the interrogator is going to do next.

The whole production was actually very disturbing like this in a rather Kafka-esque way. There were several doors onstage, out of which people would suddenly appear – they would turn the scene into a prison, a brothel or a street by their different styles. One of the most interesting things about the production for me was the way that Jonathan brought the Duke much more into the centre of the play – normally he is left hovering on the periphery.

MR You also played Helena in Jonathan's *All's Well that Ends Well* at the same time . . .

PW That's right – we performed both plays in repertory together, and they made an interesting contrast. While *Measure* was carefully updated, *All's Well* was done in seventeenth-century style. I remember Jonathan had me doing my soliloquy sitting on a bench with my chin resting in the palm of my hand. He tries to avoid people attitudinising onstage – he wants them to be simple, natural and clear. His approach is very practical and down to earth.

MR Racine has always posed problems for British actors and directors – how did Jonathan approach *Andromache* when you played Hermione for him at the Old Vic in 1988?

PW He wanted to stage it very simply to match the austerity of Racine's style. He was very successful in this. The lines are not easy, but Jonathan is

10 Janet Suzman (Andromache) and Penelope Wilton (Hermione) in *Andromache*, Old Vic 1988

very musical and would help us to phrase the lines musically to make sure that we got the tempi right.

There are lots of brief scenes and encounters in *Andromache*, and Jonathan's great skill was in having an overview of the whole piece – he could look at it and tell if all the separate elements were coming together. He's very much a collaborator in rehearsal – he doesn't tell you what to do, which is why actors like working with him so much.

Andromache showed Jonathan's strength as an interpreter – he doesn't go against a play but simply brings out its essence very accurately. It's actually very rare for him to update something – I can never understand why people brand his work 'controversial', because it is always true to the play. There's nothing at all gratuitous about his work. And when he does update something, like *Rigoletto*, for instance, his concept is always valid.

DAVID HOROVITCH

David Horovitch played Hermes in *Prometheus Bound* (Mermaid Theatre 1971), John Worthing in *The Importance of Being Earnest*, Bertram in *All's Well that Ends Well* and Claudio in *Measure for Measure* (Greenwich Theatre 1975).

Michael Romain   When Jonathan directed Aeschylus' *Prometheus Bound* at the Mermaid in 1971, did he try to get away from the traditional 'togas and sandals' style of Ancient Greek drama?

David Horovitch   Yes he did – he set the production in the seventeenth century, which he thought would boost the Greek world some way towards us. He said that the seventeenth century was like the transmitter on the Chilterns – 'It boosts the picture.'

It was one of Jonathan's more austere productions – very spare and grey. There was a chorus of six women, with three sitting on either side of the stage like secretaries, scribbling away with quill pens. One of the most innovative features of the staging was the fact that Prometheus was able to move about. I remember Jonathan telling us that Peter Brook had originally planned to direct the play with Paul Scofield in the title-role. Brook had this idea that Scofield should be chained to the rock, with the chains stretching all the way out to the back of the auditorium as if the audience were all imprisoned with him. Scofield wasn't at all keen on the idea of being confined on the stage like that, and in our production Kenneth Haigh moved around for most of the action.

MR   What ideas did Jonathan throw at you for the characterisation of Hermes?

DH   He was reading *Hope against Hope* at the time, and said that Hermes was like the 'midnight knock-on-the-door' figures in the book – cool, civil and lethal. There's a bit of him missing, but what's there is frightening enough. This characterisation was very effective, particularly for the long speech where Hermes describes the horrors that will happen to Prometheus if he doesn't toe the line. He was a very cold stage presence, and Jonathan gave me a feather stripped down to the naked quill which I played with like a little wand.

We did it all terribly quickly, with only about two weeks rehearsal for one of the most difficult plays in the repertoire.

MR How did you play John Worthing in the 1975 production of *The Importance of Being Earnest?*

DH Jonathan had the idea that John and Algy – with whom the audience must identify for the fun of the thing – were unsympathetic characters, almost club bores with not an ounce of wit between them. This was quite perverse. He wanted us to speak in a leaden, port-soaked way, which made it very difficult for the audience to delight in Wilde's delicate but deadly serious silliness. I remember Jonathan encouraging us to play the muffin scene at the end of Act 2 with a lot more venom and ill-temper – and a lot less decorum – than usual. Although this particular scene worked rather well, gathering a fierce comic momentum of its own, for the rest of the play we jettisoned this approach in favour of a lighter, more conventional tone, and the production, though not entirely successful, was not the disaster it might have been.

MR How did Jonathan deal with the difficulties of *All's Well that Ends Well* at Greenwich in 1975?

DH Jonathan cast actors of the same age as Bertram and Parolles so they could be seen as two very young men, which is most unusual. He used to say that they were like William and Ginger in the 'Just William' stories – shifty and naughty. So I played Bertram very unsympathetically as a sullen, naughty adolescent. Generally speaking, I'd say it's much more rewarding to play an unsympathetic character in one of Jonathan's productions than, say, a romantic hero. Jonathan's innate scepticism and disbelief in romantic love or altruism tend to make him convert the sympathetic into the unsympathetic. I once heard him say, 'There is no such thing as a nice person.' Thus Lorenzo becomes a prig, or John Worthing a club bore. If this is clearly against the author's intentions the actor can be left feeling very uncomfortable, both in his relation to the text and the audience. It's as if he's innocently caught up in an argument between the author and the director. Perhaps this is why Jonathan works almost exclusively with dead authors.

MR   You also played Claudio in the same season in Jonathan's *Measure for Measure* – how did his updating work?

DH   Jonathan set the play in Freud's Vienna of the 1920s, and gave it a very Kafka-esque atmosphere. The set consisted of a corridor with eight or nine doors, each of which had a different character. There were bureaucratic double-doors in the centre of the stage, a prison door for Claudio, a door to a nunnery for Isabella, a secret, concealed door used by the Duke, and so on. The whole action took place downstage of these doors, and the effect was remarkable and chilling.

Jonathan suggested that the Duke was like an analyst and the city of Vienna was his patient. He does what an analyst would do – he absents himself from the city and then, as it were, discovers what the city's problem is. He sits back and puts Vienna on the couch. All kinds of things emerge, most notably Angelo's little peccadilloes.

MR   How did Jonathan help you with Claudio?

DH   He gave me one effect that was absolutely amazing because it was so unexpected. When Isabella comes to tell Claudio that she won't sleep with Angelo in order to save his life, Jonathan suggested that I should simply yawn at the news – he said that it was a physiological reaction to an extremely stressful situation.

I remember the scene in Act Three of his *Three Sisters* where Chebutykin is washing during the fire, and crying as he talks about the life that he failed to save. There was an unforgettable moment when he left his head in the basin uncomfortably long, as if he was trying to find the courage to drown himself, and then took his head out of the water, coughing and spluttering.

There were similar touches in *Measure for Measure*. At the end of the long speech in which Claudio pleads with Isabella to save his life, Jonathan encouraged me to absolutely scream, 'Sweet sister, let me live' and then cling onto her as if we were in a rugby tackle. Dressed in grey as a very unglamorous nun, Isabella used to beat me around the head with her handbag, trying to prise herself out of my grip. Jonathan said that at that point Claudio was like someone in the water clinging onto the edge of a boat, while she is desperately trying to cut his hands off at the wrists.

The way that Jonathan handled the end of the play was tremendously effective too. He felt that, in human terms, it was just absolutely unbelievable that, after everything Isabella has seen of the Duke's manipulative nature, she could possibly want to marry him. So he had Isabella reject the

Duke – when he proposed to her, she just looked at him in horror and walked off the stage.

MAX VON SYDOW

Max von Sydow played Prospero in *The Tempest* (Old Vic 1988).

Michael Romain How did you approach the role of Prospero when Jonathan invited you to star in his production of *The Tempest* at the Old Vic in 1988?

Max von Sydow To tell you the truth, I had never actually seen *The Tempest* on stage. I had played Prospero once before, though, but that was many, many years ago in Sweden. So when I came to work on the play with Jonathan, I couldn't comment on its performing tradition. But the most intriguing thing for me about Prospero was the feeling I had that he was a man who is initially full of latent ideas of revenge. I actually think that there is a scene missing from the play, where he should tell somebody – either his daughter or Ariel – what he would like to do with the people that he has ship-wrecked on the island. But he never does. Obviously he plans to take some kind of a revenge on them. I presumed that he would just leave them there and give them the same punishment that they once gave him, and then he would go back to civilisation with Miranda and Ferdinand. But then the play becomes the story of how he somehow changes his mind and decides not to take any real form of revenge. As we worked on the play in rehearsal, I came to see him as a man who from the beginning doesn't know how the story is going to end.

MR Your Prospero appeared more of a scientist than the usual magician.

MvS Yes he was – that was part of what I will very broadly describe as the 'colonial' concept that Jonathan used for the production. This naturalised the play – the spirits, for example, were not real spirits but the natives of the island. This was a good idea, and intrigued me very much. The actors that Jonathan cast as Ariel and Caliban – Cyril Nri and Rudolph Walker – were particularly good.

MR The relationship between Prospero and Miranda was also much more intense than usual.

MvS Yes – rather more than it should be, I think. We worked hard on that in rehearsal. The problem for me was the text, which I found quite difficult. Being Swedish, I'm spoiled by our rehearsal periods, which are

11 Max von Sydow (Prospero) and Cyril Nri (Ariel), *The Tempest*, Old Vic 1988

much longer than those in Britain. For a play like *The Tempest* we would have had at least two months rehearsal. That would have been in Swedish, my mother-tongue. Doing it in London – where it was not just in English, but Shakespearian English – we had only five weeks, so it was tough going for me. But I found Jonathan a tremendous help with the verse, and an inspiring director – he's funny, charming and very generous with his knowledge, his talents and his company. The production was a great experience for me, even though it was a totally new language to work in.

DUDLEY MOORE

Dudley Moore appeared in *Beyond the Fringe* (1960–4) and later played Ko-Ko in *The Mikado* (Los Angeles Music Center Opera 1987).

Michael Romain   In the early 1960s, together with Alan Bennett and Peter Cook, you appeared in *Beyond the Fringe* with Jonathan before he became a director – what were his skills as a performer?

Dudley Moore   He was actually a marvellous performer. He stood out amongst us and attracted a lot of attention because of a certain physical angularity that he had, which is probably the least of his gifts. His general jocularity and confidence with the audience were fairly remarkable – in many respects he had a different way of performing from the rest of us. He very much 'took the audience in', and was more of an audience player even than I was – which is saying something. He was consequently very affected by audiences. At times, I remember he used to come off stage fuming about certain audiences, while I used to go on in my rather blithe way, which I think was the only way to deal with it.

I had great fun with him in *Beyond the Fringe*, even though I never performed much directly opposite him. That was because the material was written around us all by us all. I did more with Peter Cook, which led to our TV series together, and a little bit with Alan Bennett, but only bits here and there with Jonathan. I remember one sketch where I played a warder to his prisoner – that was about the sum total of our work together on stage. But it was just so enjoyable simply to be *in* the show with him.

MR   Comedy seems to be an essential component of his direction.

DM   It enlivens his approach to his work and to his life. He would be very depleted if humour was excepted from his means of expression. He sees the comedy and eccentricities of behaviour, and he loves to play on those things.

MR   To what extent do you think that *Beyond the Fringe* contributed to his career as a director?

DM   It was very important for all of us in every sense. I have a feeling that he would have done something in the arts whatever happened. But the *Fringe* did make him very widely known – though in fact he was very highly respected as a performer even before that show. I think it contributed to the desirability of a directorial career.

MR   How did you feel about his production of *The Mikado*?

DM   I loved it – what I saw of it, that is, which wasn't all that much as I was onstage most of the time. I loved the freshness of his approach to the piece. I know that some people object to precisely that, but I'm just bemused by that reaction. I'd love to see more of his opera productions – most of which I've missed because I live in America. It's funny that, of all things, he should have turned to opera, because years and years ago, back in the early 1960s, I remember him criticising music quite loudly. He once described it as 'orange-juice for the ears'. Which maybe it is – very *good* orange-juice.

MR   How would you describe his direction?

DM   Like all good directors, he gives you an area in which to play. That's very useful for actors and singers. I found him endlessly encouraging when we did *The Mikado*, even when I was having a hard time learning it – I had three weeks in which to learn the role of Ko-Ko. Working with him was always very good fun. He gave direction to people mainly by imitation – there were several occasions where he would mimic the way that he envisaged it. He creates an area where he encourages you, where he feels that something is coming along, and he'll encourage you to take it further or do it in a slightly different way. He won't say 'That was wrong', but he'll say 'That was fun – now how about doing it this way?'

MR   I remember him drawing on your musical talents on one of the programmes in *The Body in Question*.

DM   Yes – I had a small role to play. He asked me a question which greatly embarrassed me because I couldn't give him the answer. As I was reading through some Bach, he said, 'Well, how are you doing that?' I said, 'Well, I'm reading the music.' He said, 'But how are you transferring what you read to the muscular activity whereby you play it?' I confessed that I didn't know, and he said, 'That's right – that's the correct answer. As a matter of fact, we don't know how it's done.'

MR   Do you feel that he's been torn between science and the arts?

DM   I think he's often felt guilty about spending time in the theatre instead of in medical research. But I'm sure that we can all find something that we feel we should have done. I'm sure that when I do a performance with Georg Solti and the orchestra in the concert hall, my mother will roll over in her grave and think 'At last he's doing what I always wanted him to, playing a concerto or two on the bloody piano!' Maybe Jonathan would have really enjoyed a life of medical research. It's good, though, that it's fuelled everything else that he's done. It's also stopped him getting complacent about the arts.

MR   Will you work together again?

DM   If the opportunity arises, I shall grab it. I love working with him because it's such a delightful experience. He's open to all sorts of ways of doing things – you certainly never feel trapped in a corner at his rehearsals.

Directors

MAX STAFFORD-CLARK

Max Stafford-Clark is the Artistic Director of the Royal Court Theatre, where Jonathan Miller directed *The Emperor* in 1987.

Michael Romain Jonathan returned to the Royal Court in 1987 after an absence of twenty-five years to direct *The Emperor* – why was he away from the theatre for so long?

Max Stafford-Clark I think that his principal interest lies in the classical repertory, in the re-interpretation of works from the past. The Royal Court, of course, concentrates on new work, and Jonathan has never really associated himself with new writers.

MR *The Emperor* was also a return to small-scale work for Jonathan, after several years in large opera houses.

MS-C That's right – he was intrigued to work at the Court again, and found directing in the intimate space of our studio theatre very refreshing. In fact, when *The Emperor* opened and became a huge success he was rather reluctant to move it downstairs into the main auditorium, which is a proscenium arch stage and much bigger. In retrospect, he was right from an artistic point of view – it moved in the end only because we were forced to exploit its success to keep our theatre going. But I think that the small space gave him a kind of pleasure that he hadn't anticipated.

MR How did he fit in at the Court?

MS-C Very happily indeed – he enjoyed working here, he got on very well with the staff and provided us with a source of constant entertainment. The Court is a family-sized firm – it's not a big institution, and the people who work here can be entertained in one room. Jonathan likes that sort of atmosphere – if he was in a big institution, he would never be able to get acquainted with everyone who worked there. He spent a lot of time in the building, and came back to see the show once it had opened a lot more often than I believe he usually does.

MR What did you glean of his working methods?

MS-C   I didn't see him in rehearsal, but I spoke to him every lunchtime and every evening during that period. I got the impression that he worked on *The Emperor* like a film editor, editing the novel and turning it into a play as the actors went through it. The whole process was very skilfully done.

He and Michael Hastings had gathered together an extraordinary cast, and casting in general is very important to Jonathan's way of working. He often has a wonderful idea about a play, and if his actors are able to pick it up and run with it then they end up with a wonderful production. If not, then it's a much slower process. He depends – as we all do – on the actors' ability to flesh out the ideas that he gives them.

MR   What made *The Emperor* so successful?

MS-C   The marriage – which is what Jonathan does so much of the time – between the world of the novel and the Kafka-esque world of the production was fully realised on stage. There was a total fusion between the concept and its execution. Jonathan is able to do that very easily. It would take me months, for example, to construct a theory about how to direct *King Lear*. In the course of a morning's conversation when I'm trying to clean the car, Jonathan will tell me two brilliant ways in which *King Lear* could be approached, neither of which I had thought of, both of which seem absolutely superb. And then he'll say, 'Well one is not possible because of this, and the other is not possible because of that' – he can see through his own concepts to the problems underneath as well.

MR   How did people react to the production of *The Emperor*?

MS-C   Ryszard Kapúscínski felt that of all the many stage versions of his novel that had been presented around the world, Jonathan's production was the most fully realised. The critics gave it the most wonderful reviews, and for once there was no personal and antagonistic criticism levelled at him, which naturally pleased him.

MR   You knew Jonathan before *The Emperor*?

MS-C   I'd known him socially because we live opposite each other in Camden Town, but I had never worked with him. I'd always found his mind endlessly fascinating – you get a sense of that in his productions. And I admired him enormously because his knowledge of art, history, medicine and so on make him unbelievably well read. That is of great importance when you are directing a classic – when I directed *The Recruiting Officer*, I suddenly realised how little I knew about the period. Then when I came to do *Our Country's Good*, Jonathan said, 'Well, you must read Robert

Hughes' book *The Fatal Shore*, and have you read any eighteenth-century social history?' and so forth. There are always one or two books lying around my house that I've borrowed from him. He would be a wonderful librarian if he wasn't a director – his house is like a library, as it is.

MR   Jonathan is often described as a 'maverick' figure – do you agree with that term?

MS-C   Yes, absolutely. I've been married to the theatre, whereas he's had affairs with it. This is partly due to the fact that he has a very low boredom threshold – shunting between an academic life, a medical life, a theatrical life and an operatic life is something that constantly stimulates him.

What keeps him going is the fact that he is always ready to change his ideas about theatre. He's immensely open-minded, as the sheer scope of his work demonstrates – look at the way that he has really opened our eyes to European theatre in his Old Vic seasons. He's always been a strong supporter of the Royal Court – I think that if I ever needed help here at the Court, I could always count on him.

PETER JONAS

Peter Jonas is the General Director of the English National Opera, where Miller directed *Don Giovanni* (1985), *The Magic Flute* (1986), *The Mikado* (1986), *Tosca* (1987) and *The Barber of Seville* (1987).

Michael Romain   You began your first season as General Director of English National Opera in 1985 with a strong combination – Jonathan Miller and Philip Prowse collaborating on a new *Don Giovanni*.

Peter Jonas   Jonathan was very clear that he wanted Philip Prowse to design his production. By that time Philip had established himself as a director as well as a designer, and rarely designed other directors' productions – he did *Don Giovanni* as a favour to Jonathan, though, because he admired his work so much. It was unique to have two such eminent men of the theatre working together at the Coliseum.

They came up with a very clear, remarkably simple production – it was the first time I had even seen *Don Giovanni* really work on stage. That's a tremendous achievement: it's a piece which normally poses enormous logistical problems for a director – all those scene changes, for instance – and yet Jonathan's staging made the action flow very smoothly and simply. It's been a hugely successful production – both in artistic and box-office terms – and I am totally at a loss to understand why some critics misunderstood it. Jonathan drew on Goya for the style of the production, and the critics seemed unable to see the significance of this – they couldn't spot the parallels between Goya, Mozart, the Enlightenment and the Spanish origins of the Don Juan myth.

MR   Jonathan further developed Enlightenment parallels and allusions in his next Mozart at the Coliseum, his Scottish Opera production of *The Magic Flute*.

PJ   In his *Magic Flute* the Enlightenment theme was all-pervasive. The whole concept was very clearly articulated through Jonathan's use of imagery – Tamino falling asleep at the beginning, for instance, to show that the whole thing was just his dream. The audience was drawn into that eighteenth-century world by the references to the Enlightenment, the freemasons, the Church and so on – the Queen of the Night, for instance, coming on as Maria Theresa, surrounded by all her cardinals, bishops and all that hocus pocus. It was a very effective visual simile, which communicated its meaning to the ordinary public in a very direct way.

MR   You brought Jonathan's *Flute* to the Coliseum from Scottish Opera because at the time the company was unable to afford a new production – did that financial crisis also generate Jonathan's next ENO production, *The Mikado*?

PJ   That's right. The origins of *The Mikado* lie in the Camden Brasserie, where Jonathan and I had dinner one night after the *Flute* had opened. We were in a terrible fix at the Coliseum because of the Arts Council cuts in our grant, and I just had no idea what we were going to do next. I thought that what we needed most of all was a popular hit, and the idea of Gilbert and Sullivan came to mind. Jonathan was to have done a Rossini cycle for us at the time, but that had been postponed for a year, so I put the idea of *The Mikado* to him. He immediately said, 'Well of course I'd love to do it – it's pure *Duck Soup*', and began outlining ways in which he would get rid of all the Japanese business which normally swamps the piece.

He devised a very clever and witty staging that reflected perfectly what *The Mikado* is really about – the English laughing at themselves laughing at the Japanese. It's got nothing to do with the Japanese at all – it's all about the English. The rehearsal period was a very rich preparation time in the life of the Coliseum – everybody sensed that something extraordinary was happening. Looking back on the production now, I think it was one of the best things Jonathan has ever done in his career – it was spectacularly good, and proved a huge hit with our audiences. It achieved a tremendous fusion of intellectual ideas and Jonathan's particular speciality of blending diverse references into a rather rich sauce, all totally on the wavelength of every single person who comes into the theatre. Nobody could fail to be entertained by it, and there's not a moment where an allusion or a joke passes anybody by. Added to that, you had the reunification of under-graduate humour between Jonathan and Eric Idle, which provided that wonderfully daft and peculiarly English vein of nonsense.

MR   I felt that his *Tosca* at the Coliseum in 1987 had a similarly immediate effect – by updating the action from 1800 to Mussolini's Rome in 1944 he made sure that everybody could relate to the opera.

PJ   What was going on onstage in his *Tosca* was either in the experience of the audience or at the most one generation away. That was very much the case in Florence when Jonathan directed the production there – people in the chorus had actually lived through those events. Everything on the stage meant something to the audience, either from their personal experi-ences or from the general perception of a mid-twentieth-century atmo-sphere of oppression and brutality. It was a transposition that worked in every respect – it was as effective as his 'Mafia' *Rigoletto*. And like that *Rig-oletto*, his *Tosca* has since become a big hit at the box-office.

MR   What has Jonathan contributed to the English National Opera?

PJ   An immense amount. His *Rigoletto* became one of the greatest successes in the company's history. The ENO was steadily developing when Jona-than arrived at the Coliseum, and he brought to it a talent that the company was ready for. He made ENO into a wonderful laboratory of theatrical experimentation, which was not stuck in some research institu-tion but was based in a major producing-house that was operating every day and drawing the public in.

  Jonathan's *Rigoletto*, *Mikado*, and *Tosca* have not only helped to ensure the ENO's survival through the box-office but have also had far-reaching effects in popularising opera – they have all brought new audiences into the opera house. When Jonathan was directing here, you had what I think is the first example of a director actually being box-office himself. His name alone on the programme would draw people to the opera. People who groan and mutter about 'directors' theatre' are actually talking a load of rubbish. The only thing that is 'directors' theatre' about it is that Jonathan started the idea of a director being a box-office star. The first real example of this was *Rigoletto*. If we announced, for example, 'a new production of

Der Rosenkavalier directed by Jonathan Miller' it would be an instant sell-out.

MR   What are his particular strengths as a director?

PJ   Jonathan is very different indeed from most directors. His craft as a director is not methodical exercise – the muscle he has developed is in fantasy, ideas and parallels with aesthetic, visual and historical references. Those are his great skills. He is coming at it from a different school to the director who works his way up from being a stage-manager to a staff-producer and so on.

MR   How would you compare Jonathan to his counterparts in Europe?

PJ   Giorgio Strehler is much closer to Jonathan than someone like Luca Ronconi, who is much more eccentric and extravagant. With both Strehler and Jonathan, their ideas are central to their work – they both start off with very original concepts and build on these with a series of references and allusions, all backed up with tremendous imagination. Their work is always striking and immediate in a very innovative way.

Visually, they have different tastes – Strehler is very much influenced by Milanese art and the Lombardy desire for simplicity of effect; whereas Jonathan likes much more precise aesthetic detail, though at the same time drawing just as much as Strehler on art and architecture. You would never get Strehler making the sort of detailed visual references that Jonathan did in his *Mikado* or *Barber of Seville*.

Strehler is more monastic, whereas Jonathan is more worldly, more in tune with all the different aspects and movements of history and civilisation. What makes Jonathan so unique among directors is his flexibility.

TERRY HANDS

Terry Hands was Artistic Director of the Royal Shakespeare Company, where Jonathan Miller directed *The Taming of the Shrew* in 1987.

Michael Romain   What prompted you to invite Jonathan to direct for the Royal Shakespeare Company?

Terry Hands   I had always admired his work as a director very much, though we had never had the opportunity to meet frequently. But I enjoyed his company, and I remember saying to my colleagues when I proposed inviting Jonathan that, if nothing else, his presence would cheer the place up for a year.

MR   What made you offer him *The Taming of the Shrew?*

TH   It's a very difficult play to do in this day and age. So I thought that it needed somebody who was above all intelligent, not just simply modish.

MR   What impressions did you glean from the cast and crew of the way that Jonathan worked with them?

TH   From what I heard, it appears that he worked through a careful psychological analysis of each scene. It was the first time that he had come up against our kind of veteran RSC troupe – he said to me at the beginning 'Oh, I'll only need four and a half weeks' rehearsal', but as things turned out the actors demanded more from him than he had expected.

It worked out very happily in the end. When I bumped into him backstage during the previews he was full of praise for the organisational support systems that he was able to call upon. He was pleased with the production, which became a big success for us in both Stratford and London.

What I particularly admired was the economy of both movement and effect. The text emerged with great clarity and lucidity – it was a marvellously paced and beautifully unfrenetic show.

MR   Drawing on the ideas of the Annales school of French historians, Jonathan tried to reconstruct the *mentalité* of the sixteenth century in his production – what effect did that have?

TH   It set the play in context. The virtue of that approach was that Jonathan knew exactly what the effect – and the significance – of the play would have been in its own time.

MR   Which of his productions have made a particularly strong impression on you?

TH   His early work was quite extraordinary because he was a performer and writer as well as a director then. I thought his *Rigoletto* was sensational, of course, and I admired very much his *The Turn of the Screw* and *The Three Sisters*.

MR   Do you see his production style as more European than British?

TH   It depends what you mean by 'European'. I see European directors as people who re-write the plays in their productions. Jonathan doesn't do that. He respects the essence of the text, the author's intentions, and he collaborates with his actors. In that sense Jonathan is much more in the English tradition of Tyrone Guthrie.

MR   How would you sum up Jonathan's contribution to the British theatre?

TH   I think that his greatest contribution has been himself.

LORD HAREWOOD

Lord Harewood is the former General Director of the English National Opera where Jonathan Miller directed *The Marriage of Figaro* (1978), *The Turn of the Screw* (1979), *Arabella* (1980), *Otello* (1981), and *Rigoletto* (1982).

Michael Romain   What prompted you to invite Jonathan to work with English National Opera in 1978?

Lord Harewood   I had seen his production of *The Cunning Little Vixen* at Glyndebourne, which was most remarkable. He had a reputation at that time for being a tremendously avant-garde, iconoclastic director, who changed or updated things. His *Vixen* was rightly post-Felsenstein, and struck a wonderful compromise between animals and humans. Later on I saw his work with Kent Opera, including his very powerful *La Traviata*, and asked him to come to the Coliseum in 1978 to direct *The Marriage of Figaro*.

It turned out to be a wonderful *Figaro*, which absolutely fulfilled what I thought Jonathan was – a highly perceptive traditionalist who doesn't use traditions which are in reality accretions, the things that were done generations ago and gradually became a stultified orthodoxy. Jonathan isn't at all like that – he is never affected by the routine traditions of opera.

He simply went to *Figaro* and analysed what the piece was about, what the music was about, what Beaumarchais was getting at, how much of the original Mozart had left out and how much he had replaced with his own ideas, and how much the singers were going to put into it. *Figaro* was an ideal opera for Jonathan because he has a very strong sense of period – not only for its art and culture, but also for the manners of a period, particularly as related to the stage – probably stronger than anyone else I know. He loves that kind of firm basis – he's a very accurate director, and never treats a production as a mere fantasy.

MR   What made *Figaro* so successful?

LH   When he directed it, he didn't make his cast jump through hoops – rather, he discovered what kind of jumping they could do, and then used that to suit the opera. It was full of spontaneous touches – I remember Bartolo dancing the *fandango* in the third act and suddenly bumping into a chair, as if he had absolutely no idea that it would be there. That's Jonathan's great ability when working with performers – it's not so much the moves that he gives them, as their own perception of what he is asking them to do in the context of the production. And the *Figaro* turned out to be what I would call an absolute classical production, sensitively observed rather than apeing something. I don't think that Jonathan ever apes anything, except pictures. He likes to say, 'Well if that's what they did, observed in the eighteenth century by an eighteenth-century artist, that gives us our starting-point.'

MR Jonathan had previously displayed a fascination with ghosts in his film *Oh Whistle and I'll Come to You* – did this lead to his production of *The Turn of the Screw* at the Coliseum?

LH No, it was chance. On the first night of *Figaro* there was a party at the house of Charles Groves, who conducted. The performance had gone extremely well, and it seemed to me that we had a major success on our hands. As we were approaching the house, I said to Jonathan, 'Well, what next? Have you ever thought of *The Turn of the Screw?*' 'My goodness,' he replied, 'that would be wonderful. Right, I'm on!' He thought about it for a moment and then said, 'I've got lots of ideas, I know the kind of disease which would cause the Governess's condition, and I have a sense of what Henry James must have either known or half-grasped.' Within a day or two, we were already talking about how he was going to do it and who we could cast.

We gathered together a very powerful group of singers – Eileen Hannan as the Governess, Graham Clark as Peter Quint and Rosalind Plowright as Miss Jessel. The children were excellent, and Jonathan came along to the numerous auditions that we held for their roles – he was marvellous at diagnosing the right attributes in all those that we saw and heard.

The great achievement of his production was to make such an intimate piece work so well on a big stage, yet without losing any of its claustrophobic atmosphere. He evoked this claustrophobia by using slide projections taken from photographs of a Gothic mansion. One moment the whole stage would be empty, then suddenly it would all be closing in on the characters. It was a gripping event.

MR Was his next production for ENO, *Arabella*, also your suggestion?

LH No, it came from Josephine Barstow. She told us that she wanted to do a young and personable role like Arabella, so we said, 'Well, Covent Garden already owe us a production in exchange, so we'll ask them for their *Arabella*.' And Jo said, 'Oh God, must we do a warmed-up, second-hand production which is at least ten years old by now? I'd really love to work with Jonathan Miller – couldn't we ask him to come up with something?'

Jonathan said, 'Oh yes, we could do it quite inexpensively – it would cost money in any case to do up the old production.' He was very practical indeed about cost-cutting – he used a huge mirror to double everything's size and got the same staircase to serve for two different acts simply by changing its position. It may not have been one of his most important productions, but it was pretty ingenious all the same.

MR What caused the postponement of the *Rigoletto* with which Jonathan planned to follow *Arabella*?

LH We immediately agreed to do the *Rigoletto* after Jonathan had said, 'I've got this good idea ...' He explained his concept of setting it in the Mafia world of 1950s New York so logically that we knew it would work. Only one thing puzzled me – how would Monterone fit in with this, bursting in at the beginning then going off at the end to be executed? Jonathan said, 'There's no problem – it fits in perfectly with my idea.' And of course he was absolutely right – the Mafia would have thought nothing of capturing a rival and bumping him off. We all thought it was immensely exciting and began casting.

Within a short space of time, though, I found that the tenor Charles Craig was very keen to sing with us, so we offered him *Otello*. He was delighted to do this, and I asked Jonathan if he would be prepared to put *Rigoletto* back to the following season and direct Charles in *Otello* instead.

He agreed, and came up with a very schematic production based on the shape of Shakespeare's Globe Theatre, which was incorporated in the design. We were on a tight budget, as usual, so it was not an extravagant staging. All the effects were achieved very simply – I shall never forget the beautiful lighting that enveloped Desdemona when she was alone at the beginning of the fourth act. Jonathan is always good at evoking mood.

MR Did the delay in staging *Rigoletto* create any problems?

LH Initially it created one unexpected problem, yes. Once he had come up with the idea, Jonathan naturally told people about it. Soon afterwards, we heard about a production of *Rigoletto* in Switzerland which was updated to the era of Al Capone, Chicago in the early 1930s (ours was to be set in

1950s New York). We went over to see it and quickly realised that we had nothing to worry about. It was not as good as the one Jonathan subsequently did – nothing like as detailed or well-observed. Jonathan's had one central joke, but that was the only departure – everything else was exactly as it says in the libretto. The Swiss production was rather more far-fetched. We came back and said that there was no reason for any of us to be deterred because we had not been upstaged.

When we started casting the piece, Jonathan was very keen on the idea of John Rawnsley playing Rigoletto, which turned out to be a triumph because he not only had the vocal strength for the role but was also an excellent actor with just the right panache. We ran into a problem when Graham Clark, who had been cast as the Duke, had to pull out of the role. By an incredible stroke of luck, we heard about an excellent performance that Arthur Davies had given while understudying a role with Welsh National Opera, which revealed him to have a real Italianate voice, brilliant at the top. He had never done anything like it before, but we immediately offered him the role of the Duke. He did it, and with Jonathan's help transformed his career overnight.

From that point on, everything seemed to forge ahead on *Rigoletto*, and it became an extremely happy production – it was one of the most exciting things I've ever been connected with. It looked wonderful on stage. Jonathan took details from movies and taught the singers authentic American postures and gestures.

MR   Why were there objections to the production in New York?

LH   Members of the Italian community in New York objected to what they saw as the American Italian image being smirched in the production. We were actually quite gentle about it, but we eventually managed to convince them – by letter and telephone – that there was nothing for them to get upset about. I think that they decided to abandon their protest when they saw that we were not going to cut and run. We didn't alter the production at all when it arrived at the Metropolitan Opera, though I vaguely remember the word 'Mafia' being removed from a programme note.

There was one thing that we did cut. Jonathan had already filmed the production for television, without giving away any of its secrets. You never saw the sets in their entirety for any length of time on the screen. He simply suggested the settings by going in and panning out, focussing all the time on details. He would shoot these from different angles – he's a very good cameraman, with a real eye for what works on screen. Anyway, the film starts off with him talking about how the images of the Mafia world matched those of Verdi and Victor Hugo – the closed society, the power of life and death in a single man's hands, and so on – before suddenly producing New York newspapers from the 1950s with very lurid headlines and pictures of Mafia activities. When we sent a video of the film off to the Italian American protestors, we cut the whole of Jonathan's introduction! I think that it was actually the non-sensationalising of the Mafia that finally convinced them.

MR   Did you find Jonathan vulnerable to press criticism?

LH   That's his Achilles' heel, though I've never understood why he is affected by it to such a degree. A little of the criticism that he got when he was directing at the Coliseum was either dreary or snide. I don't think it can be pleasing to be referred to all the time as 'the good doctor' when you are a professional theatre man. He seemed genuinely hurt by it, but I've always thought that he is much too good to be bothered by petty criticism.

MR   It's always difficult to compare directors, but I feel that the only directors to match Jonathan's style and breadth of vision are Giorgio Strehler and Luca Ronconi – would you agree with that?

LH   I would certainly say yes to Strehler, but I think that Ronconi comes up with a kind of fantasy that isn't Jonathan's. Jonathan is capable of great fantasy in his productions, but I would call that a classical type of fantasy in the sense that to him it must always fit the facts, whereas for Ronconi it doesn't have to – I think that he bends the facts to fit his view. Strehler, on the other hand, is a classical director like Jonathan whose work fits the facts. Ronconi comes up with the most wonderful theatrical fantasy, but I think it's dottier than Jonathan would ever contemplate.

Both Strehler and Ronconi do have that great vision which Jonathan displays in his work. Jonathan is always very true to the structure of a piece, whereas Ronconi sometimes goes off in all sorts of directions. Tyrone Guthrie was more like Jonathan. He was a classicist – he would see a piece from a particular angle and often used modern dress, as with his *Hamlet* and *Troilus and Cressida*, but always kept the motivations true to the piece. That is what I mean by classical, and that is Jonathan's strength.

MR   What is his most practical asset as a director?

LH   He has a wonderful sense of scale. Looking at things with his painter's eye, he has an extraordinarily precise sense of scale – I don't think he would ever direct a production that didn't fit the frame into which it would go. If he did an opera at the Old Vic, it would fit that stage just as well as his work fitted our big stage at the Coliseum. Certainly the scale of his work for Kent Opera was very precisely right for those small theatres.

When he did his riveting *Othello* on television, the scale of the surroundings was quite small – we were in small rooms, people were mostly photographed by windows or in passages, and the scale was exactly right for the standard-sized TV screen. You expect *Othello* to be a big-scale play – partly because of the opera, partly because of productions by the big companies – so it was fascinating to see how Jonathan's instinct and intelligence had re-analysed it to bring down to the small spaces to fit the TV screen. That is what is unique about him – he rises easily to the necessarily large scale of opera, and then comes up with something as intimate as that *Othello*. To me that is admirable and excellent – it is one of his less often remarked-on qualities, and very important indeed.

Singers

ROSALIND PLOWRIGHT

Rosalind Plowright played the Messenger in *Orfeo* (Kent Opera 1976), Miss Jessel in *The Turn of the Screw* (English National Opera 1979) and Desdemona in *Otello* (English National Opera 1981).

Michael Romain When you performed in Jonathan's *Orfeo* for Kent Opera in 1976, did you find it difficult to achieve the stylised gestures and postures of the Poussin figures that Jonathan wanted for the production?

Rosalind Plowright Not at all – in fact, it was easier to do that sort of thing than naturalistic behaviour. Naturalism doesn't really come easily to a singer onstage, whereas this stylised movement gave us a lot of support. We worked on it for several weeks, and Jonathan showed us lots of Poussin paintings in the rehearsal period to convey a sense of the mood he was after. Our choreography throughout the opera was based on the movements of the figures in the pictures.

It all worked beautifully in the end – opera from Monteverdi's period is very stylised and unstated, and Jonathan's Poussin style seemed to me to be the most effective way to do it. Everything was very calm and subtle – there were no big operatic gestures or anything like that.

MR You next worked with Jonathan in 1979, when you sang Miss Jessel in his English National Opera production of *The Turn of the Screw* – did he spend much time in rehearsal discussing the ambiguities of the piece?

RP There was a lot of talking when we did that, because it's such a mysterious piece for singers to go into. We could have just sat there all day listening to Jonathan talking about the ghosts, the illness of the Governess and so on. I remember thinking to myself at such moments, 'God, I've got to try and do this now' – the way that his ideas come flowing out, you would think that you could never do justice to them onstage. But then you find that you can, simply because of the way that his words have fired your performance. That's the way that Jonathan works – through words, ideas and metaphors. But although he's a great intellectual, he would never confuse us – he has a very practical sense of the level that performers have to work on.

Because he had worked so much in the straight theatre before coming into opera, his approach tended to be quite naturalistic. A lot of opera singers are real ham actors, but nobody would ever start being 'operatic' in one of Jonathan's productions. As soon as he saw anything that was over the top, he would tell the singer so and correct it. He helped me a lot by teaching me the importance of stillness onstage. Miss Jessel is like that anyway, very poised and spooky. Jonathan managed to eliminate any 'opera business', so that *The Turn of the Screw* became very real, eerie and disturbing.

MR   When you returned to the Coliseum in 1981 to sing Desdemona in his *Otello* Jonathan brought you onstage at the beginning, a scene earlier than usual.

RP   That's right – he said it would be natural for Desdemona to rush out to greet Otello in the storm. She would obviously want to see her husband as soon as he arrived. Anyway, she would hardly be sleeping soundly in bed in the middle of a violent storm, for heaven's sake.

    She comes on during the storm in Shakespeare's play, after all. And when we did *Otello*, Jonathan had in fact just directed the play for television, so we all went to see a private viewing of it at the BBC to get an idea of the original. Although the opera is quite different to the play, it was wonderful to see how Jonathan had worked on the same characters.

MR   What were the similarities between his *Othello* and *Otello*?

RP   The most striking similarity was the 'Willow' scene, which was exactly the same in both. Jonathan had placed a candle and a skull on a table in front of Desdemona as she prepares for bed, and the flickering light created a marvellously dream-like atmosphere. Desdemona just sat there at the table, completely still, for the whole scene, which is quite long. I didn't move until the very end, where I rushed over to Emilia as she went out – the stillness with which Jonathan staged that scene was incredibly powerful, whereas all the other productions of *Otello* that I have been in have made me run madly about throughout the scene.

MR   Your Desdemona was considerably different from the passive heroine of most productions.

RP   Jonathan gave me an interpretation of Desdemona's character that I have never forgotten, and which has influenced my performance in the role ever since. He showed me that Desdemona was actually an enormously strong and defiant person. I've often been criticised because I've since played it like that in Italy – the Italians don't know the play, and see her as the beautiful, vulnerable heroine. In fact, as Jonathan showed, she stands up to Otello a great deal – that's in Verdi's music as well as Shakespeare's text. Anybody who can defy her father and go off to marry against his will must be strong. That's how it should be, and Jonathan's view of her was a revelation for me that really liberated the role from tradition.

MR Your characterisation also resulted in a much more powerful and violent death scene than usual.

RP Jonathan, the doctor/director, pointed out that if somebody is being strangled, they are instinctively going to put up a fight. So many Desdemonas in opera just lie there limply without resisting at all. Jonathan got me to have a great struggle with Otello, my legs kicking wildly and sheets flying everywhere, until I ended up with my head handing over the end of the bed. Finally I grabbed hold of the sheets and desperately tried to protect myself from Otello with them. Jonathan gives you so much to think about when you rehearse a scene like that, whereas most producers would have the soprano sitting there thinking, 'Oh, he's going to kill me, is he? Fine.'

JEAN RIGBY

Jean Rigby played Maddalena in *Rigoletto* (English National Opera 1982) Dorabella in *Così fan tutte* (BBC TV 1985) and Pitti-Sing in *The Mikado* (English National Opera 1986).

Michael Romain When you played Dorabella in Jonathan's 1985 television film of *Così fan tutte*, how did his direction in the TV studio differ from his stage work?

Jean Rigby As soon as we started rehearsals, he got rid of all the exaggerated gestures and movements that we have to do on stage, where inevitably everything has to be bigger to reach the audience. If you look at another character on stage, you have to turn your head to indicate this to the people sitting at the back of the upper circle; on TV, Jonathan showed us that we only had to move our eyes. He toned everything down in scale for the screen, and used lots of close-ups to record each little nuance.

Because he's had so much experience as a film and television director, he knows what will work in front of the cameras – he would go round peering through a lens to make sure that each shot would look right on screen. He concentrated a lot on building up the grouping in each scene, and was very careful to keep our gestures and facial expressions as naturalistic and untheatrical as possible.

MR   Your Dorabella, certainly, was much more restrained and sensitive than the standard opera house portrayal.

JR   She's normally played as simply hysterical, but I was able to avoid that as Jonathan wanted to get away from the usual histrionics. He took the opera much more seriously than it is usually taken – instead of treating it as just a comedy, he brought out all the pain that the characters go through in the course of the opera, especially Fiordiligi. She didn't run madly about – she was simply devastated at all the deception that was going on around her, and the character suddenly became terribly moving as a result.

MR   At the Coliseum you appeared in two of Jonathan's most celebrated 'updatings' – the Mafia *Rigoletto* and the 1920s *Mikado*. How did the audiences respond to these?

JR   They had never seen anything like them. Naturally they came along with preconceived ideas about how they should look – they thought that *The Mikado* should be full of kimonos, for example (though Jonathan did actually use a couple as an in-joke). But once the curtain went up, they absolutely loved the productions because they were so original. Even purists were totally convinced by the updating when they came out.

MR   How did Jonathan help you with your characterisation of Maddalena in *Rigoletto* and Pitti-Sing in *Mikado*?

JR   He wanted Maddalena to be much more sleazy than usual, so he gave me a split skirt and encouraged me to move in a very sexy way. Pitti-Sing was quite the reverse – he wanted the whole cast to sound like Jack Buchanan, or Trevor Howard and Celia Johnson in *Brief Encounter*, so I played Pitti-Sing with those clipped English vowels. Although she is a comparatively minor character, Jonathan gave the role just as much attention as the central characters – that's why his productions are seam-less onstage.

   In both *Rigoletto* and *The Mikado*, he gave every single chorus member a very distinct individual character. He would never just put a chorus onstage and let them get on with it – he gave them all sort of props (lollies, guns and dark glasses in *Rigoletto*, for instance) and built up their separate identities around them. And he always knew the name of every single chorus member, which is rare among directors. He's particularly good at choreographing crowd scenes, and the chorus would always busy themselves for him – he used to encourage them to come up with all kinds of business, and they were very responsive to this.

MR   How does he approach an opera?

JR   Probably in the same way that he would approach a play – he views it as a whole, and comes up with all-embracing idea to work from. He always leaves a lot of room for humour once we start rehearsals, because it's precisely by telling the cast jokes every day that he gets the best out of them. The mood of the rehearsals is so important, and he always gives us time to relax.

He never has a rigid concept, but just waits to see what evolves once we start work – he'll watch how the different personalities of the cast spark each other off, and then build on that. He's always very quick to seize on little moments that he's noticed, even if they have happened out of rehearsals.

Throughout the rehearsal period, he is always open to suggestions, and we felt that we could freely discuss things with him. His way of working with performers is very much give-and-take: if you say to him, 'I do find that difficult, but I'll try it all the same', then he'll say, 'Well have a go, and if it doesn't work we'll scrap it.' He's never dogmatic about anything, and he's well aware of a singer's limitations – he knows, for instance, that there are several positions in which a singer can't sing. So he will go out of his way to avoid making you feel uncomfortable onstage. And that is very reassuring.

JONATHAN SUMMERS

Jonathan Summers played the title role in *Rigoletto* (Kent Opera 1975) and Ford in *Falstaff* (Kent Opera 1980).

Michael Romain   What were your first impressions of Jonathan when he invited you to work with him at Kent Opera?

Jonathan Summers   Being an Australian, newly arrived in Britain, I didn't really know who Jonathan Miller was before I met him, but I had been told that he was this hugely accomplished figure. When I knocked on the door of his house in Camden Town, I was met by this tall, gangling streak of a man who was so gentle and quietly spoken that I was completely disarmed. I shall never forget walking in and seeing the place literally lined with books. They were everywhere – in piles down the hall, all over the living-room table, overflowing on shelves, lying on chairs, and so on. To offer me a seat, he had to move a pile of books. I asked him, 'With such a busy life as yours, when do you get a chance to read all these books?' 'Oh,' he said, 'I spend 80 or 90 per cent of my time reading.'

MR   What do you remember of his direction?

JS   What impressed me more than anything was the fact that he was never authoritarian and never tried to impose his ideas on the singers. In fact, he sometimes referred to himself as parasitic – he fed from the talents of his performers. We came up with something that was initially his conception and which he moulded, but he had this knack of making us feel terrific by drawing on everything that we had to offer. This had a knock-on effect – because he made us so confident, we would be ready to do anything for him, however difficult or bizarre.

MR   The roles you played for him at Kent Opera – Rigoletto, and Ford in *Falstaff* – offer tremendous comic scope – did he give you any guidelines for comedy?

JS   Jonathan regularly said that good comedy always comes from the seriousness with which you apply yourself to it. He hated the idea of going for cheap gags. He felt that if you play something for laughs, then people won't laugh; but if you play a comic situation seriously and really believe in it, then you will make the audience laugh. His other great rule was 'Less is more.' 'You don't need to do that – that's operatic. Less is more', he would always say.

RICHARD VAN ALLAN

Richard Van Allan played Leporello in *Don Giovanni* (English National Opera 1985) and Pooh-Bah in *The Mikado* (English National Opera 1986).

Michael Romain   What was the starting-point for Jonathan's *Don Giovanni* at the Coliseum in 1985?

Richard Van Allan   He always had this very strong image of the death of the Don at the climax. His idea was that the Don's hell was for him to have to make love to women, at their demand, for eternity. So once he was in his hell, the roles were reversed – instead of the Don taking his pleasure with women at will, he was damned to have women taking their pleasure at will with him forever.

Jonathan initially wanted to have an older Don, but William Shimell, who had been cast in the role, was such a young and virile figure that he couldn't use the idea. But he originally intended to portray the Don as ageing and world-weary, unhappily compelled to go seducing women because his reputation makes people expect it of him. Having been the predator for most of his life, as it now draws towards a close the Don is becoming the victim of his own reputation. That idea would have made Jonathan's ending all the more ironic: the Don would almost greet the Commendatore with open arms as a welcome release from his life of constantly having to satisfy women, only to find that what awaits him is an infinitely worse fate.

MR Your Leporello was the first I've seen that was actually similar in build to the Don, which made the deception of Elvira credible for once.

RVA Jonathan was very precise about that, otherwise it would have made Elvira look such a fool. What he tried to achieve by making the trick plausible was a sense of Elvira's utter shame, disbelief and horror when her partner is revealed as Leporello in disguise. She's probably thinking about what they've just been doing together – 'Oh my God – and with a servant!' It really is devastating for her, which makes her return at the climax to try and save the Don seem even more sensitive and noble.

Elvira is always a problem character, and Jonathan tried to flesh out her scenes as much as possible. I remember him saying to the Don, 'Don't be so glib with your replies to her – it's almost as if you can't quite remember what the circumstances were.' At one rehearsal, we were doing the scene where the Don says, 'My dear Donna Elvira, please calm yourself.' Bill Shimell hesitated slightly after 'My dear Donna ...' so I added 'Elvira, Elvira.' Jonathan loved this and kept it in – it said a lot about both characters that the Don had obviously forgotten the name of the woman, in spite of the fact that she had been pursuing him all over the country. Jonathan is very good at picking up on little moments like that.

MR How did you arrive at the characterisation of Pooh-Bah in Jonathan's 1986 production of *The Mikado*?

RVA As with his *Rigoletto*, Jonathan had thought out *The Mikado* very carefully and set it in a twenties world with overtones of Marx Brothers films, like *Duck Soup*. He saw Pooh-Bah as a laid-back, sophisticated figure, rather like George Sanders. This didn't work for me, so Jonathan told me to experiment. At one rehearsal I tried playing him as a sergeant-major, and Jonathan said, 'Well, that's sort of it, but it needs to be more like an officer.' In the end I based Pooh-Bah on a very colonial upper-class Lieutenant-Commander that I knew, and Jonathan immediately saw that this type of characterisation would work for me. This is typical of the flexibility of his approach – he will never impose anything on his performers, but always adapts to them so that they will be fully comfortable in their roles.

MR Jonathan's *Mikado* proved an enormous hit with audiences – what was it like for the performers?

RVA By the time that it opened, Jonathan had produced such a slick, polished show that we all got a tremendous kick out of the performances. We had great professional pride in that show – it was so well-crafted that even the occasional mistake was covered up with real aplomb. The knowledge that we were in a real hit went through the chorus as well as the principals, so morale was very high.

There was always a good working atmosphere on that show, because Jonathan's direction instilled a lot of enthusiasm and excitement in the cast. He's very good in that respect because he's naturally gregarious and enjoys being with performers – while he was at the Coliseum, he would always spend a lot of time in the canteen or the dressing-rooms. Singers like him for that and find him easy to get on with – he's basically a rather humble person, despite his intellect and the fact that he can concentrate on six things at the same time.

MR Jonathan came to opera from a background in straight theatre – how does he react to the special demands of singers?

RVA He has complete understanding of the problems faced by singers which actors rarely encounter. You won't find him trying to distort the vocal line, or saying, 'Oh, why can't you do it at a different speed?' If you say to one of his ideas, 'We can't do it that way, because ...' there is no impatience or anything like that from him – he immediately sees the problem, and comes up with another idea to replace it with. He knows how to handle singers, and is extremely responsive himself to music – he's very adept at matching the action onstage to the music.

ROGER DALTREY

Roger Daltrey played Macheath in *The Beggar's Opera* (BBC TV 1984).

Michael Romain   After seeing you play the title-role in the film *McVicar*, Jonathan asked you to play Macheath in his BBC TV production of *The Beggar's Opera* – what was your initial reaction to his offer?

Roger Daltrey   I was completely taken aback, mainly because I was a bit in awe of Jonathan – he's one of those people who, no matter how successful you are in life, you will always be looking up to. I'd never met him before, and was just astounded at the offer.

   The only recording of the piece I could get hold of was by D'Oyly Carte, and I found that horrendously twee – I thought that Jonathan must be going crazy if he wanted me to do that. But when I went to see him he said, 'No, no, we won't do it like that at all – we'll bring it down to earth and make it much more realistic.' I told him that as a rock singer I was fairly new to acting, but he said, 'Don't worry – you'll really be good in it.' So I promised him that I would go off and listen to it again, and see if I could sing it in a way that would add something new to the role. Although I'd never done anything like that eighteenth-century dialogue before, I told him that I would take the part if I felt that I could sing it.

   When I listened to the recording again, I realised that if you take away the D'Oyly Carte plushness and plums-in-the-mouth style and instead simply play the songs for what they are you are left with these very melodic old English folk-songs with great lyrics about subjects which are timeless. So I decided to use a very strong Cockney accent for the songs, and let them ring out as if they were being sung in the East End. This added a richness to the songs which was missing from the D'Oyly Carte version.

MR   You also went against tradition by bringing out very powerfully the dangerous side to Macheath's character.

RD   Macheath is a thug – a murderer and a highwayman – but because the piece is so often played as a 'jolly jape' that fact gets completely overlooked. It's precisely because he's such a thug that he has this fatal attraction for Polly, Lucy and the other women in the piece. Jonathan encouraged me to strip away all that D'Oyly Carte jollity from the role, and make him totally amoral and self-centred. Yet in a curious way, because Macheath is so self-centred he's actually more honest than everyone around him. And Jonathan's direction gave me a lot of opportunities for humour in the role.

MR   Did you find that Jonathan gave you a lot of freedom in rehearsals?

RD   Yes I did. One of his strokes of genius was the way that he mixed the rough and the smooth in the cast – real opera singers like Rosemary Ashe with people like myself, Bob Hoskins and Peter Bayliss. Jonathan was very brave in letting styles develop spontaneously, because everybody came from different areas. Somehow this mix of totally different performers gave the society in the opera a sense of reality – you felt that these were real people in real situations in the underworld of eighteenth-century London.

MR   How did Jonathan tackle the transition from dialogue to song?

RD   In a very daring way. One of the first things that struck me about the opera was the strange way that everything stopped for the songs. Jonathan suggested that as this was an 'anti-opera' opera, the action should just carry on as the songs jumped in. This completely solved the problem of 'What do you do during an eight-bar introduction?' Songs would literally start on the pull of a collar. We did it live, too, with John Eliot Gardiner conducting the orchestra in the next studio as he watched the action on a monitor. We achieved something quite extraordinary, and for me that was one of the things that made the production so exceptional. I think it was the best performance that particular music had ever received.

MR   Jonathan's principal visual reference for the piece was Hogarth – did you find this useful?

RD   Immensely, because those paintings portray the world of *The Beggar's Opera* very vividly. The sets for the production were absolutely stunning, and Jonathan was able to conjure up this Hogarthian world against them. The scenes in the prison were literally like animated Hogarth pictures – we even froze into postures from the paintings at various moments.

   I don't think that television could accommodate everything that Jonathan is able to give to *The Beggar's Opera* – he really needs the scope and resources of film. He used darkness and shadow in the most amazing way in the production – the effect would have been even stronger on film, but I'm sure that television equipment restricts him to a certain degree.

MR   Jonathan gave the ending a wonderfully innovative twist by having Macheath hung by mistake as the order comes through that he has been reprieved.

RD   It was a nice, witty touch. The Player and the Beggar are arguing away together, while Macheath is being strung up in the background – when the Player finally gives the order to reprieve him, it is mistaken for the order to

hang him. You get a great reaction-shot of their faces as they realise this –
'Oh, no!' It's theatrical licence. In fact, I've just played the Street Singer in
a film of *The Threepenny Opera*, and after seeing what Brecht did to John
Gay's Macheath I was shouting, 'Hang the swine – let him swing!' Brecht's
character is just unbearable – *The Beggar's Opera* is wonderful, and I think
that Brecht just ruined it.

MR What struck you most about Jonathan's direction?

RD His care for detail, and his incredible flexibility – he's willing to discard
a really good idea if necessary and start all over again. Not many directors
do that – they generally get hooked on an idea and insist that it is the only
way of doing the scene. Jonathan was never like that – even up to the last
rehearsal he'd make changes to accommodate the performers. At least four
different versions of some scenes evolved in rehearsals before Jonathan
decided that they would work for everyone – that's the mark of a great
director. He's not at all afraid to take chances.

Conductors

Kent Nagano conducted *Mahagonny* (Los Angeles Music Center Opera 1989).

Michael Romain   Did you know Jonathan before you conducted his production of *Mahagonny* at the Los Angeles Music Center Opera in 1989?

Kent Nagano   I knew him by reputation, but not personally – I'd wanted to work with him for a long time.

MR   How did you feel about his staging, which was a radical departure from the Brechtian tradition?

KN   I think that Jonathan was interested in staging it in a much more original way than usual. It's become limited in its effect because of all the clichés that audiences have become used to and have come to expect – Jonathan's approach was much more fresh and up to date. That's why he set it in this timeless space somewhere in California around the 1920s. Of course we were in LA, so the Hollywood setting was very apt and Robert Israel had a lot of experience in that area of set design. It was interesting for me to spend an extended period in LA working on such a production – although I'm a Californian born and bred, I'd always lived in the northern part rather than the southern. So my experiences of discovering *Mahagonny* through Jonathan's Hollywood eyes and simultaneously looking at Hollywood through contemporary eyes complemented each other ideally. Jonathan caught that style of early movies in the staging very accurately – we all sat around in rehearsals one day watching Chaplin movies to get the spirit of the thing.

MR   What were Jonathan's rehearsals like?

KN   Wonderful – in fact, there are very, very few people whom I've enjoyed working with as much as Jonathan. It was one of those rare collaborative efforts that really worked from the very beginning. Jonathan works in a very refreshing way. Some directors turn up at the first rehearsal with all the blocking and scene-plots entirely worked out, but Jonathan doesn't work like that. He told me quite bluntly early on that he didn't read music so I shouldn't expect him to approach it in the way that a musician would.

Everything was highly improvised – a lot of the improvisation was generated by the atmosphere Jonathan created. He incorporated a lot of methods from the straight theatre into the overall design: even though he had the basic framework and conception worked out in a very defined way, he left precise detail and precise action to evolve through the performers, and he would add to it by drawing on their individual characteristics to the maximum. That's why when you looked at the stage you saw such well-defined characters. He looked at the people playing those roles and incorporated their personal traits into the characterisation. This was marvellous for the comic side of the piece. One of the recurring effects was Fatty's constant biting of his finger-nails – the singer himself had this habit offstage, and Jonathan picked up on that at the first rehearsal. He saw the singer, Greg Fedderly, standing in a corner gnawing at his finger-nails, and quickly magnified that so it could be incorporated into Greg's character, Fatty. As a result, it became very funny indeed.

MR How did you feel the production worked onstage?

KN I was very pleased with it. The interesting thing was how well it worked in a space as large as the Los Angeles Music Center. Sometimes you run the risk of having the intensity of the rehearsal period diminished by the jump in scale on stage, but in this case Jonathan had already built the larger movements into the initial rehearsals so it went smoothly onto the stage.

MR What do you consider to be Jonathan's strengths as a director?

KN His background, his knowledge and his keen intelligence all combine to create a very invigorating atmosphere in rehearsals. That's the overwhelming thing that he brings to opera. A lot of stage directors are very conservative, and know only about the theatre and not too much about anything else. Jonathan knows a lot about everything. That's what he brings into his productions – a sense of everyday life.

MR Will you work together again?

KN I'd like to, yes. I want to do *Wozzeck* with him – as a doctor, he's the ideal director for it.

ROGER NORRINGTON

Roger Norrington conducted all of Jonathan Miller's productions for Kent Opera – *Così fan tutte* and *Rigoletto* (1975), *Orfeo* (1976), *Eugene Onegin* (1977), *La Traviata* (1979), *Falstaff* (1980) and *Fidelio* (1982).

Michael Romain   How did you bring Jonathan to Kent Opera?

Roger Norrington   I knew his work from the Cambridge Footlights – I can
remember seeing him do sketches barefoot at the Oxford Playhouse when
he was about nineteen. Then in 1974, when I was Music Director of Kent
Opera, I saw his production of *Noah's Flood* at the Roundhouse. He was
obviously a very important director, but I didn't know whether he would be
interested in doing opera. At that time I had moved into a house just down
the road from him near Regent's Park, and he happened to come round for
a party. We got talking and he said that he was very keen to direct Mozart,
so I immediately invited him to do *Così fan tutte* for Kent Opera in 1975.
That became the first of seven productions which we would work on
together for the company.

MR   What sort of conductor–director relationship did you have?

RN   It was very much a partnership. He was very interested in the music,
while I was very interested in the stage. Although he doesn't read music,
he is nevertheless extremely responsive to it, and he would make many
suggestions as to musical phrasing and so on.

   Jonathan doesn't come to rehearsals with set ideas about the piece, so
there was always a lot of spontaneity. He's surprisingly flexible. We
meshed so well together that one singer turned round to us in the second
week of *Così* rehearsals and said, 'Which of you is producing and which is
conducting?' The correct answer would have been both – it was a real
marriage of minds.

   One of the reasons that we worked so well together was because we both
used humour as a working-tool – it made rehearsals much easier. When
we were rehearsing *Fidelio*, or the death scene from *La Traviata*, the whole
cast would be in stitches – you could be forgiven for thinking that you had
wandered in to a rehearsal of *Die Fledermaus*. Humour allowed us to strip
the tragedies of their pomposity and left us free to get on with the serious
bits.

   Another thing that Jonathan and I had in common was a very positive
approach – we never said, 'That was terrible', but always said, 'That was
good – now what else can we do with it?' This gave rise to a very good
working atmosphere and a strong sense of a supportive community.

MR   Another aim that you both shared was to get to the heart of the opera
from a historical perspective.

RN   We both shared a belief in – not a reverence for – the past. He tried to recreate a sense of the age which produced these operas, while I tried to show how the music originally sounded – with *Fidelio*, for example, the score should sound light, more like Mozart, not slow and boring as it does when people try to turn it into Mahler and Wagner.

MR Which of the productions that you worked on with Jonathan gave you the most satisfaction?

RN They were all remarkable – Jonathan rethought each piece on its own terms so it had a new-minted feel. *Eugene Onegin* was very suitable for him as it is such a poetic piece, very inward with extremely subtle relationships. It has been ruined by grandiose productions in big opera houses – Tchaikovsky wanted it performed in a Conservatory instead. That's what Jonathan achieved – a wonderfully intimate, small-scale production, with almost no set so that the concentration was firmly on the cast.

Jonathan's *Falstaff* was absolutely stunning. It was set in the world of Bruegel, a sort of 'continental' version of Shakespeare, which set it somewhere between Verdi's Italy and Shakespeare's England, and gave it a wonderfully deft character. One night I didn't conduct the production and slipped into the dress circle to watch it instead – I don't think I stopped laughing until the end of the performance.

ZUBIN MEHTA

Zubin Mehta conducted *Tosca* (Maggio Musicale, Florence 1986), *Tristan and Isolde* (Los Angeles Music Center Opera 1987) and *Don Giovanni* (Maggio Musicale, Florence 1990), the first in a Mozart/da Ponte cycle with Miller.

Michael Romain How did your association with Jonathan begin?

Zubin Mehta I'd always known about him and his many facets, and often seen him on television – I'd also heard a lot about his *Rigoletto*. One day we literally bumped into each other at the Philharmonic Hall in New York. I can't remember how the subject of *Tosca* came up, but I said to him that I'd always wanted to do the opera in the contemporary setting of the Second World War. He replied, 'That's *exactly* how I've always thought about it!' So we hit it off then and there, and at the first opportunity I had the Teatro Communale contact him about making *Tosca* happen at the 1986 Maggio Musicale in Florence. As of the end of the first act on the opening night, the production was an unmitigated success. Of course, I think it's a production that an Italian audience will probably relate to more than anyone else, unless they know a lot about conditions in Rome during the Second World War. But even if you were to take away that background from the production, it would still be very strong on a dramatic level. But naturally it had a very great resonance for the Italian audience, because they identified with the period and with the pros and cons of those events. Italy was not just a one-faceted nation – there were divisions amongst them too, and Jonathan brought that out in the social realism of his staging.

MR Was it the success of the *Tosca* that prompted you to embark on your current Mozart/da Ponte cycle with Jonathan at the Maggio Musicale?

ZM Absolutely. We had talked a lot about Mozart, and I was very struck by Jonathan's love for the composer and his work. At first, we just thought that we'd do *Don Giovanni*. But when I decided to do the whole Mozart/da Ponte trilogy, I suggested to the theatre that it would be a good idea to have the same team for all three. In fact, in many instances we have the same singers too, doing corresponding roles. Jonathan and I are also going to do *The Magic Flute* together in Israel, but that will obviously have different economics behind it – I've always wanted him to do something in Israel.

MR What were your initial aims for *Don Giovanni*, which began the cycle in 1990?

ZM I didn't want to do *Don Giovanni* in a modern setting, and Jonathan absolutely agreed with me on this – he has never wanted to update Mozart. We're doing it in Mozart's own time. Jonathan and I share the same view of Don Giovanni – we don't look at him as an Errol Flynn figure. In our interpretation his weaknesses come through as well as his charms – his weaknesses as a human being are set against his strengths as the super-charmer of all time. And Jonathan has made sure that the ranks of the bourgeoisie around him are also very well composed. Rehearsals have been hugely productive, and I've had a wonderful time – the city has given me one theatre for *Il Trovatore* and another for *Don Giovanni*, and I swing between rehearsals.

MR How do you work together as conductor and director?

ZM I prepare the music completely, and I'm at nearly all of his staging rehearsals. If I have a suggestion here and there, Jonathan is always very flexible and accommodating towards it. I have to have a deep understanding of what is going on onstage. I'm directing the direction of the drama from the pit – as in the second act of *Tosca* – and therefore I have to be in complete agreement with what is going on, I have to go along with every word. In *Tosca* and *Don Giovanni* every word is reflected in the score. And in Italy, singing recitative is really different from anywhere else because the people want to hear and understand every word. If you gave an English audience *South Pacific*, for example, and they didn't understand the dialogue, then they wouldn't like that at all, even though they love the songs. They want to understand the dialogue too. Well, recitative is dialogue in that sense – it's the grandfather of dialogue – and it has to be done clearly. We are so used to non-Italian singers doing recitative as fast as they can. I remember that at the Vienna Opera Don Giovanni and Leporello used to have a race as to who could speak Italian faster – you couldn't understand a thing, and nothing made sense. So you just closed your ears and read your programme during the recitatives while you waited for the next aria or ensemble. But that's not what these Mozart operas are for. They are literally theatrical masterpieces, and Jonathan and I are both striving to do justice to this onstage. He shares my view on the importance of the recitative – in fact, he's the one who's telling the singers to speak the recitative even slower sometimes, like that whole recitative where Don Giovanni seduces Zerlina. There are no props on stage, so they can't sit at a table or anything like that – it's just the two of them. I remember how Jonathan explained to Samuel Ramey how just one finger down Zerlina's cheek is more sensual than all the gesticulations that one normally gets.

MR What do you consider to be Jonathan's principal strength as a director?

ZM His strength is his inventiveness. Constantly. If Jonathan were to start rehearsing *Don Giovanni* from scratch again tomorrow with the same cast, all the details would probably be different. That's his strength. He doesn't come to rehearsals with a set text-book and say, 'On the D major chord the left hand goes up.' He doesn't work that way. His work is in a state of constant evolution, and that's what happens at his rehearsals. Whenever I'm present at them, I'm always giving and learning at the same time.

MR How would you rank Jonathan amongst the other international directors that you've worked with?

ZM Jonathan is in the Strehler mould. Strehler improvises a lot, like Jonathan. I did *Fidelio* here at the Maggio Musicale with Strehler, and he had never done it before – although he had obviously studied it in advance, everything evolved during the rehearsals, *everything*, and Jonathan is absolutely of that way of thinking and working too. Above all, Strehler and Jonathan both share a sense of drama and humour – absolutely.

Writers

ERIC KORN

Eric Korn translated Racine's *Andromache* for Jonathan Miller's production at the Old Vic in 1988.

Michael Romain   Before your translation of *Andromache*, for the Old Vic season in 1988, Racine had never really worked in English – what did you and Jonathan aim for in the translation?

Eric Korn   The main thing was accessibility. We initially discussed patterns of verse, and whether one could conceivably do alexandrines in English or whether one should do it in prose. I was looking for a slightly sedate, mandarin turn of speech, definitely rather prosaic, but couched in blank verse which seemed to be the normal elevated speech of the English stage.

   Jonathan talked a great deal about the play to the cast once I'd finished the translation, and he was dazzling in his exposition – I'd never seen him in action as a director before, and he simply drew diagrams and talked off the cuff about seventeenth-century France and the psychology of human passions. Then he more or less stopped talking about it until the actors had worked themselves into the play.

   Although Jonathan had very clear ideas about it, it came as a surprise to both of us to see just how bizarre the characters' behaviour was, and the fact that they get away with it in French – this can be quite unsettling for audiences unused to the extraordinary ironic depth of the play, and the grotesque, almost surreal passions it expresses.

MR   During rehearsals, Jonathan described Racine as a 'Cartesian geometer who proposes a sort of Newtonian diagram of the moral universe'.

EK   Yes indeed, because of the symmetry of the disposition of the characters' emotions. He emphasised the contrast between, on the one hand, the orderliness and sedateness of the stage, dress and style, the mechanics of the plot and its formal layout (you could easily represent it in diagram form) and, on the other hand, what is being said by the characters, the fact that everyone is behaving so monstrously, and the fact that they are all literally the creators of their own fates and yet the puppets of their own emotions.

MR   What did you observe of Jonathan's direction?

EK   As with the best directors, Jonathan is a kind of polymorphously perverse actor who wants to take every part and can. He does this constant mimicry – not only of the characters, but also of the audience, the critics and so on. He has a tremendous ability to adjust to the comprehension of different members of the cast; he's very helpful to people in the minor roles still learning their lines, while able to challenge the leading actors at the same time.

   A lot of his direction is instinctive and intuitive, and a lot also comes out of his collaboration with the designer. The designs help the thing to take shape in his head – with *Andromache*, he knew where he wanted it to sit and how the actors would appear on the stage, battling against this incredibly steep rake designed by Richard Hudson. There's a proscenium arch in Jonathan's head, and he moves figures about in that to generate the tempo of the action. He's not a puppet-master in any sense at all, but he has a firm grasp of the shape and appearance of the piece, within which he gives the cast a lot of freedom to experiment.

MR   As a scientist yourself, how much do you feel Jonathan's scientific background informs his work?

EK   Immensely. He's able to get the chronological framework of a piece. He can relate Racine to the intellectual climate of his day, which was very much occupied with scientific revolutions of thought. Jonathan has always been very concerned with the seventeenth and eighteenth centuries anyway. But because England is still so profoundly philistine about science, all the critics go, 'Titter, titter – here's Dr Miller on mesmerism again', or, 'Titter, titter – what have gravity or optics got to do with it?' Quite clearly, what they have to do with it is to show how the world was structured in the minds of the seventeenth century.

   I love the fact that his productions very often illustrate scientific paradigms. You see it in his *Lear*, you see it in his *Tempest*, which was full of sociology and even had a telescope standing in Prospero's cell. There's a sense in his work that ideas are current – they're in the wind, and inform everything.

MR   Does Jonathan's work in psychology help him to illuminate character in rehearsal?

EK   Yes it does – his skill at characterisation arises simultaneously from mimicry – not in the superficial sense – and from analysis of motivation. It is quite extraordinary to see him directing when he hops about improvising, and stops at any moment to deliver a lecture.

He's not governed by any one school of thought – he'll draw on Freud, for example, to cast some light on a certain role in a certain context, but he'll approach another character from a completely different point of view. He's a very flexible thinker – he uses whatever is appropriate, which is where the man of the theatre predominates over the man of science. He is able to pass joyfully among a dozen theories, rather than tying himself down to one in particular. Erving Goffman, for instance, has provided him with a tremendous number of examples and case histories, but he is a reference for him rather than an influence – in no sense is Jonathan anyone's disciple.

MICHAEL IGNATIEFF

Michael Ignatieff is the author of *Dialogue in the Dark*, which Jonathan Miller directed for BBC TV in 1989.

Michael Romain   Jonathan directed your philosophical conversation-piece *Dialogue in the Dark* for television in 1989 – had he been involved with the project from its inception?

Michael Ignatieff   Yes he was – he had already directed two similar pieces for television, *The Drinking Party* and *The Death of Socrates*, and he was keen to do more. He'd read the chapter on Boswell and Hume in my book *The Needs of Strangers*, and when we were at a conference together in 1985 he said to me, 'You know, that would make an amazing two-hander.' So the whole idea was initially his. We first conceived it as a short film, and then it rapidly seemed to me to be more plausible as a piece of television.

MR   How did you collaborate as writer and director?

MI   I did a couple of drafts which he read, and he was very non-interventionist – he'd just say, 'Yes, it's coming along.' He had a nice way of indicating that it wasn't quite there, so I kept on going.

I'd initially envisaged something a little more elaborate, involving Johnson and Boswell on one side and Boswell and Hume on the other. I somehow had it in my mind that I wanted to have Boswell and Johnson rowing across the Thames at night with a boatman behind them, which I suppose in a rather stagey way was an anticipation of death, a way of evoking Charon the Ferryman. And I remember Jonathan saying very firmly, 'Oh God, not a night shoot! I can't stand those!' He wanted to keep it very simple.

MR   With the exception of Michael Hastings, you were the first living playwright that Jonathan had worked with for almost fifteen years.

MI   Yes, but I'm surprised to hear myself referred to as a living writer. I feel that I'm a sort of dead writer in this case, because one of the key things about the piece is that it's very textual. About 65 per cent of the text is directly taken from various pieces of Hume's and Boswell's writing, although in every case I slightly re-worked it to return it to some approximation of eighteenth-century speech. So I felt as if I was serving the dead.

MR   How did you find the rehearsals?

MI   The most enjoyable moment for me in the whole process was the very first read-through – it was the first play I'd written, and I'd never heard the lines spoken before. Jonathan just looked up at the end and said, 'There – it's fine.'

He didn't monkey around with the text, or play games with it or ask me to rewrite it substantially. The text that I wrote was the text that came out.

Jonathan wanted to play it very fast, because he aimed – quite rightly – to keep it conversational and avoid the potential ponderousness of a philosophical dialogue. So he used – very successfully – the technique of overlapping the lines, which he'd previously used in his *Long Day's Journey into Night*. He tried to make it very pacey without losing any of the edge of the argument. It had to be fast, Boswell had to be very drunk, but also the viewers had to be able to understand in broad terms the issues that were at stake – Jonathan and the actors ultimately brought all this off.

MR   The encounter between Hume and Boswell is ideal subject-matter for Jonathan, not least because of his strong historical empathy.

MI   He has enormous empathy with the eighteenth century in particular. He is completely at home when it comes to directing all that business with rouge and powdered wigs. That's why I don't really count myself a modern writer with this piece – in that sense, it was really a project between two eighteenth-century historians working together to do a twentieth-century play. It all stemmed from our mutual passion for the eighteenth century, and we've since discussed the idea of doing similar projects from that period.

MR   What impressions did you form of Jonathan's direction?

MI   It seems to me to be very non-directional directing – he knows how to let a cast get comfortable with things. The most interesting thing about him as a director is his incredible sense of humour – I've seen him use it brilliantly to take the tension out of a rehearsal and help the actors loosen up.

He's highly inventive in rehearsal – in *Dialogue in the Dark*, he suddenly came up with a couple of bits of business at the end which worked terribly well. And he was very interesting about the woman servant – I had written dialogue for her in some versions, and it was his idea to have her as a completely silent third party. She did it all with her eyes – disapproving looks, and so on – and it proved remarkably effective. He really understands television – what to do with it, how to make it work. As soon as he saw the set they had built in the studio, he just stripped about half of it – he knows just how he wants things to look on the screen.

The three days that we took to shoot it in Glasgow was one of the happiest periods of my life – it was hard work, very concentrated, but above all the most wonderful fun.

MR   What do you think makes Jonathan such a unique director?

MI   I don't think anyone else could direct Mozart as well as he can – nobody could equal his understanding of the eighteenth-century context. There are all sorts of touches in his Mozart productions that you won't find anywhere else – his treatment of the masonic themes, for instance; or that quite unforgettable backward glance of the ensemble at the very end of his *Magic Flute*, conjuring up that incredible sense of 1789 looking forward to our own time. There's also the amazing imaginary library of the *Flute*.

People often think of him as a primarily intellectual director, but I'm always struck by how much of his inspiration comes from his prowling around art galleries and museums. Clearly it's the influence of the painter Edward Hopper that makes his *Rigoletto*, and Jonathan was the first person to see Hopper's possibilities from a directorial point of view. Similarly, some of his fascist imagery came from complex sources like Bertolucci and Rossellini movies.

I'd sum up his strengths in three ways. One, he has an amazing mimic's ear for speech, so he can really do conversations in a very interesting way. In *Long Day's Journey*, for instance, he took this rather grand, formal O'Neill language and just subverted it so that it became startlingly realistic, like a genuine family quarrel. Two, his incredible sense – literally a historian's grasp – of the eighteenth century. Three, his very strong visual ability and photographic memory for pictures. He works with designers in a very precise way. People think that he works for some big concept in the German sense of *Der Begriff*, but I've often seen him work from simply a painting or an image.

MR   Why does his work frequently provoke such hostile criticism in Britain?

MI   A lot of it is anti-intellectualism – this is the only culture that has the phrase 'too clever by half'. Jonathan is definitely too clever by half – that's what makes his work so unique. But the culture takes its revenge on him.

MICHAEL HASTINGS

Michael Hastings adapted Kapúscínski's novel *The Emperor* for the stage at the Royal Court in 1987.

Michael Romain   How did Jonathan become involved in the stage version of Ryszard Kapúscínski's novel about the downfall of Haile Selassie in Ethiopia, *The Emperor*?

Michael Hastings   When I was based at the Royal Court as a Script Associate in 1986, I wrote several letters to Kapúscínski asking him if I could adapt *The Emperor* for the stage. One day he phoned from Warsaw to tell me that other people were also interested in dramatising the book, including Jonathan Miller. But he hadn't heard from Jonathan for some time – he always has so many different projects going at once that he picks things up and pursues them if he can, but puts them on pause if he can't – so we were able to secure the book for the Royal Court.

Then months went by, as the Court's contract system is pretty chaotic, until we finally signed a contract with Ryszard. Shortly after that, Max Stafford-Clark, the Court's Artistic Director, said to me, 'I am a neighbour of Jonathan and we were talking the other day. I told him that you had arranged with Kapúscínski for us to have *The Emperor*, and Jonathan said, "Well that is odd – I know Ryszard and I have told him that I would love to do it myself."' So Max suggested that I should meet Jonathan to discuss the project – although we now owned the rights, it seemed a wonderful opportunity to tempt Jonathan back to the Court.

MR   Although the Royal Court was the scene of Jonathan's directorial debut in 1962 with *Under Plain Cover*, he had not been back there since – why did it take him so long to return?

MH Once William Gaskill, Lindsay Anderson and Anthony Page were running the Court in the late sixties, there was simply no room for anyone else. Jonathan would no doubt have loved to work there, but, like a large number of directors and writers (myself included), he was frozen out.

After an absence of twenty-five years, I think Jonathan was pleased to get back inside the building with *The Emperor* – the Royal Court is rather like a little palace that you always want to conquer from time to time. Even if you fail there, it is a right, not a crime.

MR How did you both approach the task of dramatising the novel?

MH When we first talked about it, Jonathan was quite emphatic that the work had to be left in its original form – what we had to do was to find a way of making the words fit the stage, not interpose ourselves between Ryszard's lines. The result was that every line we used was Ryszard's, apart from a little bit of juxtaposition and a few comic touches that simply arose out of the exuberance of the rehearsal period.

First of all I did a workshop on the play with Jonathan, and then we sat down to do the casting. Neither of us was quite sure at that point what we really wanted – I think we were looking for a typical African feeling about the actors' faces. Once we'd found the right actors, though, Jonathan said, 'Now we've got this wonderful group together, we don't really need to worry about being extraordinary – the subject and the writing are extraordinary.'

He was quite right – with material that original, it was unnecessary to redecorate it. I know Jonathan thought *The Emperor* is possibly a rather elliptic analogy of Polish politics under Gierek in the 1970s – he said that it would be much simpler to put the actors in very grey suits, give them a grey dustiness and allow the language to do it all.

We were fortunate to have a sensitive translation, which Ryszard said acquired a 'highly poetic tone' which was true to his text. When the actors spoke, it sounded theatrical in a way that normal prose doesn't necessarily, and that worked well onstage.

We fiddled about with the speeches for a time – Jonathan asked at one point, 'There are forty voices here – how do we fit them all in?' The cast solved the problem for us – they started by keeping to one particular speech, then moved to another, and so on. Jonathan saw the part of the Emperor moving back and forth between them, so we decided to break it up and let the voices of the five actors naturally select the parts. In the end, what we were doing was dramatising the text but keeping the weight of Ryszard's words exactly as he wrote them.

MR   Jonathan said that he wanted 'language to do it all' – how did he create this narrative style?

MH   He built up a 'theatre of telling' with the actors. He could do that with *The Emperor* because the words are dream-like and sonorous. Ryszard essentially wrote it out of a deliberate dramatic conceit, and all Jonathan and I did was to pick that up and realise it theatrically on stage. There was a melancholic quality in the writing that Jonathan picked up on, a deep sadness that you can remember the past but little has been learned from it – Jonathan was attracted to this because he has a deep-rooted interest in the nature of loss. He built up a sense that the characters speak not in the present but out of the past – they have no life except for that of leaning beneath the shadow of his imperial highness, Haile Selassie.

MR   What background did Jonathan envisage for the action?

MH   He stuck to his plan where he said, 'Let's not have all this nonsense about people in strange garments and things – let's just have suits, rather badly-fitting grey suits, with plain ties and white shirts.' He went back to the designer Richard Hudson with this, and Richard came up with a box-like world of secrets, whispers, hidden doors, and the silence of innuendo.

We had a low budget, and I remember Richard's face going white when I said to him, 'Well I'm awfully sorry – the Theatre Upstairs is not like any other theatre, and we've got £900 for the set and the lighting.' That's peanuts in comparison to the opera houses he was used to. He went away, then came back a few days later with this atmospheric set design that perfectly matched the evolving ideas.

MR   I felt that his designs contributed very powerfully to one of the most remarkable features of the production, its surrealism.

MH   I think that *The Emperor* was one of the first total pieces of social surrealism that has worked from beginning to end. That's a rarity in contemporary theatre – you can get wonderful bits of surrealism on the fringe, but they are only isolated moments. *The Emperor* worked entirely from start to finish from the correct proposition of surrealism, Breton's idea that surrealism is a re-analysis of all our normal functions. Jonathan and I admire a clear, surreal conceit, that is *The Bedbug* by Mayakovsky. The spirit of a work like that is something he wanted to achieve in *The Emperor*.

MR   How did Jonathan direct the play?

12 Scene from *The Emperor*, designed by Richard Hudson, Royal Court 1987

MH   Each section of the text was taken out like a movement of voices, then it was a matter of giving the actors little moments to come in and out on, always built around a central section like 'Waiting for the Emperor to Arrive' or 'Going to the Ceremonial Starting-Up of the Nation's First Tractor'. His prime view was that the timbre of the piece was continuous – it doesn't go up or down.

He was coming out with ideas off the top of his head, thinking on his feet all the way. There was a moment in the middle of Act 2, where the actors were playing the Swedish physicians brought to Ethiopia by Selassie, and Jonathan said to them, 'I want you to come in looking like very gloomy Swedish physicians.' So the actors did that, and when they came to do their callisthenics Jonathan encouraged them to look as absurd as possible. I asked them to lie on the ground wriggling their legs and arms in the air like dying flies – we were gently laying onto the text East European parallels which go back to Čapek and *The Insect Play*.

During those weeks of rehearsal we felt that we had made contact with the same dialectic in our discussion and ideas as they had in the twenties and thirties in Prague and Berlin. Jonathan needs to identify with other times and cultures – if you don't have that, you will go through life thinking that a potato-soup diet of *Look Back in Anger*, *The Norman Conquests* and *Serious Money* is all there is to the British theatre.

MR   There is a strange musicality to the text of *The Emperor* – with his wide experience of opera, Jonathan must have been very receptive to this.

MH   Very much so – he frequently used musical terms in rehearsal. I remember an actor asking one day, 'Do you think there is too much of this one sound in my voice?' Jonathan replied, 'If you treat it as one tone in the orchestra, you'll find that the other actors have the musical difference to produce a kind of vibrato effect to balance it.'

MR   Jonathan said at the time that *The Emperor* was the best thing he had done for fifteen years.

MH   He turned round to me at the end of rehearsals and said, 'That was the happiest rehearsal period I've ever had.' He was surprisingly happy – he felt that we had worked together with a deal of sympathy and connection, and come up with something exceptional as a result. He thought *The Emperor* was his best work since his *Three Sisters* fifteen years before. He sees those two as his most crucial productions, shows that were excellent, but remained very un-English.

MR   What was the response when *The Emperor* opened?

MH   It was very generous. What Jonathan usually gets from the critics is 'Oh, here comes another bit of cleverness from Dr Miller', but on this occasion they agreed that it was fresh and quite unlike anything he had done before. In a sense it was unrepeatable, because it is such an exceptional book. The production sold out at the box office two days after the reviews came out; and that year it was subsequently transferred onto the main stage of the Court, and was later filmed for television by Jonathan, who shot it as it was designed for the stage.

MR   What do you think guides Jonathan's direction?

MH   His European outlook. He's very much aware that the axis of real art in the twentieth century belongs somewhere in that middle East European section of the twenties and thirties, whereas this country has always been remarkably slow in gauging what was coming out of Europe, and indeed parts of Russia. The whole event of *The Emperor* was induced by social melancholia. After what has happened to Stalinism in Europe, there remains the dust of the dead, memory without redemption, and fall. And a certain anger at the foolishness of a century. Something along those lines, scenes to that effect, keep Miller going.

ROBERT BRUSTEIN

Robert Brustein is the Artistic Director of the American Repertory Theatre at Harvard, where Jonathan Miller directed *The School for Scandal* in 1982. He was previously the founding director of the Yale Repertory Theatre, where Miller directed *Prometheus Bound* in 1967. He is also the drama critic of the *New Republic*.

Michael Romain   Was *The Old Glory* at the American Place Theatre in 1964 your first encounter with Jonathan's work?

Robert Brustein   That's right – the only thing of his I'd seen before that was his own performance in *Beyond the Fringe*, and I'd met him once when he came to a party at my house in New York. Then I had the great pleasure of seeing *The Old Glory*, which just knocked my socks off because it came after years of very arid American theatre.

MR   You reviewed it in the *New Republic* along with a disastrous revival of *The Changeling* at Lincoln Center.

RB   In that article I was announcing a new theatre heralded by *The Old Glory* and denouncing the old represented by *The Changeling*. *The Old Glory* seemed to me like the beginning of a renaissance for the American theatre, especially if we could have persuaded Jonathan to stay – he would have had a very deep influence. And he did to an extent with this one production alone.

What made such an impact was the way that Jonathan allowed the play to breathe. Robert Lowell, who was not essentially a dramatist, had written a poem based on a Melville novel about the sea, and about racial oppression, and Jonathan simply let it breathe, allowing it to pause at the right moments. He did things in his direction that Robert Wilson was later to do, and his production cast an extraordinary hypnotic web over the audience.

In the first part of *The Old Glory*, *My Kinsman, Major Molineux*, Jonathan's direction was very stylised – the characters wore white masks and black costumes, and everything seemed to be taking place in the infernal regions. Jonathan used the primary colours of black and white in a very striking way – I think my own production of *Don Juan* at Yale several years later must have been influenced by that.

You felt that a mind was at work on *The Old Glory* – a mind that was equal to the mind that had conceived the play for a change, instead of a mind that was setting out to vulgarise the play. And Jonathan gathered a marvellous team around him – the designer Willa Kim, and actors like Frank Langella whom most of us had never seen before.

MR Did *The Old Glory* lead to Jonathan directing Robert Lowell's version of Aeschylus' *Prometheus Bound* for you at Yale in 1967?

RB Yes – I'd heard that Cal had written a Prometheus play, influenced and stimulated by the Vietnam War, and I thought that no one but Jonathan could direct it.

MR How did he work at the Yale Repertory Theatre?

RB Very happily. He had recruited a very strong cast – Irene Worth as Io, Kenneth Haigh as Prometheus – and Michael Annals designed a remarkable set. We had a lot of time to do it, and it turned out to be a very enjoyable rehearsal period. Jonathan lectured daily to our students, Irene came to talk to our acting class, and Ken Haigh gave verse courses – they all functioned pedagogically as well as artistically.

MR Jonathan set *Prometheus Bound* in a seventeenth-century limbo ...

RB Jonathan found a metaphor for *Prometheus Bound* rather than taking the easy option of just updating the production, which is done so often these days by young directors – because *Much Ado About Nothing* reminds them of life on a Texas ranch, they'll set it on a Texas ranch. Jonathan would find not a simile like this, but a poetic metaphor – the seventeenth-century limbo for *Prometheus* – that reverberated and resonated in the minds of the audience, and left them thinking more and more about it.

The setting for *Prometheus* was like a Spanish Inquisition prison – it wasn't that specific, but Jonathan had that image in mind. He basically created an atmosphere of repression, in which Prometheus was imprisoned on a level of this massive structure that looked like a Pharos lighthouse – it went up as far as the eye could see, and equally far down. It was rather like *Marat/Sade* in that the characters enacted their oppression. It was a brilliantly metaphorical production, and still haunts me to this day.

MR   Jonathan went very much against the traditional style of frills, fans and silk handkerchiefs in his production of *The School for Scandal* at Harvard in 1982.

RB   That was the beauty of it – he brought a realistic historical overview of the period to the play. He fulfils Brecht's dictum about making the familiar strange and the strange familiar. He will use realism where appropriate, and it worked brilliantly with *The School for Scandal*. For the first time you felt this real Hogarthian society coming alive onstage. The sets were spectacularly dank, and the production was absolutely inspired on a physical level – Lady Sneerwell removed her wig at her dressing-table mirror to reveal a totally bald pate, the servants were pregnant, and the aristocracy didn't wash. The sense of reality was almost overpowering.

MR   You've also seen much of Jonathan's work in your role as drama critic of the *New Republic* – what has made a particular impression on you?

RB   I was very impressed by his production of *The Malcontent* at the Nottingham Playhouse in 1973. I'd written my doctoral dissertation on Marston, so he was someone I was very familiar with, but Jonathan staged the play in a way that totally surprised me. I'd never seen a production of *The Malcontent* before, and had always regarded it as a tragicomedy. Jonathan, however, directed it as a screaming comedy, and it was hilarious. Jonathan has a unique ability to see the comic side of tragedy – I remember him talking about doing *King Lear* with Jack Lemmon in the title role at one time. Then of course he went and did *Long Day's Journey into Night* with Lemmon as James Tyrone.

The *Malcontent* is a good example of what Jonathan has done for world theatre – he has rescued the great plays which nobody ever touched. They were just sitting there mouldering until Jonathan blew the cobwebs off them and brought them back to life. And that encouraged the rest of us to follow his lead.

MR   You've followed Jonathan's career right from the beginning with *The Old Glory* back in 1964 – how have you seen his work develop?

RB   His visual style was always free and surrealist in his early work like *The Old Glory* and *Prometheus Bound*, and now it has become much more so. In the most recent production of his that I've seen, *The Liar* at the Old Vic, he used the designs quite brilliantly to express the theatrical side of the play, showing the bare flats and the unfinished structures of the set.

One thing that has remained consistent is his way of reappraising the classics. He's written brilliantly on this subject, and justified the whole notion through this marvellous idea he has of the 'afterlife' of a work of art. He's completely convincing about that, and has given us all an intellectual construction for doing what we do.

MR   Where does he stand in world theatre?

RB   Jonathan is a world figure – he's one of our leading international directors. There's no insularity about him whatsoever – he's completely open to what's happening everywhere. He doesn't fit into anybody's style or preconceptions.

The vast range of knowledge that he brings to bear on his work makes him unique as a director. He can take scientific theories – whether physiological or psychological – and absorb and recreate them in artistic terms. That's what gives such distinction to his work.

Index